THE
OLDER
SOPHISTS

THE
OLDER
SOPHISTS

EDITED BY
ROSAMOND KENT SPRAGUE

A COMPLETE TRANSLATION

BY SEVERAL HANDS

OF THE FRAGMENTS IN

DIE FRAGMENTE

DER VORSOKRATIKER

EDITED BY DIELS-KRANZ

AND PUBLISHED BY

WEIDMANN VERLAG

(VADUZ, LIECHTENSTEIN)

(by whose permission the translations have been made)

WITH A NEW EDITION OF

ANTIPHON AND OF *EUTHYDEMUS*

UNIVERSITY OF SOUTH CAROLINA PRESS
COLUMBIA, SOUTH CAROLINA

International Standard Book Number: 0–87249–192–7
Library of Congress Catalog Card Number: 71–120587

CONTENTS

Intro on all
(2 pp. each)

Contents

PREFACE

The ancient material concerning the older sophists has not been easily accessible to English readers. Kathleen Freeman's *Ancilla to the Pre-Socratic Philosophers: A Complete Translation of the Fragments in Diels' "Fragmente der Vorsokratiker"* (Oxford, 1948) included a certain amount of sophist material, but the longer extracts from Gorgias and Prodicus were summarized rather than translated, and the same procedure was followed in the case of the two concluding essays, the one by the Anonymus Iamblichi, and the *Dissoi Logoi*. Of Diels-Kranz' text of this latter, in fact, there appeared to be no complete translation anywhere, with the exception of the Italian versions by M. Timpanaro Cardini (*I Sofisti* [Bari, 1923], corrected and enlarged 1954) and M. Untersteiner (*I Sofisti, testimonianze e frammenti* [Florence, 1949–62]).

To present a complete English translation of the sophist material in Diels-Kranz therefore needs no apology; this volume attempts to do for English readers what was done for Italian readers by Timpanaro Cardini as long ago as 1923. To this last statement, however, there are two exceptions. The translator of Antiphon, J. S. Morrison, had become convinced that, contrary to the opinion of Diels, the sophist Antiphon was one with and the same as the orator Antiphon of Rhamnus. He did not feel justified, therefore, in simply translating the text of Diels-Kranz. What he has done is to re-edit the material completely so as to produce a reunited Antiphon. In this section of the book, then, a sophist has been freshly edited rather than directly translated from the arrangement of Diels-Kranz. The second exception is the appearance, in an appendix, of the sophist Euthydemus. As is there explained, Euthydemus is a historical person, so that there seems no reason why he should not have a section to himself.

In other respects the book is, and was intended to be, a handbook rather than an edition. As Diels-Kranz was the standard text, its arrangement and numbering was naturally followed. In actual form the following changes have been made: the names of authors and of titles of works cited have usually been expanded and anglicized, and most of the italics employed by Diels for the purpose of differentiating an author's words from the surrounding text have been eliminated. In editing the work of ten different translators, I would be surprised if I had caught all typographical inconsistencies; there are a goodly number in *DK* itself. I can only hope that none of those remaining will seriously mislead.

Thanks are due to Professor Gilbert Ryle for permission to reprint my translation of the *Dissoi Logoi* from *Mind*, n.s. 306, LXXVII (Apr. 1968), pp. 155–67, and to the Bobbs-Merrill Company for permission to quote from my translation of the *Euthydemus* (Indianapolis, 1965). My student, Edwin L. Green III, contributed many long hours to the index of passages. Permission to use the seventh edition of H. Diels and W. Kranz, *Die Fragmente der Vorsokratiker* (Berlin, 1951–54) was given by the publisher, Weidmann.

ROSAMOND KENT SPRAGUE

University of South Carolina

ABBREVIATIONS

A	*Suidae Lexicon (Suda)*, ed. A. Adler, 5 vols. (Leipzig, 1928–38).
ALG	*Anthologia Lyrica Graeca*, ed. E. Diehl, 2 vols. (Leipzig, 1925).
BA	*Anecdota Graeca*, ed. I. Bekker, 3 vols. (Berlin, 1814–21).
CAG	*Commentaria in Aristotelem Graeca* (Berlin, 1892–1909).
CMG	*Corpus Medicorum Graecorum* (Leipzig, 1908——).
D	*Doxographi Graeci*, H. Diels (Berlin, 1879).
Diels	*Poetarum Philosophorum Fragmenta*, H. Diels (Berlin, 1901).
DK	*Die Fragmente der Vorsokratiker*, H. Diels and W. Kranz, 7th ed., 3 vols. (Berlin, 1951–54).
Etym. Gen.	*Etymologicum Genuinum* Ineditum; cf. R. Reitzenstein, *Geschichte der Griechischen Etymologika* (Leipzig, 1897).
FGrHist	*Die Fragmente der Griechischen Historiker*, F. Jacoby (Berlin, 1923——).
FHG	*Fragmenta Historicorum Graecorum*, C. Müller, 5 vols. (Paris, 1841–70).
HSCP	*Harvard Studies in Classical Philology* (Cambridge, Mass., 1896——).
Loeb	Loeb Classical Library (London and Cambridge, Mass., various dates).
LSJ	*A Greek-English Lexicon*, H. G. Liddell and R. Scott, 9th ed., rev. by H. S. Jones and R. McKenzie (Oxford, 1940).

Orat.Att.	*Oratores Attici*, J. G. Baifer and H. Sauppe (Zurich, 1839–50).
PLG	*Poetae Lyrici Graeci*, T. Bergk, 4th ed., 3 vols. (Leipzig, 1882).
POxy	*Oxyrhynchus Papyri*, B. P. Grenfell and A. S. Hunt (London, 1898——).
RE	*Pauly's Realencyclopädie der classischen Altertumswissenschaft*, ed. Wissowa, Kroll et al. (Stuttgart, 1894——).
Rh.Gr.	*Rhetores Graeci*, L. Spengel, 3 vols. (Leipzig, 1853–56).
SEG	*Supplementum Epigraphicum Graecum*, ed. J. J. E. Hondius et al. (Leyden, 1923——).
Suidas	[Suidae] Lexicon, ed. G. Bernhardy (Halle, 1853).
TGF	*Tragicorum Graecorum Fragmenta*, ed. A. Nauck, 2d ed. (Leipzig, 1889).
Th.	Antiphontis orationes et fragmenta post Fredericum Blass edidit Theodorus Thalheim ed. stereotypa editionus primae (MCMIV), repr. 1966.
Untersteiner	*I Sofisti, testimonianze e frammenti*, M. Untersteiner, 4 vols. (Florence, 1949–62).
Zeller-Nestle	*Die Philosophie der Griechen*, E. Zeller, 1. Teil, 1. Hälfte (7th ed., 1923) and 2. Hälfte (6th ed., 1920), ed. W. Nestle, Leipzig.

THE
OLDER
SOPHISTS

79. NAME AND NOTION

translated by WILLIAM O'NEILL

1. ARISTIDES *Orations* 46 [II 407 Dindorf] . . . they do not at all seem to me even to know what the very term "philosophy" meant for the Greeks, or that it did not even have any of the meanings associated with this subject. Did not Herodotus call Solon a "sophist" [I 29, 1], and in turn Pythagoras [IV 95, 1]? Did not Androtion [fr. 39 *FHG* I 375] call the Seven (I mean the Seven Wise Men) "sophists," and Socrates in turn, that famous individual, a "sophist"? Again, did not Isocrates term "sophist" those concerned with disputation and the self-professed dialecticians [13, 1], but "philosophers" himself and the orators and those concerned with political skill? Some of his pupils, too, use the same terminology. Does not Lysias [fr. 281 *Orat.Att.* II 212a9] call Plato a "sophist," and again Aeschines? By way of reproach in the case of Lysias, one might say. But the rest of the authors at any rate were not reproaching those other distinguished individuals; nevertheless, they called them by this same name. And further, although it was possible to call Plato a "sophist" by way of reproach, why should anyone speak of those others so? No, I think that "sophist" was probably a general term, and "philosophy" had this meaning: a sort of love of the beautiful and study concerning discourse, and not this modern usage of the word, but culture in the universal sense . . . since he always somehow seems to be reviling the sophist, and the person who most of all rebelled against the term seems to me to be Plato. The reason for this is his contempt both for the masses and for his contemporaries. But he seems also to have used this form of address in an entirely auspicious sense. At any rate, the god whom he considers to be wisest and the receptacle of all truth, him indeed he has called "a perfect sophist" [*Cratylus* 403E].

2. PLATO *Sophist* 231D   First, he [viz., the sophist] was discovered to be a mercenary hunter after the young and rich . . . secondly, a sort of wholesaler of learning for the soul . . . and thirdly, was he not shown up as a retailer of the same goods? . . . and fourthly, a salesman of his own products of learning to us . . . but fifthly, . . . he was a sort of master in the art of combat about words, appropriating to himself the eristic technique . . . now the sixth instance was disputed, but nevertheless we agreed to assign him the role of a purifier, as regards the soul, of opinions that obstruct learning. Cf. *Protagoras* 317B [*DK* 80 A 5].

2a. XENOPHON *Memorabilia* I 1, 11   [Socrates] did not even discuss the origin of the universe, as the majority of other thinkers did, nor examine how the so-called cosmos of the "sophists" arose[1] and by what necessities each set of heavenly bodies is born.   6, 13 . . . the same with wisdom: those who sell it to anyone for money are called "sophists," just like prostitutes.   *On Hunting* 13, 8 But the "sophists" talk to deceive and write for their own gain and are of no benefit to anyone; for none of them is wise or ever became so, but it is enough for each one of them to be called a "sophist," which is an insult, at least to men of sound understanding. So I exhort you to beware of the instruction of the "sophists," but not to disregard the considerations of the philosophers.

3. ARISTOTLE *On Sophistical Refutations* I 165a21   For the sophist's craft is an apparent wisdom but not a real one, and the sophist is a money-maker by apparent but not real wisdom.

[1] Reading ἔφυ: FLc & *Loeb* ed.

8o. PROTAGORAS

translated by MICHAEL J. O'BRIEN

Protagoras, the oldest of the sophists, was born about 490 B.C. and
died about 420. A native of Abdera in Thrace, he is known to have
ranged in his travels as far as Sicily, and he visited Athens more than
once. In Athens he came to know Pericles, and their acquaintance
was marked by mutual esteem. The appointment of Protagoras to
write laws for the Athenian colony of Thurii in 444 no doubt reflected
Pericles' judgment. Protagoras was a successful and respected teacher,
and one who demanded for his services a large fee. Plato, no partisan
of his views, portrays him as courteous and eloquent and makes it
clear that he was admired and sought out in Athens by the cultivated
rich. The range of his interests was wide, extending to ethics, politics,
theology, education, cultural history, literary criticism, linguistic
studies, and rhetoric. He was both teacher and writer. It is not possible
to say whether each of the titles of "works" ascribed to him (and
listed separately in section B below) actually designates a separate
work; moreover, the subject matter of some of these—let alone their
contents—is disputable (e.g., 8b) or unknown (e.g., 8f). His most
famous dicta are those with which he began his two works *Truth* and
On the Gods (B 1 and B 4). Legend and error have tainted some accounts of his life. His biographical tradition therefore contains several
colorful details that are unverifiable (magian influence on his philosophy), or false (his studies under Democritus, his death at ninety),
or unlikely (his trial and banishment from Athens). Against this last
report stands Plato's testimony (A 8) that he died with honor
undiminished.

A. LIFE AND TEACHINGS

1. DIOGENES LAERTIUS IX 50   Protagoras, the son of Artemon or of Maeandrius (the latter, according to Apollodorus [*FGrHist* 244 F 70 II 1040] and the fifth book of Dinon's *Persian History* [fr. 6 *FHG* II 90; cf. A 2]), was a native of Abdera, as Heraclides Ponticus says in his *Laws* [fr. 21 Voss]. Heraclides also says that he wrote laws for Thurii. On the other hand, the *Flatterers* of Eupolis [fr. 146 I 297 Kock] makes him a native of Teos, in the line "Inside is Protagoras of Teos." He and Prodicus of Ceos collected money for their lectures, and Plato says in the *Protagoras* [316A] that Prodicus had a deep voice. Protagoras was a student of Democritus (he was called "Wisdom," as Favorinus says in his *Miscellaneous History* [fr. 36 *FHG* III 583, viz., Democritus; cf. *DK* 68 A 2 and A 18]). (51) Protagoras was the first to say that on every issue there are two arguments opposed to each other [B 6a]; these he made use of in arguing by the method of questioning, a practice he originated. One of his works, moreover, begins in this way: "Of all things the measure is man, of things that are, that they are, and of things that are not, that they are not" [B 1]. He said too that soul was nothing apart from its sensations, according to Plato's *Theaetetus* [152ff.], and that all things are true. Elsewhere he begins a work in this fashion: "Concerning the gods, I cannot know either that they exist or that they do not exist; for there is much to prevent one's knowing: the obscurity of the subject and the shortness of man's life" [B 4].   (52) Because he began his book in this way he was expelled by the Athenians, and they also burned his books in the marketplace, having first collected them by public messenger from all who owned copies.

Protagoras was the first man to exact a fee of a hundred minas. He was also the first to distinguish the tenses of the verb, to expound the importance of the right moment, to conduct debates, and to introduce disputants to the tricks of argument. Moreover, in neglecting meanings and concerning himself with mere words, he fathered the present shallow tribe of quibblers—to the point that Timon can speak of him as "Protagoras who mixes in,[1] master of wrangling" [fr. 47 *Diels*]. (53) He it was who first introduced the Socratic type of argument. And he was the first to adopt in discussion the argument of Antisthenes which attempts to prove that contradiction is impossible: so says Plato in the *Euthydemus* [286c]. And he was first to introduce the methods of attacking any thesis, as Artemidorus the dialectician says in his work *Against Chrysippus*. He invented as well the so-called shoulder pad, on which porters carry their loads, according to Aristotle in his work *On Education* [fr. 63 Rose]. For he used to be a porter, as Epicurus says somewhere [see *DK* 68 A 9]; indeed this was the occasion of his having been adopted by Democritus, who observed him tying up bundles of wood. He first divided speech into four modes: entreaty, question, answer, and command (54) (according to others he recognized seven: narration, question, answer, command, report, entreaty, and invitation), and these he called the basic parts of speech. But Alcidamas [fr. 8 *Orat.Att.* II 155b36] makes the forms of speech four: affirmation, negation, question, and address. The first of his works that he read publicly was that called *On the Gods*, the opening words of which we have quoted above. Cf. B 4. He read it at Athens in the house of Euripides or, some say, in the house of Megacleides. According to others, the place was the Lyceum, and his pupil Archagoras, son of Theodotus, lent his voice for the readings. He was laid under accusation by the son of Polyzelus, Pythodorus, one of the Four Hundred (Aristotle says it was Euathlus [fr. 67; see B 6]). (55) The works of Protagoras which survive are these: * * * *The Art of Debating, On Wrestling, On Mathematics, On Government, On Ambition, On the Virtues, On the Original State of Things, On Those in Hades, On Human Errors, Direction, Trial over a Fee, Contradictory Arguments in Two Books*. So ends the list of his works.

Plato, moreover, has a dialogue about him. Philochorus says [fr. 168 *FHG* I 412] that while he was voyaging to Sicily the ship he was on sank, and that Euripides makes an oblique reference to this in his *Ixion* [performed 410–408, p. 490 Nauck (2d ed.)]. Some say he died

---

[1] Probably "avid in combat," possibly "sociable." See *Untersteiner* I, 18n.

on a journey at the age of about ninety.   (56) Apollodorus [*FGrHist* 244 F 71 II 1040] says he died at seventy, adding that he was a sophist for forty years and in his prime in the eighty-fourth Olympiad [444–441]. [There follows an epigram of Diogenes.]

A story is told of the time he demanded his fee from Euathlus, a pupil of his. Euathlus refused to pay, saying, "But I haven't won a victory yet." Protagoras replied, "But if I win this dispute I must be paid because I've won, and if you win it I must be paid because you've won." Cf. B 6.

There was another Protagoras too, an astronomer, for whom Euphorion [p. 31 Scheidweiler] wrote a dirge; and a third, a Stoic philosopher.

1a. PLUTARCH   so-called   *Lamprias Catalog* [Bernardakis VII 476] no. 141 *On the First Things by Protagoras.*

2. PHILOSTRATUS *Lives of the Sophists* I 10, 1. Cf. *DK* 68 A 9. Protagoras of Abdera, the sophist, became a disciple of Democritus while in his own town and also made the acquaintance of Persian magi at the time of Xerxes' invasion of Greece. For his father was Maeandrius, a man of extraordinary wealth among the Thracians, one who entertained Xerxes himself in his house and by means of gifts won from him for his son the privilege of associating with the magi. (The Persian magi do not teach those who are not Persians, except by command of the king.)   (2) I think it was from his Persian instruction that Protagoras derived the unorthodox view that one cannot say whether the gods exist or not; for the magi acknowledge the gods in their secret rites but try to do away with the public belief in divinity, since they do not wish to give the impression that their power is from that source.   (3) For this reason the Athenians banished him from all their territory. Some say this was a court-judgment, others that he was merely the object of a voted decree. Between island and mainland he moved, in his attempt to keep ahead of the Athenian triremes that were scattered over every sea, until a small vessel on which he was sailing sank.   (4) He invented the practice of speaking for a fee and ⌐

was the first to introduce it to Greece. He merits no reproach on this account, for we are more enthusiastic about pursuits which cost us money than about those which cost us nothing. Plato, having observed that Protagoras not only expounded his views in a pompous way but took pride in being pompous, and moreover that he was sometimes unduly verbose, gave a sample of his style in a long myth [C 1].

3. HESYCHIUS *Onomatologus* in SCHOLIA on PLATO *Republic* 600C Protagoras of Abdera, son of Artemon. He was a porter, but after meeting Democritus he became a philosopher and turned to oratory. He was first in inventing eristic arguments and first to charge his pupils a fee of one hundred minas. On this account he was nicknamed "Calculation." He had as pupils Isocrates the orator and Prodicus of Ceos. His books were burned by the Athenians, for he said, "Concerning the gods I cannot know either that they exist or that they do not exist" [B 4]. Plato wrote a dialogue about him. He died in a shipwreck on a voyage to Sicily at the age of ninety, having been a sophist for forty years. SUIDAS s.v. "Protagoras" [a blend of A 1 and 3]

4. EUSEBIUS *Chronicle* according to Jerome   Euripides . . . is held in renown, and so is Protagoras the sophist, whose books the Athenians burned in accordance with a public decree in the eighty-fourth Olympiad [444–441].   APULEIUS *Florida* 18 Protagoras was a sophist of very wide knowledge and a man of exceptional eloquence among the first inventors of rhetoric. He was also a contemporary and fellow townsman of Democritus the natural philosopher (it was from him that he got his learning). This Protagoras, they say, contracted for too large a fee with his pupil Euathlus, and with a rash stipulation, etc. Cf. B 6.

5. PLATO *Protagoras* 317B [Dramatic date about 431] [Protagoras:] Therefore I have taken a course entirely different from theirs [the disguised sophists like Orpheus], and I admit that I am a sophist and that I teach men. . . . c And yet it has been many years now that

I have practiced this art, for I have had many years of life. As far as age goes, there is not one in this whole group whose father I might not be. . . . 318A Young man, if you associate with me, you shall, on the first day you enter my company, go home a better man for it, and so too on the next day; and every day you shall unfailingly improve. . . . 318D For the others mistreat the young: when these have fled from the arts, their teachers lead them back against their wills and plunge them once more into the arts, teaching them calculation and astronomy and geometry and music (as he said this he looked at Hippias), whereas a pupil coming to me will learn only the subject he has come to learn. By this I mean prudence in his own affairs, so that he may manage his own household in the best way, and prudence in the affairs of the city, so that he may be most effective in action and in speech in matters concerning the city. . . . 319A [Socrates:] I take it that you refer to the political art and that you promise to turn men into good citizens. —— That is exactly the profession that I make, Socrates. 349A [Socrates:] Whereas you, openly advertising yourself throughout Greece under the title of sophist, have proclaimed yourself a teacher of culture and virtue, and you are the first man to think he is entitled to a fee for this.

6. —— —— 328B [Protagoras speaks] For this reason I have fixed upon this method of exacting the fee. A pupil of mine pays, if he wants to, the amount I charge. But if he is unwilling, then he puts down instead whatever amount he has declared, under oath in a temple, the lessons are worth.

7. —— —— 329B But Protagoras here is able to speak at length and nobly too, as is now clear, and able as well to respond briefly to questions, or, when he is the questioner, to wait and listen to the answer. These are rare gifts. Cf. 334Dff.

8. —— *Meno* 91D For I know of one man, namely Protagoras, who has got more money from this wisdom we speak of than Phidias, so renowned for the beautiful works he has turned out, and any ten

other sculptors. . . . E Whereas Protagoras, you ask me to believe, hoodwinked all of Greece for more than forty years, corrupting his associates and sending them away in worse condition than he had found them. For I think he died when he was close to seventy, after forty years spent in his profession. And in all this time, down to the present day, his reputation has not faded.

9. ——— *Hippias Major* 282DE [Hippias speaks; see *DK* 86 A 7] But I arrived once in Sicily while Protagoras was there on a visit, and though he had a great reputation and was a much older man than I . . . etc.

10. PLUTARCH *Pericles* 36 [from STESIMBROTUS *FGrHist* 107 F 11 II 5 19] For, he said, when a competitor in the pentathlor, without meaning to, struck and killed Epitimus of Pharsalus with a javelin, [Pericles] spent a whole day with Protagoras trying to decide whether, according to the most correct judgment, one ought to regard as the cause of the mishap the javelin or the man who threw it rather than the directors of the games. Cf. ANTIPHON *Second Tetralogy* 87 B III.

11. ATHENAEUS V 218B Then again, the conversation in the *Protagoras*, which takes place after the death of Hipponicus, when Callias has already come into his inheritance, mentions Protagoras as having come to town for the second time not many days before [*Protagoras* 309D]. But Hipponicus, while serving as general in the archonship of Euthydemus [in 431?], was a comrade of Nicias in fighting the Tanagraeans and their Boeotian allies, a battle in which he was victorious. He died in all likelihood [at Delium in 424] not long before the presentation, in the archonship of Alcaeus [in 421], of the *Flatterers* of Eupolis. . . . Now in this play Eupolis introduces Protagoras as being in town. [See above A 1.] On the other hand, Ameipsias in the *Connus* [1 673 Kock], presented two years before [in 423], does not number him in the chorus of "Thinkers." So it is clear that he arrived in the interval. XI 505F But Pericles' sons, Paralus and Xanthippus, whose father died in the plague, could certainly not have conversed with Protagoras during his second visit to Athens, since they had died before their father. Cf. EUSTATHIUS on HOMER *Odyssey* V 490 1547, 53. Eupolis is said to exhibit the natural philosopher Protagoras in a satirical light in the words, "The scoundrel puts on false airs about what's in the sky, but eats what comes from the earth" [fr. 146b I 297 Kock; see above A 1]. Cf. fr. 147 "Protagoras bade him [Callias] drink, so that he might have his lung well washed out before the dog days came."

12. SEXTUS *Against the Schoolmasters* IX 55, 56 [following *DK* 88 B 25] Theodorus the atheist agrees with these men [Euhemerus, Diagoras, Prodicus, Critias] and, according to some, so does Protagoras of Abdera . . . who has clearly stated in one of his works: "Concerning the gods I am unable to say whether they exist or what they are like, for there are many things that hinder me" [B 4]. It was for this that the Athenians voted the death penalty against him. He fled and died in an accident at sea. This story is also mentioned by Timon of Phlius in the second book of his *Lampoons* [fr. 5 *Diels*]. His account follows:

. . . afterwards, too, to Protagoras among the sophists, a man with clear voice, eye straight on the mark, and able for any work. They made up their minds to make ashes of his books because he put it in writing that he did not know nor could he perceive what or who the gods are. His words were cautious and reasonable. When this did him no good he made a run for it, hoping to avoid the cold drink of Socrates and a trip to Hades.

13. PLATO *Cratylus* 385Eff. As Protagoras meant when he said that of all things the measure is man [B 1], that as things appear to me, then, so they actually are for me, and as they appear to you, so they actually are for you.

14. SEXTUS *Outlines of Pyrrhonism* I 216 Protagoras, too, will have it that of all things the measure is man, of things that are that they are, and of things that are not that they are not [B 1], meaning by "measure" the standard of judgment, and using the word *chremata* rather than *pragmata* for "things." So he says, in effect, that man is the standard of judgment of all things, of those that are that they are, and of those that are not that they are not. And for this reason he posits only what appears to the individual, thus introducing relativity. . . . (217) Now what he says is that matter is in a state of flux, and that as it changes there is a continuous replacement of the effluvia which it gives off; that, moreover, one's sensations undergo change and alteration in accordance with one's age and other aspects of one's bodily condition. (218) He says too that the reasons [*logoi*] of all the appearances are present in the matter, so that the matter is capable, as far as lies in its own power, of being everything that appears to everybody. Men, however, apprehend different things at different times according to their various dispositions. For the man whose condition is natural grasps, out of what is contained in matter, what can appear to those in a natural condition, whereas the man whose condition is not natural grasps what can appear to those in his condition. (219) The same account, moreover, must be given of differences in age, the question whether one is asleep or awake, and every type of variation in one's condition. And so, according to him, man becomes the standard of judgment of things that are. For all things that appear to men also exist, but things which appear to no man do not exist either. We see, therefore, that he dogmatizes not only about the flux of matter, but also about the presence in it of the reasons [*logoi*] of all appearances, although these are obscure matters on which we suspend judgment.

15. ——— *Against the Schoolmasters* VII 389 It could surely not be maintained that every appearance is true, because that argument can be turned back upon itself, as Democritus and Plato [*Theaetetus* 171A] showed when they took issue with Protagoras: for if every appearance is true, then the belief that not every appearance is true—once this belief takes the form of an appearance—will also be true, and so the belief that every appearance is true will become false. [Democritus against Protagoras; *DK* 68 A 113; B 11, B 69, B 156 and n.]

16. HERMIAS *Pagan Philosophers Derided* 9 (D 653) But Protagoras tries to draw me to the other side, where he stands, with the statement:

Man is the standard and judge of things, and whatever comes before the senses is a thing, but that which does not is not among the forms of being. Cf. *DK* 70 B 1.

17. ARISTOTLE *Metaphysics* IX 3, 1046b29 There are some, the Megarians for example, who say that a thing can act only when it is acting, and that when it is not acting, it cannot act. For example, the man who is not building cannot build, but only the man who builds and only when he is building. The same is alleged of other things too. It is not hard to see the strange consequences of this view. For it is clear that a man will also not be a builder unless he is building, since to be a builder is to be able to build. The same applies to the other arts. Now if it is impossible to possess such arts without ever learning[2] them and having acquired them, and impossible not to possess them 1047a1 without ever having lost them (whether by forgetfulness, mishap, or the passage of time; for it is surely not by the destruction of the thing itself,[3] since that is always in existence), once a man stops acting he will not possess the art, and yet he may start to build again without delay—how then has he acquired the art? The same applies to inanimate things. For nothing which is not being perceived will be cold or hot or sweet or in any way perceptible. And so it will turn out that those who believe this are upholding the view of Protagoras. In fact, nothing will possess the power of perception either unless it is perceiving and acting.

18. TERTULLIAN *On the Soul* 15 [Location of the soul in the breast; from *DK* 31 B 105] Protagoras and Apollodorus and Chrysippus know this too.

19. PLATO *Euthydemus* 286BC I must say that I always wonder at this argument [viz., that contradiction is impossible], which I have

---

[2] μανθάνοντα. However, μαθόντα ("having learned"), the reading in Alexander's commentary, is preferable.

[3] I.e., the form.

heard from many people and on many occasions—for Protagoras'
circle made great use of it, as did others even before him. Cf. *DK* 22
A 7. But to my mind the argument always seems extraordinary in
the way it overthrows not only other arguments but itself too. [See
above A 1 (53).] ARISTOTLE *Metaphysics* IV 4, 1007b18 Moreover, if
contradictory statements are all true at the same time about the same
thing, it is clear that all things will be one. For the same thing will be
a trireme and a wall and a man, if it is permissible either to affirm or
to deny anything of everything, as those who uphold the argument of
Protagoras must admit. For if anyone thinks that a man is not a trireme,
it is clear that he is not a trireme. Therefore he *is* one too, if the contradictory statement is true. Cf. 5, 1009a6; SEXTUS VII 389 [*DK* 68 A 114].
ARISTOTLE *Metaphysics* XI 6, 1062b13 He [Protagoras] said that of all
things the measure is man, meaning simply that what appears to each
person also *is* positively the case. But once this is taken to be so, the
same thing turns out both to be and not to be, and to be bad as well
as good, not to mention the other opposites, since often what seems
beautiful to this group of people will seem the opposite to that group,
and since what appears to each man is taken to be the measure.

20. CLEMENT *Miscellanies* VI 65 [II 464, 14 Stählin] Every argument
has an opposite argument, say the Greeks, following Protagoras.
SENECA *Letters* 88, 43 Protagoras says that one can argue equally well
on either side of any question, including the question itself whether
both sides of any question can be argued. Cf. B 6a.

21. ARISTOTLE *Rhetoric* II 24, 1402a23 And this is what one means
by "making the weaker argument stronger" [B 6b]. And for this
reason men were justly offended by what Protagoras professed to do,
for it is a falsehood and is not a true, but only an apparent, probability.
It belongs, moreover, to no art except rhetoric and eristic. STEPHANUS
BYZANTIUS, under the entry "Abdera": Protagoras, who, according to
Eudoxus [*Elements* fr. 4 VI 78 Gisinger], created the weaker and
stronger argument and taught his pupils to blame and praise the same
person. Cf. C 2.

21a. PLATO *Theaetetus* 166Dff. [Apology of Protagoras] For I say that the truth is as I have written: each one of us is the measure of what is and of what is not, yet one man differs vastly from another—the difference being just this: that different things are and appear to different men. And I am far from denying the existence of wisdom and of wise men; it is rather that I call "wise" precisely that man who, by working a change in us, makes what is good appear and be to any one of us to whom what is evil appears and is. 167B But, I think, when a man's soul is in an evil state, and so has thoughts which suit that state, then a good state of soul makes him think other thoughts, natural to that state, which some men ineptly call "true," whereas I call them better than the former kind but in no way truer. And the wise . . . in matters that concern the body I call physicians, and in matters that concern plants, husbandmen. I maintain, you see, that the latter produce in plants, instead of the harmful sensations which attend sickness in any of them, beneficial and healthy sensations, and true ones;[4] and the wise and good orators make what is beneficial rather than what is harmful appear just to the cities. For whatever sort of thing appears just and honorable to each city *is* so for that city for as long as it so deems. But the wise man makes what is beneficial rather than what is harmful for them in any particular case appear and be just. On the same principle the sophist too, capable as he is of educating in this way those under his instruction, is wise and worth a great deal of money as well to those he has taught. And so it is that some are wiser than others, and no one holds false opinions, and that you, whether you want to or not, must put up with being a measure. For with these arguments this doctrine is saved.

22. ——— *Protagoras* 333D Are then . . . those things good which are beneficial to men? —— Yes, by Zeus, said [Protagoras], and even if things are not beneficial to men I call them good. 334A Do you . . .

---

[4] The text is uncertain. The phrase "and true ones" cannot be correct. A. Diès in *Rev. Phil.*, XXXVII (1913), p. 67, conjectured ἕξεις ("states") in place of ἀληθεῖς ("true ones").

mean, Protagoras, things that are beneficial to no man, or things that are not beneficial at all? And do you call such things as these good? —— Not at all, he said, but I know of many things which are harmful to men, foods and drinks and drugs and countless other things, while others are beneficial; and others are neither beneficial nor harmful to men, but are one or the other to horses, etc. Cf. *DK* 22 B 61; 68 B 172; 90, 1.

23. —— *Theaetetus* 162D [Protagoras speaks] Noble boys and elders, there you sit together ranting and bringing the gods in, the question of whose existence or nonexistence I exclude from my speeches and writings. Cicero *On the nature of the gods* 1 23, 63 When Protagoras of Abdera . . . the very greatest sophist of those times, began a book with the words, "Concerning the gods I am able to say neither that they exist nor that they do not exist," he was banished by order of the Athenians from city and countryside, and his books were burned in public assembly. 12, 29 (*D* 535) Nor indeed does Protagoras, who denies that he has any clear knowledge of the gods, whether they exist or do not exist, and what their nature is, seem to have any conception of the nature of the gods. [From the same source] Philodemus *On Piety* col. 22 p. 89 Gomperz [*Herkulanische Studien* II (Leipzig, 1866)] . . . or those who say that it is unknowable whether any gods exist or of what sort they are. Diogenes of Oenoanda [fr. 12, col. 2, line 1, p. 19 William] Protagoras of Abdera maintained an opinion identical in meaning to that of Diagoras, although he expressed it differently in order to avoid putting it in too forceful a way. For he said that he did not know whether gods exist. But this amounts to saying that he knows they do not exist. Cf. B 4.

24. Plato *Cratylus* 391BC [Socrates to Hermogenes] These are the sophists. To these your own brother Callias paid a great deal of money, and he now enjoys the reputation of wisdom. But since you are not master of your inheritance, you must entreat your brother and ask him to teach you the correctness [viz., of names] in such matters which he learned from Protagoras. —— It would be an odd request indeed on my part, Socrates, if I, who reject altogether the *Truth*[5] of Protagoras, should prize as if they were worth something statements characterized by that kind of truth.

25. —— *Protagoras* 339A It is my view that ... the greatest part of a man's education is skill in poetry, that is to say, being able to understand the utterances of the poets, whether correctly or incorrectly expressed, as well as knowing how to distinguish between them and give an account when questioned. [There follows the interpretation of Simonides.] GNOMOLOGIUM VATICANUM 743 no. 468 [Sternbach *Wiener Studien*] When a maker of verses cursed Protagoras because he would not approve of his poems, his answer was, "My good sir, I am better off enduring your abuse than enduring your poems."

26. PLATO *Phaedrus* 266Dff. [Socrates and Phaedrus] That first of all, at the beginning of the speech, one must have an introduction. I suppose this is what you mean, isn't it, the fine points of the art? —— Yes. —— And secondly, of course, a narration, and testimonies after that, thirdly proofs, and fourthly probabilities. And confirmation and supplementary confirmation: that outstanding word-craftsman, the man from Byzantium, mentions those, I think. —— You mean the admirable Theodorus? [See *DK* 82 A 30.] —— Indeed I do. And how one must carry out refutation and supplementary refutation whether accusing or defending. But shall we not bring on the illustrious Evenus of Paros [*PLG* II 269; *ALG* I 78], who invented insinuation and oblique commendation? Others say that he even recites his oblique reprobations in verse as an aid to memory, wise man that he is. As for Tisias [see *DK* 82 A 7; 85 A 2] and Gorgias, shall we let them rest, the ones who have perceived that the likely is more commendable than the true? Moreover, they use the power of language to make the small seem great and the great seem small, to put the new in an old light and the old in a new, and have invented, for speeches on all subjects, the methods of brevity and uncircumscribed prolixity.

[5] I.e., the work by that title.

Prodicus [see *DK* 84 A 20] laughed once when he heard me say this and said that he alone had discovered the art of appropriate speech: that what one needs is not length or brevity but due measure. —— Very wisely put, Prodicus. —— Aren't we going to mention Hippias [*DK* 86 A 12]? For I think the man from Elis would cast his vote with Prodicus. —— By all means. —— And turning to Polus and his *Word Sanctuaries of the Muses,* what shall we say of them, repetition, for example, and sententiousness, and the figurative style, not to speak of the terms Licymnian which he got as a gift from their inventor for the making of elegant speech? —— Come now, Socrates, didn't Protagoras have some things of the same sort? —— Yes, he had propriety of phrase, my boy, and many other fine things. But in the matter of tearful speeches applied to the aged and the poor, the mighty Chalcedonian [Thrasymachus; see *DK* 85 B 6] has to my mind won the victory with his art, and the man is adept as well not only in enraging the multitude but also in beguiling it again, once angered, with his incantations, as he put it; while in creating and dissipating calumny, whatever its source, he is a master. The last part of a speech—to go on to the next point — seems to be a matter of common agreement among all, though some call it recapitulation and others something else.

27. ARISTOTLE *Rhetoric* III 5, 1407b6   Fourthly, distinguish words by gender, the way Protagoras does, into masculine, feminine, and neuter.

28. —— *On Sophistical Refutations* XIV 173b17   (Solecism) One can have the error itself, the mere appearance of the error, and the mere appearance of avoiding it, as one has, for example, if—as[6] Protagoras used to say—the words "wrath" and "helmet" are masculine;[7] for then someone who says "accursed" in the feminine form (to qualify these nouns) is guilty of solecism according to him, although it seems correct to others, whereas someone who uses the masculine form

---

[6] Read ὅ instead of ὁ. See W. D. Ross, ed., *Aristotelis Topica et Sophistici Elenchi* (Oxford, 1958).

[7] The two words in question are actually feminine.

seems to, but does not, commit a solecism. Cf. C 3; PLATO *Cratylus* 430Dff.

29. —— *Poetics* 19, 1456b15 For why should one assume that Protagoras is right in criticizing as faulty the phrase "Sing, goddess, the wrath . . ." on the grounds that it is a command purporting to be a request? For, he says, to bid someone to do or not to do something is a command. Cf. above A 1 (53).

30. AMMONIUS SCHOLIUM on HOMER [*POxy* II no. 68] col. XII 20 on *Iliad* XXI 240 Protagoras says that the next episode, the fight between Xanthus and a mortal, is meant to divide the battle, in order to make a transition to the battle of the gods; perhaps also in order to glorify Achilles and . . . the dangers . . . catching . . . leaped no longer in the stream bed but on the plain.[8]

B. FRAGMENTS

PROTAGORAS' *TRUTH* OR *REFUTATIONS*

1. SEXTUS *Against the Schoolmasters* VII 60 Some also reckoned Protagoras of Abdera in the company of those philosophers who do away with the standard of judgment, since he says that all appearances and opinions are true and that truth is a relative matter because a man's every perception or opinion immediately exists in relation to him. At any rate, he begins the *Refutations* with the following pronouncement: "Of all things the measure is man, of things that are that[9] they are, and of things that are not that they are not." Cf. above A 1 (51), A 13, A 24; opposed in PLATO *Laws* IV 716C.

---

[8] The text is mutilated.

[9] The Greek word ὡς ("that"), used here and in other quotations of this statement, also means "how," and some prefer to translate it so. For discussion of this problem, see Kurt von Fritz, *RE*, s.v. "Protagoras."

PLATO *Theaetetus* 151E–152A [Socrates and Theaetetus] It seems to me that this account you've given of knowledge is not a bad one at all; in fact, it was also Protagoras' version of the matter. But he expressed the same view in rather different words. For he says somewhere that of all things the measure is man, of things that are that they are, and of things that are not that they are not. You've read it, I suppose? —— I've read it many times. —— Now doesn't he say[10] something of this sort, that as each thing appears to me, so it is for me, and as it appears to you, so in turn it is for you, you being a man, and I too? . . . Isn't it true that at times, when the same wind is blowing, one of us will be cold and the other will not, or the one slightly and the other extremely so? —— Indeed it is. —— Now in that case shall we say that the wind is cold in itself or not cold, or shall we agree with Protagoras that it is cold to the man who feels cold but not so to the other? —— We shall agree with him, it seems. —— It also "appears" so to each one, doesn't it? —— Yes. —— And "it appears" surely is the same as "he perceives"? —— It is. —— Appearance, then, and perception are equivalent when one is speaking of warmth or anything of that sort. Then things are, I venture, for each person just as he perceives them. 161C [Socrates:] On the whole I'm quite delighted with his statement that what appears to each man also *is*. But I'm surprised at the way he started his account, that he didn't say at the beginning of his *Truth* that of all things the measure is the pig or the baboon or some other even more outlandish choice from among creatures endowed with sensation, so that he might have commenced speaking to us with an air of magnificence and utter disdain, demonstrating that, whereas we stood in awe of him as of a god because of his wisdom, he was in fact no more intelligent than a tadpole, to say nothing of other men. Cf. A 21a.

ON BEING

2. PORPHYRY, from Book 1 of the *Lecture on Literature*, in EUSEBIUS *Preparation of the Gospel* x 3, 25 Books written by Plato's predecessors

[10] Possibly "mean."

are scarce; otherwise one might perhaps have detected more of the philosopher's ⟨plagiarisms⟩. In a passage that I came upon by chance while reading Protagoras' book *On Being*, I do find Protagoras using similar counterarguments against those who propose being as one. For I took pains to memorize the passage word for word. [Eusebius adds:] And having said this much he sets out his proofs at some length.

THE GREAT SPEECH

3. ANECDOTA PARISIENSIA I 171, 31 *On Hippomachus* B 3 [ed. A. Bohler, *Sophistae anonymi Protreptici fragmenta* (Leipzig, 1903), p. 46, 5] In the work entitled the *Great Speech* Protagoras said: "Teaching requires natural endowment and practice," and "They must learn starting young." He would not have said this if he had himself been a late learner, which was the opinion that Epicurus held and expressed about Protagoras [fr. 173 Usener; *DK* 68 A 9].

ON THE GODS

4. EUSEBIUS *Preparation of the Gospel* XIV 3, 7   For Protagoras, the disciple of Democritus, acquired the reputation of an atheist. He is said, at any rate, to have begun his treatise *On the Gods* in this fashion: "Concerning the gods I do not know . . . form they might have." DIOGENES LAERTIUS IX 51 [above A 1 (51)] "Concerning . . . man's life." Cf. A 2, A 3, A 12, A 23.

"Concerning the gods I cannot know either that they exist or that they do not exist, or what form they might have,[11] for there is much to prevent one's knowing: the obscurity of the subject[12] and the shortness of man's life."

---

[11] "Or what form they might have" is omitted in Diogenes.
[12] Possibly "the imperceptibility [of the gods]." See Theodor Gomperz, *Die Apologie der Heilkunst*, Sitzungsberichte Kaiserl. Akad. Wien, Philos.-Hist. Classe, 120 (1889), IX. Abhandlung, 143.

CONTRADICTORY ARGUMENTS, IN TWO BOOKS
[See above A 1 (55).]

5. DIOGENES LAERTIUS III 37 Euphorion [fr. 152 Scheidweiler] and Panaetius [fr. 50 Fowler] have stated that the opening words of [Plato's] *Republic* were found set out in many different arrangements, and Aristoxenus [fr. 33 *FHG* II 282] claims that almost the whole of the *Republic* can be read in the *Contradictory Arguments* of Protagoras. (57) The *Republic* . . . which, according to the second book of Favorinus' *Miscellaneous History* [fr. 21 *FHG* III 580], is also found almost in its entirety in the *Contradictory Arguments* of Protagoras.

DOUBTFUL TITLES

THE ART OF DEBATING [See above A 1 (55).]

6. CICERO *Brutus* 12, 46 (from ARISTOTLE *Compilation of "Arts"* fr. 137 Rose) . . . and that Protagoras wrote down and prepared disputations on notable subjects, which are now called "general arguments (*loci communes*)." QUINTILIAN III 1, 10 Protagoras of Abdera, from whom Euathlus [see above A 1 (54), (56), A 4] is said to have learned, for a fee of ten thousand denarii, the art which he had created. 1, 12 (*DK* 84 A 10) Of these Protagoras and Gorgias are said to have been the first to discuss general arguments (*loci communes*), and Prodicus, Hippias, Protagoras again, and Thrasymachus the first to discuss the emotions.

6a. DIOGENES LAERTIUS IX 51 [See above A 1 (51).] [Protagoras] was the first to say that on every issue there are two arguments opposed to each other. Cf. A 20.

6b. ARISTOTLE *Rhetoric* II 24, 1402a23 Cf. A 21. . . . making the weaker argument stronger.

ON MATHEMATICS [See above A 1 (55).]

7. ARISTOTLE *Metaphysics* III 2, 997b32   Nor is it true to say that
mensuration has for its object perceptible magnitudes which are also
perishable, for then it would perish when they did. But on the other
hand astronomy surely does not have for its object perceptible magnitudes nor does it deal with the heaven that we see. For perceptible
lines are not such as the geometer speaks of either, for nothing perceptible is straight or round in that way; for the circle touches the
straightedge not at a point, but as Protagoras said it did when he
refuted the geometers, nor. . . . Cf. A 5 and A 15.

7a. PHILODEMUS *On Poetry*, according to J. Heidmann, *Der Papyrus
1676 der Herculanensischen Bibliothek: Philodemus περὶ ποιημάτων* (Diss.
Bonn, 1937) C I 12ff.   . . . that the subject matter is unknowable
and the terminology repugnant, as Protagoras says of mathematics.

ON WRESTLING [See above A 1 (55).]

8. PLATO *Sophist* 232DE   Moreover, concerning the arts in general
and every art in particular, there have been committed to writing and
published somewhere, for those who wish to learn them, the arguments
to be used in controversy with the actual practitioners of each art.
—— I suppose you mean the writings of Protagoras about wrestling
and the other arts. . . . 233A Then how could someone who was himself ignorant ever have anything worthwhile to say in opposition to
a man with knowledge? —— He could not.

8a. ON GOVERNMENT [See above A 1 (55).] Cf. B 5.

8b. ON THE ORIGINAL STATE OF THINGS[13]
[See above A 1 (55).] Cf. C 1.

[13] Possibly *On the Original Social* [or *Political*] *Structure*. Some connection is
likely between this title and the subject matter of the *Protagoras* myth (C 1).

8c. ON AMBITION [See above A 1 (55).]

8d. ON THE VIRTUES [See above A 1 (55).]

8e. ON HUMAN ERRORS [See above A 1 (55).]

8f. DIRECTION [See above A 1 (55).]

8g. TRIAL OVER A FEE [See above A 1 (55).] Cf. A 1 (56); B 6.

8h. ON THOSE IN HADES [See above A 1 (55).][14]

FROM UNSPECIFIED WRITINGS

9. [PLUTARCH] *Letter of Consolation to Apollonius* 33 p. 118E   Pericles was called "the Olympian" because of his extraordinary powers of speech and understanding. The story is told that when he learned that both his sons, Paralus and Xanthippus, had perished (as Protagoras says in the following passage: "For though his young. . . . in like circumstances"); for,[15] right after the message about his two sons, Pericles, wearing a crown in spite of all, in accordance with ancestral custom, and clad in white, addressed the people, "taking the lead in good counsels" [HOMER *Iliad* II 273] and rousing the Athenians more than ever for the war.

"For though his young and beautiful sons had died within a period of only eight days he bore it without grieving. For he maintained his tranquillity of mind, a fact which served him well every day by bringing good fortune, calming distress, and raising his reputation

---

[14] A work by this title is also ascribed to Democritus. *DK* 68 B 0 cff.

[15] The long inserted quotation has altered the syntax of the sentence.

among the people. For at the sight of the manly way he endured his sorrows all judged him high-minded and brave and superior to themselves,[16] knowing well their own helplessness in like circumstances."

10. STOBAEUS III 29, 80   Protagoras said that art was nothing without practice and practice nothing without art.

11. [PLUTARCH] *On Practice* 178, 25 [*Rheinisches Museum*, XXVII (1872), p. 526]   Protagoras has said, furthermore: Education does not sprout in the soul unless one goes to a great depth.[17]

POORLY ATTESTED

12. GRAECO-SYRIAN TEXTS trans. into German by Ryssel[18] [*Rheinisches Museum*, LI (1896), p. 539, n. 32]   Protagoras has said: Toil and work and instruction and education and wisdom are the crown of glory which is woven from the flowers of an eloquent tongue and placed on the heads of those who love it. The tongue's use is not effortless, to be sure, yet its blossoms are abundant and ever fresh, and the on-lookers and those who applaud and the teachers rejoice, and the students make progress and the fools are annoyed—or perhaps they are not even annoyed, since they are not intelligent enough.

C. IMITATION

1. PLATO *Protagoras* 320C [Myth of Protagoras]   There once was a time when there were gods but no mortal creatures. But when   D the appointed time came for these too to have their beginnings, the gods

---

[16] Possibly "master of himself."

[17] The English version of this fragment is simply a translation of a German version (by J. Gildemeister and F. Bücheler, reproduced in *DK*) of a Syriac translation of the lost Greek original.

[18] The English translation is from the German.

molded them within the earth from a mixture of earth and fire and whatever is compounded with fire and earth. When they were about to lead them forth to the light, they bade Prometheus and Epimetheus fit them out and distribute to each suitable powers. Epimetheus asked Prometheus whether he might himself distribute. "And when I have distributed," he said, "inspect." And so he persuaded him and made his distribution. And as he distributed, to some   E he allotted strength but not speed, while the weaker ones he equipped with speed. Others he armed, while for those whom he had left unarmed he devised some other endowment to keep them safe. To those invested with smallness of frame he allotted winged flight or a home in the earth, but those whom he made large   321A found safety in size itself. It was in this same fashion that he upheld equality among the others too as he distributed. All this he devised as a precaution lest any kind of creature should suffer destruction. But when he had furnished them with ways to escape mutual death-dealing, he devised ready protection against Zeus' seasons by clothing them in thick hair and firm hides, ample defense against winter but effective against summer's heat as well. These were also meant to provide bedding, appropriate and   B self-grown, for each creature's repose. Some he shod with hooves, others with stiff and bloodless nails. He then gave to each its own type of nourishment, to some earth's pasture, to others the fruit of trees, to others roots; and some he allowed to prey on other animals for food. And to some he gave meager progeny, while those others whom they ate he made prolific, so preserving their stock. Now Epimetheus, who was not nearly clever enough, unwittingly   C squandered on the dumb beasts all the endowments he had to give. There was left to him, then, still unequipped, the race of men, and he was at a loss what to do with it. In his perplexity Prometheus came to him to oversee the distribution. He saw the other animals fittingly provided in every way, but man he saw naked and unshod and unbedded and unarmed. And the appointed day was already at hand, too, on which man, like the others, must emerge from the earth into the light. At a loss as to what means he could find of saving   D man, Prometheus stole from Hephaestus and Athena their technical wisdom and with it fire (for without fire no one could have acquired it or used it), and so it was that he gave man this gift. Now in this way man got the wisdom required to live, but political wisdom he did not have, for it was in Zeus' possession. It was not now possible for Prometheus to enter the citadel where Zeus had his home (moreover, Zeus' sentinels were terrible), but he did enter E secretly into the common dwelling-place of Athena and Hephaestus, in which they practiced their arts. Having stolen the fiery art of Hephaestus along with Athena's art, he gave them to man. Hence it was that man won ease of livelihood, whereas, 322A the story goes, Prometheus later underwent prosecution for theft. Since man had won a share in what was properly divine, he became, to begin with, by virtue of his kinship with the god, the only animal to worship gods, and he undertook to build altars and statues of the gods. Then too, he soon devised, through his skill, articulate speech and names for things, and invented houses and clothing and footwear and beds and nourishment from the earth. Thus provided, men at first lived scattered, B and there were no cities. As a result, they were being destroyed by the wild beasts, because they were in every respect weaker than these. Their skill as craftsmen was sufficient to help them get food, but it failed them in their warfare against the beasts; for they did not yet possess the political art, of which the art of war is a part. So they sought safety in numbers by founding cities. Now whenever they formed communities they would wrong one another, lacking as they did the political art, with the consequence that they would disperse again and be destroyed. Zeus, therefore, C fearing that our race might be destroyed altogether, sent Hermes to bring to men reverence and justice, in order that there might be governments for the cities and bonds to join men in friendship. Now Hermes asked Zeus how he should go about giving justice and reverence to men. "Shall I distribute these in the same way that the arts have been distributed? For example, one physician is enough to treat many laymen, and it is the same with other craftsmen. Shall I place justice and reverence among men in this same fashion, or shall I distribute them to everyone?" D "To everyone," said Zeus, "and let everyone have a share in them, for cities would not come into being if only a few shared in these as they do in the other arts. And lay down this law by my order: let them put to death as a plague on the city the man who cannot share in reverence and justice." Cf. MOSCHION fr. 6 *TGF* p. 813; and ARISTOTLE *On the Parts of Animals* IV 10, 687a23: Those who say that man is not well put together, but in fact worse than any other animal (for they say he is unshod and naked and without armor for defense), are wrong. Cf. also *DK* 88 B 25.

2. ARISTOPHANES *Clouds* 112ff. Cf. A 21. They say that both arguments can be found among them, the stronger, whoever he is, and the weaker. Of these two arguments, the one—the weaker—(115) wins out, they claim, by saying what is more unjust. Cf. the Agon of the Just and the Unjust Argument 889ff.

3. ——— ———658ff. [Socrates and Strepsiades] Cf. A 28. But you must learn other things before these, like which quadrupeds are properly masculine. (660) —— But I know the masculine ones, unless I'm out of my mind: ram, billy goat, bull, dog, fowl [*alektryon*]. —— Do you see what's happening? You're calling the female a "fowl" and the male the same thing. —— How? Tell me. —— How? Like this: "fowl" and "fowl." (665) —— By Poseidon, I do! But now what should I call them? —— "She-fowl" [*alektryaina*] for one. For the other, "he-fowl" [*alektor*]. —— "She-fowl"? By the air above, that's superb! For this lesson alone I'll fill your barley bowl to the brim. (670) —— There! You've done it again. You call the bowl [*tēn kardopon*] (671) masculine though it's feminine . . . (677) But what must I call it from now on? —— Call it a "she-bowl" [*tēn kardopēn*], the way you call Sostrate "she." —— The "she-bowl"—feminine? —— Right you are.

4. EURIPIDES *Bacchae* 199 [Cadmus and Tiresias] Cf. B 1. I am a mortal and do not despise the gods. (200) —— No, and we do not practice cleverness on divine beings. The traditions of our fathers, a

27

legacy as old as time itself—no argument will overthrow[19] those, in spite of the wisdom invented by subtle brains.

5. (?) AESCHINES THE SOCRATIC *Callias* fr. 16 p. 50 Krauss   Cf. *DK* 84 A 4b.

---

[19] The verb used here, καταβάλλω ("overthrow," "refute"), may be an allusion to Protagoras' book entitled *Truth* or *Refutations* (καταβάλλοντες). Cf. B 1.

81. XENIADES

translated by WILLIAM O'NEILL

Xeniades was a native of Corinth, presumably somewhat earlier than Democritus, who mentions him. (Cf. *Zeller-Nestle* I [6th ed.] p. 1369 n. 2; M. Untersteiner, *The Sophists*, trans. K. Freeman [Oxford, 1954], pp. 162–63.)

SEXTUS *Against the Schoolmasters* VII 53[1] And Xeniades the Corinthian, whom Democritus [DK 68 B 163] mentions, said that everything is false, that every sense-image and opinion lie, and that everything which comes to be, comes to be from the nonexistent, and everything which passes away, passes away into the nonexistent. Virtually he holds the same opinion as Xenophanes.[2] Cf. *Outlines of Pyrrhonism* II 18, 76 (*Rheinisches Museum*, LXIV [1909], p. 262).

[1] Cf. Sextus *Against the Schoolmasters* VII 388.
[2] Cf. *DK* 21 A 1, A 12, A 28, A 31–35, A 49; B 27, B 34.

82. GORGIAS

translated by GEORGE KENNEDY

Gorgias was born shortly before 480 B.C. in Leontini in Sicily and lived there for much of his life. He may have studied with Empedocles and certainly was familiar with the philosophy and rhetoric of the time. His only definite philosophical work, *On the Nonexistent or On Nature*, is to be dated to the late 440s. In 427, he was sent as an ambassador by Leontini to Athens, and subsequently he seems to have visited the city repeatedly or even to have settled there. His extant rhetorical pieces and fragments date from the late fifth and early fourth centuries. Sometime after 380, he removed to the court of Jason at Pherae in Thessaly, where he died at the age of at least one hundred and five.

A. LIFE AND TEACHINGS

1. PHILOSTRATUS *Lives of the Sophists* I 9, 1 Leontini in Sicily was the birthplace of Gorgias, a man to whom as to a father we think it right to refer the art of the sophists. For if we consider how much Aeschylus contributed to tragedy by adorning it with costume and the high buskin, and types of heroes, and messengers from abroad or from the house, and with the distinction between suitable onstage and offstage action, Gorgias would correspond to this in his contribution to his fellow artists. (2) For he was an example of forcefulness to the sophists and of unexpected expression and of inspiration and of the grand style for great subjects and of detached phrases and transitions, by which speech becomes sweeter than it has been and more impressive, and he also introduced poetic words for ornament and dignity. (3) It was said at the beginning of my discussion [A 1a]

that he also improvised easily, and it is no wonder if he was admired by many when he spoke in Athens, although by then an old man, and I understand that he attracted the attention of the most admired men, Critias and Alcibiades who were young, and Thucydides and Pericles who were already old. Agathon too, the tragic poet, whom Comedy regards as wise and eloquent, often Gorgianizes in his iambic verse. (4) He was conspicuous also at the festivals of the Greeks, declaiming his *Pythian Speech* [B 9] from the altar at the temple of the Pythian god, where in addition a golden statue of himself was set up. His *Olympic Speech* [B 7, 8a] dealt with political matters of the greatest importance, for seeing Greece involved in civil dissension, he became a counselor of concord to her inhabitants, turning their attention against the barbarians and persuading them to regard as prizes to be won by their arms, not each other's cities, but the territory of the barbarians. (5) The *Funeral Oration* [B 6], which he delivered at Athens, was spoken over those who fell in the wars, whom the Athenians bury at public expense with eulogies, and it is composed with surpassing cleverness. For though inciting the Athenians against the Medes and Persians and contending for the same idea as in the *Olympic Speech*, he mentioned nothing about concord with the Greeks, since he was addressing the Athenians, who were eager for empire, which could not be obtained unless they adopted extremism, but he dwelt on praise of the victories over the Medes, showing them that victories over the barbarians require hymns of celebration, victories over the Greeks require laments [B 5b]. (6) It is said that Gorgias lived to the age of one hundred and eight years without suffering physical incapacity from old age but sound of body to the end and with the mind of a young man.

1a. ———— ———— 11 Gorgias of Leontini was the founder of the older type [i.e., of sophistry] in Thessaly. . . . Gorgias [seems] to have begun extemporaneous oratory. For coming into the theater of the Athenians he had the boldness to say "suggest a subject," and he was the first to proclaim himself willing to take this chance, showing apparently that he knew everything and would trust to the moment to speak on any subject.

2. SUIDAS   Gorgias, son of Charmantides, of Leontini, orator, student of Empedocles, teacher of Polus of Acragas and Pericles and Isocrates and Alcidamas of Elaea, who also took over direction of his school. He was the brother of the physician Herodicus [A 2a].

Porphyry places him in the eightieth Olympiad [460–457], but it is necessary to regard him as older.

He was the first to give to the rhetorical genre the verbal power and art of deliberate culture and employed tropes and metaphors and figurative language and hypallage and catachresis and hyperbaton and doublings of words and repetitions and apostrophes and clauses of equal length. He charged each of his students a hundred minas. He lived one hundred and nine years and wrote a great deal.

2a. PLATO *Gorgias* 448B   If Gorgias happened to be acquainted with the art of his brother Herodicus, by what name would we appropriately call him?

3. DIOGENES LAERTIUS VIII 58, 59 Cf. *DK* 31 A 1 (58).   [Empedocles] was both a physician and the finest orator. At least, Gorgias of Leontini was his student, and a man outstanding in rhetoric and the author of an Art. Satyrus [III fr. 12 p. 162] claims that he said he was with Empedocles when the latter played the wizard.

4. DIODORUS SICULUS XII 53, 1   [In the archonship of Eucles, 427 B.C.] At this time in Sicily the people of Leontini, who were colonists of the Chalcideans but relatives of the Athenians, happened to be involved in war with the Syracusans. Being hard pressed in the war and in danger of being forcibly overrun because of the numerical superiority of the Syracusans, they sent ambassadors to Athens, asking the democracy to come to their aid as quickly as possible and to rescue their city from its dangers.   (2) The chief of the delegation was the orator Gorgias, in power of speech by far the most eminent of the men of his time. He was the first to invent rhetorical techniques and so surpassed others in sophistry that he received a fee of one hundred minas from students.   (3) When he had arrived in Athens and been brought before the people, he addressed the Athenians on the subject of an alliance, and by the novelty of his style he amazed the Athenians, who were cultivated and fond of letters. (4) He was the first to use extravagant figures of speech marked by deliberate art: antithesis and clauses of exactly or approximately equal length and rhythm and others of such a sort, which at the time were thought worthy of acceptance because of the strangeness of the method, but now seem tiresome and often appear ridiculous and excessively contrived. (5) Finally, after persuading the Athenians to make an alliance with the Leontinians, and having himself won admiration in Athens for his rhetorical art, he returned home to Leontini. [Derived from Timaeus; cf. DIONYSIUS OF HALICARNASSUS *Lysias* 3.] Gorgias of Leontini illustrates this, making the style in many places very labored and bombastic and declaiming some passages "not unlike certain dithyrambs" [PLATO *Phaedrus* 238D], and among his associates those like Licymnius and Polus do the same. Poetic and figurative style captured the Athenian orators, according to Timaeus [fr. 95 *FHG* 1 216], beginning when Gorgias on an embassy to Athens amazed his hearers in the assembly, but in truth it was always somewhat admired even earlier. Cf. *Prolegomenòn Syllaloge Rhetores Graeci* XIV 27, 11ff. Rabe.

5. XENOPHON *Anabasis* II 6, 16ff. Proxenus of Boeotia, when he was just a lad, wanted to be a man who could do great things, and because of this desire he paid a fee to Gorgias of Leontini.

5a. ARISTOPHANES *Birds* 1694

> There is in Phanae by the
>   Waterclock a rascally race
>   Of those who live by their tongues,
> Who reap and sow
> And gather in and play the sycophant
>   With tongues. They are
>   Barbarians by birth,
> Gorgiases and Philips,
> And when these Philips

Who live by their tongues
Are sacrificed, everywhere in Attica
The tongue is cut from their bodies.

—— *Wasps* 420

By Heracles they have stings too. Don't
you see, O master?

——Stings by which in a lawsuit they killed
Philip, the offspring of Gorgias.

6. [PLUTARCH] *Lives of the Ten Orators* p. 832F   [Antiphon of Rhamnus] was born during the Persian wars [that is, 480 B.C.] and about the time of Gorgias the sophist, but a little later than he. Cf. *DK* 41, 1a.

7. PAUSANIAS VI 17, 7ff. It is possible also to see the statue of Gorgias of Leontini. Eumolpus, a descendant in the third generation of Deicrates, who married Gorgias' sister, claims on the inscription that he dedicated the statue at Olympia. This Gorgias was the son of Charmantides and is said to have been the first to rescue care for speech, which had been generally neglected and had almost been forgotten among men. They say that Gorgias was famous for the speeches he gave at the Olympic games and when he came on an embassy to the Athenians with Tisias. . . . (9) But Gorgias acquired greater honor than the latter among the Athenians, and when Jason was ruling in Thessaly [± 380–370], though the school of Polycrates had acquired by no means little fame in Athens, he preferred Gorgias to Polycrates. They say that Gorgias lived five years beyond the century mark. X 18, 7 [Delphi] The golden statue, a dedication of Gorgias of Leontini, is Gorgias himself. Cf. ATHENAEUS XIX 505D; [DIO] 37, 28. CICERO *On the orator* III 32, 129 For whom [Gorgias] so great honor was held by Greece that to him alone of all those at Delphi not a gilded but a golden statue was erected. PLINY *Natural History* XXXIII 83 Gorgias of Leontini was the first man to dedicate a solid gold statue of himself, which he did around Olympiad LXX [?] in the temple at Delphi. So great was the profit from teaching the art of oratory.

8. EPIGRAMMATA GRAECA 875a [p. 534 Kaibel] [Beginning of the fourth century, found in 1876 in Olympia]

Charmantides' son, Gorgias of Leontini.
a. Deicrates married the sister of Gorgias.
  And from her was born to him Hippocrates.
Hippocrates' son was Eumolpus, who dedicated this statue
  For two reasons, learning and love.
b. No one of mortals before discovered a finer art
  Than Gorgias to arm the soul for contests of excellence;
His statue stands as well in the vale of Apollo
  Not as a show of wealth, but of the piety of his character.

8a. PLATO *Apology* 19E It seems to me [Socrates] a good thing, however, if someone be able to educate men as can Gorgias of Leontini and Prodicus of Ceos and Hippias of Elis.

9. AELIAN *Miscellaneous History* XII 32 The story is forgotten that Hippias and Gorgias appeared in purple clothes.

10. APOLLODORUS [*FGrHist* 244 F 33; see *DK* 31 A 1 (58).] He lived nine years past the century mark. PORPHYRIUS (See above A 2.) OLYMPIODORUS on PLATO *Gorgias* [*Neue Jahrbuch* Supplement 14 (1848) ed. A. Jahn, p. 112] Secondly, we shall say that they flourished at the same time: Socrates in the third year of the seventy-seventh Olympiad [470–469], and Empedocles the Pythagorean, the teacher of Gorgias, studied with him.[1] It is well known also that Gorgias wrote a fine treatise *On Nature* in the eighty-fourth Olympiad [444–441]. So that Socrates was earlier by twenty-four years or a little more. Moreover, Plato says in the *Theaetetus* [183E; cf. 28 A 5], "When I [Socrates] was quite young I met Parmenides, who was very old, and found him a most profound man." This Parmenides was the teacher of Emped-

---

[1] Or, adopting the conjecture of Cousin, "with Parmenides."

ocles, the teacher of Gorgias. And Gorgias was rather old; for, as has been said, he died at the age of one hundred and nine. Thus they lived about the same time. Cf. 82 B 2.

11. ATHENAEUS XII 548CD   Gorgias of Leontini, about whom the same Clearchus says in book eight of his *Lives* [fr. 15 *FHG* II 308] that because he lived sensibly he survived with all his faculties for nearly eighty [?] years. And when someone asked him what regimen he observed to live such a great length of time so pleasantly and with perception he said, "By never doing anything for the sake of pleasure." Demetrius of Byzantium in the fourth book *On Poems* says "Gorgias of Leontini, when asked what was the cause of his living more than a hundred years, said 'Never doing anything for the sake of anybody else. [?]' "

12. CICERO *Cato* 5, 12   His [Isocrates'] teacher Gorgias of Leontini lived a hundred and seven years and never relaxed in his effort and labor. When he was asked why he wanted to remain alive so long he said, "I have no cause for complaint against old age."

13. PLINY *Natural History* VII 156   It is beyond doubt that Gorgias of Sicily lived a hundred and eight years.   [LUCIAN] *Long-Lived Men* 23 Among the orators, Gorgias, whom some call a sophist, lived a hundred and eight years and died by abstaining from food. They say that when he was asked the reason for his prolonged old age and health with all his faculties he said it was because he never attended other people's parties. Cf. CENSORINUS 15, 3; see 68 A 6.

14. QUINTILIAN III 1, 8ff.   The earliest writers of Arts were the Sicilians, Corax and Tisias. They were followed by a man from the same island, named Gorgias of Leontini, said to have been a pupil of Empedocles. Because of his very long life (for he lived one hundred and nine years) he had many different contemporaries and thus was both a rival of those of whom I spoke above and survived to the time of Socrates.

15. AELIAN *Miscellaneous History* II 35   Gorgias of Leontini at the end of his life and in advanced old age, overtaken by a feeling of weakness, lay down and was gradually slipping off into sleep. When one of his friends came over to see him and asked what he was doing, Gorgias answered, "Sleep already begins to hand me over to his brother Death."

15a. ATHENAEUS XI 505D   It is said that also Gorgias himself, having read the dialogue which bears his name, said to his friends, "How well Plato knows how to satirize!"

16. QUINTILIAN III 1, 13   Many followed them, but the most famous of the students of Gorgias was Isocrates. Although authorities do not agree about his teacher, we follow the view of Aristotle [fr. 139 Rose]. Cf. A 12.

17. [PLUTARCH] *Lives of the Ten Orators* p. 838D   [Tomb of Isocrates as described by the guidebook writer Heliodorus] Near it was a tablet showing poets and his teachers, among whom is Gorgias looking at an astronomical globe and Isocrates himself standing by.

18. ISOCRATES 15, 155   Of the sophists whom we call to mind, Gorgias of Leontini acquired the most money. After spending his time in the neighborhood of Thessaly when its inhabitants were the most prosperous of the Greeks and after living a very long life and being engaged in the making of money (156) and since he did not inhabit any one city steadily, not spending money for public benefits nor being required to pay a tax, moreover neither marrying a wife nor begetting children but being free of this continual and most expensive demand, after having all these advantages in acquiring more than other men, he left behind him only ten thousand staters.

19. PLATO *Meno* 70AB   O Meno, in the past, Thessalians were fortunate among the Greeks and were admired for their horsemanship and wealth, but now, it seems to me, also for their wisdom, and not the least admired are the Larisians, the fellow citizens of your companion Aristippus. You can thank Gorgias for this. For after arriving in the city he made the leading Aleuadae, of whom your lover Aristippus is one, and the other Thessalians into lovers of wisdom. And moreover, he has accustomed you to the custom of answering fearlessly and haughtily if someone asks something, as is right for those who know, just as he makes himself available to any of the Greeks to ask anything he wishes and there is no one he does not answer. ARISTOTLE *Politics* III 1, 1275b26   [Definition of civic rights] Gorgias of Leontini, partly at a loss what to say, partly in irony, said that just as things made by mortar-makers are mortars, so also Larisians are those made by public servants, for they are a group of Larisofiers.

20. PLATO *Gorgias* 447C   I wish to learn from the man [Gorgias] what is the function of his art and what it is he proclaims and teaches: let him postpone other demonstration to another time, as you say. ——— There is nothing like asking him, O Socrates. For this was part of the demonstration. At least he urged those inside the house to ask what anyone wanted and said he would answer all questions.   449C [Gorgias speaks] And again this is one point of those that I am making, that no one speaks the same things in fewer words than I do. ——— This is what we need, O Gorgias. Make me a demonstration of this thing, that is, of speaking briefly, and of speaking extensively on another occasion.

21. ——— *Meno* 95C   I most admire Gorgias for this, O Socrates, that one never heard him promising this [i.e., to be a teacher of excellence], but he even laughs at others when he hears them so promising. Rather he thinks it is his duty to make clever speakers.

22. ——— *Gorgias* 456B   It has often happened that I [Gorgias] have gone with my brother [A 2, 2a] with other physicians to the bedside of a sick man who was unwilling to drink medicine or allow the doctor to cut or cauterize him, and though the doctor could not persuade him, I did persuade by means of no other art than rhetoric.

23. ARISTOTLE *Rhetoric* III 3, 1406b14   The remark of Gorgias to the swallow, when it flew over him and let go its droppings, is in the best tragic style. He said, "Shame on you, Philomela." If a bird did it there was no disgrace, but it was shameful for a girl. His reproach was clever, therefore, since he called the bird what it was rather than what it is.

24. PHILOSTRATUS *Lives of the Sophists* p. 4, 4 Kayser   Gorgias, laughing at Prodicus for speaking what was old-fashioned and had often been said before, turned his own attention to what was timely. Yet he did not escape spite. For there was a certain Chaerephon at Athens. . . . This Chaerephon, carping at Gorgias' seriousness, said, "Why, Gorgias, do beans inflate the belly but do not fan the fire?" Gorgias was not disturbed by the question and said, "I leave this to you to consider; for my part I have long known that the earth produces reeds for such ends."[2]

25. PLATO *Phaedrus* 267A   [See *DK* 80 A 26.] CICERO *Brutus* 12, 47   Commonplaces [80 B 6]   [They say] that Gorgias did the same in that he wrote passages of praise and blame of individual things because he believed the most characteristic task of the orator was to be able to amplify a subject by praise and, on the other hand, to deflate it by vituperation.

26. PLATO *Philebus* 58A   I often heard Gorgias say that the art of rhetoric differs from all other arts. Under its influence all things are willingly but not forcibly made slaves. CICERO *On invention* 5, 2   Gorgias of Leontini, almost the earliest rhetorician, thought that an orator ought to be able to speak best on all subjects.

27. PLATO *Gorgias* 450B   [Gorgias is speaking] In the case of the other arts, knowledge is, so to speak, concerned with handicrafts and similar activities, but there is no such handiwork of rhetoric, but all

---

[2] I.e., as blowpipes for fires and as rods to beat the insolent.

activity and effect comes through words. For this reason I think the art of rhetoric is concerned with words, defining it correctly as I claim. OLYMPIODORUS on this passage p. 131 Jahn [Jahn's *Archiv* Supplement 14, 131] Those clever about words criticize the two words "handiwork" and "effect" as not in good usage, for in truth they are not found. We conclude, therefore, that since it is Gorgias who says them, Plato is borrowing from him words which are localisms, for Gorgias came from Leontini.

28. PLATO *Gorgias* 453A If I understand at all, you [Gorgias] are saying that rhetoric is the artificer of persuasion and all its business and its real essence is directed toward this goal. 455A Rhetoric is then, as it seems, the artificer of persuasion which is credible but not instructive, concerned with the just and the unjust.

29. ARISTOTLE *Rhetoric* III 1, 1404a24 Since, though speaking absurdities, the poets seemed to have acquired their present fame through their style, for this reason prose style was in the first instance poetic, like that of Gorgias. And even now, many uneducated people think such stylists express themselves best. SYRIANUS *On Hermogenes* I 11, 20 Rabe [DIONYSIUS OF HALICARNASSUS *On Imitation* 8 p. 31, 13 Usener] Gorgias transferred poetic expression to civic discourse because he did not think it right for the orator to be like private citizens. But Lysias did the opposite, etc. [Similarly I 10, 13 Rabe; 7 p. 30, 20 Usener]

30. CICERO *Orator* 12, 39 They say that Thrasymachus of Chalcedon [85 A 2, 3] and Gorgias of Leontini were the first to have tried these figures [antithesis, parison, etc.], and after them Theodorus of Byzantium and many others whom Socrates in the *Phaedrus* calls "skilled in tricking out a speech." Cf. 80 A 26 [266 E].

31. ———— ———— 49, 165 We have learned that Gorgias was the leader in pursuit of this concinnity.

32. —— —— 52, 175 [Of rhythm] the first discoverer was Thrasymachus, all of whose almost too rhythmical writings survive. For Gorgias was the first to employ like joined to like with similar endings and, conversely, opposites balanced with opposites, phrases which usually come out rhythmically even if one does nothing to make them do so, but he uses them excessively. . . . (176) Gorgias, however, is rather partial to this sort of thing and immoderately abuses these "festive decorations," as he regards them. Isocrates managed them with greater restraint, although in Thessaly when a young man he had been a student of the already aged Gorgias. DIONYSIUS OF HALICARNASSUS *Isaeus* 19 But keeping in mind that no one was better than Isocrates in this poetical style and elevated and pompous way of speaking, I have intentionally omitted those whom I knew to be less successful in these particular forms, regarding Gorgias of Leontini as one who was exiled from his native country and became repeatedly puerile.

33. ATHENAEUS V 220D His [Antisthenes'] dialogue *The Statesman* contains an attack on all the demagogues at Athens, and his *Archelaus* an attack on Gorgias the orator.

34. CLEMENT *Miscellanies* VI 26 [II 443, 4 Stählin] Gorgias of Leontini and Eudemus of Naxos [*FHG* II 20], the historians, and, in addition to these, Bion of Proconnesus [*FHG* II 19], stole from Melesagorus [*FHG* II 21].

35. PHILOSTRATUS *Epistle* 73 [II 257, 2d Teubner edition] The admirers of Gorgias were noble and numerous: first, the Greeks in Thessaly, among whom "to be an orator" acquired the synonym "to Gorgianize," and secondly, all Greece, in whose presence at the Olympic games he denounced the barbarians, speaking from the racecourse belonging to the temple. Aspasia of Miletus is said to have sharpened the tongue of Pericles in imitation of Gorgias, and Critias and Thucydides were not unaware of how to acquire from him glory and pride, converting it into their own work, the one by careful choice

of word and the other by vigor. Aeschines the Socratic, in whom you [Julia is being addressed] were recently interested on the ground that he was clearly criticizing dialogues, did not hesitate to Gorgianize in the speech for Thargelia. For at one point he says [fr. 22 Dittmar; cf. Münscher in *Philologus*, Supplement x 536], "Thargelia the Milesian, coming to Thessaly, lived with Antiochus the Thessalian, who was king of all Thessaly." The digressions and transitions of Gorgias' speeches became the fashion in many circles and especially among the epic poets.

B. FRAGMENTS

GORGIAS' *ON THE NONEXISTENT OR ON NATURE*

1. ISOCRATES 10, 3   For how could one outdo Gorgias who dared to say that of existing things none exists or Zeno who tried to prove the same things to be possible and again impossible?   15, 268 ... the theories of the early sophists, of whom one said the number of existing things is limitless ... but Parmenides and Melissus said it is one and Gorgias none at all.

2. OLYMPIODORUS on PLATO *Gorgias* p. 112 Jahn [See A 10.] Of course Gorgias, too, wrote an elegant treatise *On Nature* in the eighty-fourth Olympiad [444–441].

3. SEXTUS *Against the Schoolmasters* VII 65 Gorgias of Leontini began from the same position as those who have abolished the criterion, but did not follow the same line of attack as the school of Protagoras. In what is entitled *On the Nonexistent or On Nature* he proposes three successive headings: first and foremost, that nothing exists; second, that even if it exists it is inapprehensible to man; third, that even if it is apprehensible, still it is without a doubt incapable of being expressed or explained to the next man.

(66) Now he concludes in the following way that nothing exists: If ⟨anything⟩ exists, either the existent exists or the nonexistent or both the existent exists and the nonexistent. But, as he will establish, neither does the existent exist nor the nonexistent, as he will make clear, nor the existent and ⟨the⟩ nonexistent, as he will also teach. It is not the case then that anything exists.   (67) More specifically, the nonexistent does not exist; for if the nonexistent exists, it will both exist and not exist at the same time, for insofar as it is understood as nonexistent, it will not exist, but insofar as it *is* nonexistent it will, on the other hand, exist. It would, however, be entirely absurd for something to exist and at the same time not to exist. The nonexistent, therefore, does not exist. And to state another argument, if the non-existent exists, the existent will not exist, for these are opposites to each other, and if existence is an attribute of the nonexistent, non-existence will be an attribute of the existent. But it is not, in fact, true that the existent does not exist. ⟨Accordingly⟩, neither will the non-existent exist.   (68) Moreover, the existent does not exist either. For if the existent exists, it is either eternal or generated, or at the same time eternal and generated. But it is neither eternal nor generated nor both, as we shall show. The existent therefore does not exist. For if the existent is eternal (one must begin with this point) it does not have any beginning.   (69) For everything which is generated has some beginning, but the eternal, being ungenerated, did not have a begin-ning. And not having a beginning it is without limit. And if it is without limit it is nowhere. For if it is somewhere, that in which it is, is something other than it, and thus if the existent is contained in something it will no longer be without limit. For the container is greater than the contained, but nothing is greater than the unlimited, so that the unlimited cannot exist anywhere.   (70) Moreover, it is not contained in itself. For in that case container and contained will be the same, and the existent will become two things, place and body (place is the container, body the contained). But this is absurd. Ac-cordingly, existence is not contained in itself. So that if the existent is eternal it is unlimited, and if it is unlimited it is nowhere, and if it is nowhere it does not exist. Accordingly, if the existent is eternal, it is

not existent at all. (71) Moreover, neither can the existent be generated. For if it has come into being, it has come either from the existent or the nonexistent. But it has not come from the existent. For if it is existent, it has not come to be, but already exists. Nor from the nonexistent. For the nonexistent cannot generate anything, because what is generative of something of necessity ought to partake of positive existence. It is not true either, therefore, that the existent is generated. (72) In the same way it is not jointly at the same time eternal and generated. For these qualities are mutually exclusive of each other, and if the existent is eternal it has not been generated, and if it has been generated it is not eternal. Accordingly, if the existent is neither eternal nor generated nor both at once, the existent should not exist. (73) And to use another argument, if it exists, it is either one or many. But it is neither one nor many, as will be set forth. Therefore, the existent does not exist. For if it is one, it is an existent or a continuum or a magnitude or a body. But whatever of these it is, it is not one, since whatever has extent will be divided, and what is a continuum will be cut. And similarly, what is conceived as a magnitude will not be indivisible. And if it is by chance a body it will be three-dimensional, for it will have length, and breadth and depth. But it is absurd to say that the existent is none of these things. Therefore, the existent is not one. (74) And moreover it is not many. For if it is not one, it is not many either, since the many is a composite of separate entities and thus, when the possibility that it is one was refuted, the possibility that it is many was refuted as well. Now it is clear from this that neither does the existent exist nor does the nonexistent exist. (75) It is easy to conclude that both the existent and the nonexistent do not exist either. For if the nonexistent exists and the existent exists, the nonexistent will be the same thing as the existent as far as existence is concerned. And for this reason neither of them exists. For it is agreed that the nonexistent does not exist, and the existent has been shown to be the same as the nonexistent and it accordingly will not exist. (76) Of course, if the existent is the same as the nonexistent, it is not possible for both to exist. For if both exist, they are not the same, and if the same, both do not exist. To which the conclusion follows that nothing exists. For if neither the existent exists nor the nonexistent nor both, and if no additional possibility is conceivable, nothing exists.

(77) Next it must be shown that even if anything exists, it is unknowable and incomprehensible to man. For, says Gorgias, if things considered in the mind are not existent, the existent is not considered. And that is logical. For if "white" were a possible attribute of what is considered, "being considered" would also have been a possible attribute of what is white; similarly, if "not to be existent" were a possible attribute of what is being considered, necessarily "not to be considered" will be a possible attribute of what is existent. (78) As a result, the statement "if things considered are not existent, the existent is not considered" is sound and logically follows. But things considered (for this must be our starting point) are not existent, as we shall show. The existent is not therefore considered. And moreover, it is clear that things considered are not existent. (79) For if things considered are existent, all things considered exist, and in whatever way anyone considers them. Which is absurd. For if one considers a man flying or chariots racing in the sea, a man does not straightway fly nor a chariot race in the sea. So that things considered are not existent. (80) In addition, if things considered in the mind are existent, nonexistent things will not be considered. For opposites are attributes of opposites, and the nonexistent is opposed to the existent. For this reason it is quite evident that if "being considered in the mind" is an attribute of the existent, "not being considered in the mind" will be an attribute of the nonexistent. But this is absurd. For Scylla and Chimaera and many other nonexistent things are considered in the mind. Therefore, the existent is not considered in the mind. (81) Just as objects of sight are said to be visible for the reason that they are seen, and objects of hearing are said to be audible for the reason that they are heard, and we do not reject visible things on the grounds that they are not heard, nor dismiss audible things because they are not seen (since each object ought to be judged by its own sense, but not by another), so, too, things considered in the mind will exist even if they should not be seen by the sight nor heard by the hearing, because they are perceived by their own criterion. (82) If, therefore, someone

But some things considered do exist

45

considered in the mind that chariots race in the sea, even if he does not see them, he should believe that there are chariots racing in the sea. But this is absurd. Therefore, the existent is not an object of consideration and is not apprehended.

(83) But even if it should be apprehended, it would be incapable of being conveyed to another. For if existent things are visible and audible and generally perceptible, which means that they are external substances, and of these the things which are visible are perceived by the sight, those that are audible by the hearing, and not contrariwise, how can these things be revealed to another person? (84) For that by which we reveal is *logos*, but *logos* is not substances and existing things. Therefore we do not reveal existing things to our neighbors, but *logos*, which is something other than substances. Thus, just as the visible would not become audible, and vice versa, similarly, when external reality is involved, it would not become our *logos*, (85) and not being *logos*, it would not have been revealed to another. It is clear, he says, that *logos* arises from external things impinging upon us, that is, from perceptible things. From encounter with a flavor, *logos* is expressed by us about that quality, and from encounter with a color, an expression of color. But if this is the case, *logos* is not evocative of the external, but the external becomes the revealer of *logos*. (86) And surely it is not possible to say that *logos* has substance in the way visible and audible things have, so that substantial and existent things can be revealed from its substance and existence. For, he says, even if *logos* has substance, still it differs from all the other substances, and visible bodies are to the greatest degree different from words. What is visible is comprehended by one organ, *logos* by another. *Logos* does not, therefore, manifest the multiplicity of substances, just as they do not manifest the nature of each other.

(87) Such being, in Gorgias' view, the problems, insofar as they are valid, the criterion is destroyed. For there would be no criterion if nature neither exists nor can be understood nor conveyed to another. Similar summary in [ARISTOTLE] *Melissus, Xenophanes, and Gorgias* 5, 6, 979a11–980b21. Aristotle himself wrote a monograph *In Reply to the Opinions of Gorgias*. See DIOGENES LAERTIUS V 25.

4. PLATO *Meno* 76Aff. [Meno and Socrates are speaking] How do you define color, Socrates? —— You really are a troublemaker, Meno. You tell an old man what he must answer, but you yourself don't want to remember and tell what Gorgias says virtue to be. . . . c Do you want me to answer you in the manner of Gorgias, in a way that you could most easily follow? — Yes, of course. —— Then you two [Meno and Gorgias] following Empedocles, say, don't you, that existing things have some effluences? —— Certainly. —— And pores into which and through which the effluences are carried? —— Yes. —— And some of the effluences fit some of the pores, but some D are smaller or larger? —— That is so. —— Isn't there also something you call sight? —— Yes. —— From these premises "grasp what I say," in Pindar's words [fr. 105/6 Schroeder 3d ed.]. Color is an effluence of things commensurate and perceptible to sight. —— You seem to have spoken this answer very well, Socrates. —— Probably it was spoken in accordance with your expectation. And I suppose you understand also that you could define what voice is, as well, in this way E and smell and many other similar things? —— Certainly. —— The answer, Meno, is in the grand style.

5. THEOPHRASTUS *On Fire* 73 p. 20 Gercke (*Progr. Gryph.* 1896) And that they[3] kindle the light from the sun by reflection from smooth surfaces (and the fuel mingles together), but they do not kindle the light from a fire, the reason is the existence of small particles in the former case and the fact that the light becomes dense the more it is reflected, but the other light cannot become dense because it consists of dissimilar elements. Thus the one, melting into fuel by means of condensation and smoothness, is able to catch fire, but the other, lacking these characteristics, is not able to. Combustion from a mirror and from bronze and silver surfaces polished in some way does not take place, as Gorgias says and some others believe, "by means of the fire passing away through the pores."

[3] I.e., burning glasses or mirrors.

FUNERAL ORATION Cf. A 1 (5); B 27.

5a. Athanasius *Introduction to Hermogenes, Rh.Gr.* xiv 180, 9 Rabe [I call] the third kind of rhetoric that which is concerned with something ridiculous, awakening the guffaws of the young and being basically a shameless flattery. The circle of Thrasymachus and Gorgias practiced this in style and in their invalid arguments, making use of many equal clauses and failing to understand when this figure is appropriate. Many also have displayed it in figures of thought and tropes, but especially Gorgias, since he was the most affected; during the course of the very narrative in his *Funeral Oration*, not venturing to say "vultures" he spoke of "animate tombs." In the thought he falls below what is necessary, as Isocrates also testifies when he says, "For how could one. . . ." [B 1] [Longinus] *On the Sublime* 3, 2 In this way also the writings of Gorgias of Leontini are laughed at, since he called Xerxes "the Persians' Zeus" and vultures "living tombs."

5b. Philostratus *Lives of the Sophists* i 9, 5 [See above A 1 (5).] "Victories over the barbarians require hymns of celebration, over the Greeks laments."

6. Planudes on Hermogenes *Rh.Gr.* v 548 Walz Dionysius the elder in the second book *On Kinds of Style*, speaking of Gorgias, says as follows: "I have not met with judicial speeches by him, but with a few deliberative speeches of a sort and technical treatises and numerous epideictic speeches. The following is an example of the style of his speeches (he is praising those of the Athenians who were distinguished for their bravery in war): 'What was absent to these men of that which should be present to men; and too, what was present of that which should not be present? Would that I can speak what I wish and would that I wish to speak what I should, avoiding divine displeasure and escaping human envy. For these men attained an excellence which is divine and a mortality which is human, often preferring gentle fairness to inflexible justice, often straightness of speech to exactness of law, believing that the most godlike and universal law was this: in time of duty dutifully to speak and to leave unspoken, to act ⟨and to leave undone⟩, cultivating two needed qualities especially, judgment ⟨and strength⟩, one for deliberating, the other for accomplishing, giving help to those unjustly afflicted and punishment to those unjustly flourishing, determined in regard to the expedient, gentle in regard to the fitting, by the prudence of the mind checking the irrationality ⟨of the body⟩, insolent with the insolent, decent with the decent, fearless with the fearless, terrible among terrors. As evidence of these qualities they set up a trophy over their enemies, an honor to Zeus, an ornament to themselves; not inexperienced were they in native valor or legitimate passions or armed strife or honorable peace, reverent to the gods by means of justice, respectful to parents by means of care, just to fellow citizens by equality, loyal to friends by faithfulness. Wherefore, though they have died, desire for them has not died, but lives on immortal among bodies not immortal, though they do not live.' "

SPEECH AT THE OLYMPIC GAMES Cf. A 1.

7. ARISTOTLE *Rhetoric* III 14, 1414b29   The source of prooemia in epideictic speeches is praise or blame, as for example, Gorgias in the Olympic speech: "They deserve to be admired by many, O men of Greece." For he praises those who create the national assemblies.

8. CLEMENT *Miscellanies* I 51 [II 33, 18 Stählin]   According to Gorgias of Leontini, "A contest such as we have requires two kinds of excellence, daring and skill; daring is needed to withstand danger, and skill to understand how to trip the opponent [?]. For surely speech, like the summons at the Olympic games, calls him who will, but crowns him who can."

8a. PLUTARCH *Advice to Bride and Groom* 43 p. 144BC   When Gorgias the orator read a speech at Olympia about concord among the Greeks, Melanthius said: "This fellow advises us about concord, though he has not persuaded himself and his wife and his maid, only three in number, to live in private concord." For it seems that Gorgias had a passion for the little maid and his wife was jealous. Cf., however, A 20.

SPEECH AT THE PYTHIAN GAMES

9. Philostratus *Lives of the Sophists* 1 9, 4 [See A 1 (4).]

ENCOMIUM FOR THE PEOPLE OF ELIS

10. Aristotle *Rhetoric* III 14, 1416a1 Gorgias' *Encomium for the People of Elis* is of this sort. For without any preliminary skirmishing or prelude he begins immediately, "Elis, happy city."

GORGIAS' ENCOMIUM OF HELEN

11. (1) What is becoming to a city is manpower, to a body beauty, to a soul wisdom, to an action virtue, to a speech truth, and the opposites of these are unbecoming. Man and woman and speech and deed and city and object should be honored with praise if praiseworthy and incur blame if unworthy, for it is an equal error and mistake to blame the praisable and to praise the blamable. (2) It is the duty of one and the same man both to speak the needful rightly and to refute ⟨the unrightfully spoken. Thus it is right to refute⟩[4] those who rebuke Helen, a woman about whom the testimony of inspired poets has become univocal and unanimous as had the ill omen of her name, which has become a reminder of misfortunes. For my part, by introducing some reasoning into my speech, I wish to free the accused of blame and, having reproved her detractors as prevaricators and proved the truth, to free her from their ignorance.

(3) Now it is not unclear, not even to a few, that in nature and in blood the woman who is the subject of this speech is preeminent

---

[4] Accepting Diels's "sense" as given in the *apparatus criticus*.

among preeminent men and women. For it is clear that her mother was Leda, and her father was in fact a god, Zeus, but allegedly a mortal, Tyndareus, of whom the former was shown to be her father because he was and the latter was disproved because he was said to be, and the one was the most powerful of men and the other the lord of all.

(4) Born from such stock, she had godlike beauty, which taking and not mistaking, she kept. In many did she work much desire for her love, and her one body was the cause of bringing together many bodies of men thinking great thoughts for great goals, of whom some had greatness of wealth, some the glory of ancient nobility, some the vigor of personal agility, some command of acquired knowledge. And all came because of a passion which loved to conquer and a love of honor which was unconquered. (5) Who it was and why and how he sailed away, taking Helen as his love, I shall not say. To tell the knowing what they know shows it is right but brings no delight. Having now gone beyond the time once set for my speech, I shall go on to the beginning of my future speech, and I shall set forth the causes through which it was likely that Helen's voyage to Troy should take place.

(6) For either by will of Fate and decision of the gods and vote of Necessity did she do what she did, or by force reduced or by words seduced ⟨or by love possessed⟩. Now if through the first, it is right for the responsible one to be held responsible; for god's predetermination cannot be hindered by human premeditation. For it is the nature of things, not for the strong to be hindered by the weak, but for the weaker to be ruled and drawn by the stronger, and for the stronger to lead and the weaker to follow. God is a stronger force than man in might and in wit and in other ways. If then one must place blame on Fate and on a god, one must free Helen from disgrace.

(7) But if she was raped by violence and illegally assaulted and unjustly insulted, it is clear that the raper, as the insulter, did the wronging, and the raped, as the insulted, did the suffering. It is right then for the barbarian who undertook a barbaric undertaking in word and law and deed to meet with blame in word, exclusion in law, and punishment in deed. And surely it is proper for a woman raped and

robbed of her country and deprived of her friends to be pitied rather than pilloried. He did the dread deeds; she suffered them. It is just therefore to pity her but to hate him.

(8) But if it was speech which persuaded her and deceived her heart, not even to this is it difficult to make an answer and to banish blame as follows. Speech is a powerful lord, which by means of the finest and most invisible body effects the divinest works: it can stop fear and banish grief and create joy and nurture pity. I shall show how this is the case, since   (9) it is necessary to offer proof to the opinion of my hearers: I both deem and define all poetry as speech with meter. Fearful shuddering and tearful pity and grievous longing come upon its hearers, and at the actions and physical sufferings of others in good fortunes and in evil fortunes, through the agency of words, the soul is wont to experience a suffering of its own. But come, I shall turn from one argument to another.   (10) Sacred incantations sung with words are bearers of pleasure and banishers of pain, for, merging with opinion in the soul, the power of the incantation is wont to beguile it and persuade it and alter it by witchcraft. There have been discovered two arts of witchcraft and magic: one consists of errors of soul and the other of deceptions of opinion.   (11) All who have and do persuade people of things do so by molding a false argument. For if all men on all subjects had ⟨both⟩ memory of things past and ⟨awareness⟩ of things present and foreknowledge of the future, speech would not be similarly similar, since as things are now it is not easy for them to recall the past nor to consider the present nor to predict the future. So that on most subjects most men take opinion as counselor to their soul, but since opinion is slippery and insecure it casts those employing it into slippery and insecure successes.   (12) What cause then prevents the conclusion that Helen similarly, against her will, might have come under the influence of speech, just as if ravished by the force of the mighty? For it was possible to see how the force of persuasion prevails; persuasion has the form of necessity, but it does not have the same power.[5] For speech constrained the soul, persuading

---

[5] Accepting Diels's "sense" as given in the *apparatus criticus*.

it which it persuaded, both to believe the things said and to approve the things done. The persuader, like a constrainer, does the wrong and the persuaded, like the constrained, in speech is wrongly charged. (13) To understand that persuasion, when added to speech, is wont also to impress the soul as it wishes, one must study: first, the words of astronomers who, substituting opinion for opinion, taking away one but creating another, make what is incredible and unclear seem true to the eyes of opinion; then, second, logically necessary debates in which a single speech, written with art but not spoken with truth, bends a great crowd and persuades; ⟨and⟩ third, the verbal disputes of philosophers in which the swiftness of thought is also shown making the belief in an opinion subject to easy change. (14) The effect of speech upon the condition of the soul is comparable to the power of drugs over the nature of bodies. For just as different drugs dispel different secretions from the body, and some bring an end to disease and others to life, so also in the case of speeches, some distress, others delight, some cause fear, others make the hearers bold, and some drug and bewitch the soul with a kind of evil persuasion.

(15) It has been explained that if she was persuaded by speech she did not do wrong but was unfortunate. I shall discuss the fourth cause in a fourth passage. For if it was love which did all these things, there will be no difficulty in escaping the charge of the sin which is alleged to have taken place. For the things we see do not have the nature which we wish them to have, but the nature which each actually has. Through sight the soul receives an impression even in its inner features. (16) When belligerents in war buckle on their warlike accouterments of bronze and steel, some designed for defense, others for offense, if the sight sees this, immediately it is alarmed and it alarms the soul, so that often men flee, panic-stricken, from future danger ⟨as though it were⟩ present. For strong as is the habit of obedience to the law, it is ejected by fear resulting from sight, which coming to a man causes him to be indifferent both to what is judged honorable because of the law and to the advantage to be derived from victory. (17) It has happened that people, after having seen frightening sights, have also lost presence of mind for the present moment;

in this way fear extinguishes and excludes thought. And many have fallen victim to useless labor and dread diseases and hardly curable madnesses. In this way the sight engraves upon the mind images of things which have been seen. And many frightening impressions linger, and what lingers is exactly analogous to ⟨what is⟩ spoken. (18) Moreover, whenever pictures perfectly create a single figure and form from many colors and figures, they delight the sight, while the creation of statues and the production of works of art furnish a pleasant sight to the eyes. Thus it is natural for the sight to grieve for some things and to long for others, and much love and desire for many objects and figures is engraved in many men. (19) If, therefore, the eye of Helen, pleased by the figure of Alexander, presented to her soul eager desire and contest of love, what wonder? If, ⟨being⟩ a god, ⟨love has⟩ the divine power of the gods, how could a lesser being reject and refuse it? But if it is a disease of human origin and a fault of the soul, it should not be blamed as a sin, but regarded as an affliction. For she came, as she did come, caught in the net of Fate, not by the plans of the mind, and by the constraints of love, not by the devices of art.

(20) How then can one regard blame of Helen as just, since she is utterly acquitted of all charge, whether she did what she did through falling in love or persuaded by speech or ravished by force or constrained by divine constraint?

(21) I have by means of speech removed disgrace from a woman; I have observed the procedure which I set up at the beginning of the speech; I have tried to end the injustice of blame and the ignorance of opinion; I wished to write a speech which would be a praise of Helen and a diversion to myself.

A DEFENSE ON BEHALF OF PALAMEDES
BY THE SAME AUTHOR

11a. (1) Prosecution and defense are not a means of judging about death; for Nature, with a vote which is clear, casts a vote of death against every mortal on the day on which he is born. The danger relates to dishonor and honor, whether I must die justly or whether I must die roughly with the greatest reproaches and most shameful accusation. (2) There are the two alternatives; you have the second within your power, I the first; justice is up to me, roughness is up to you. You will easily be able to kill me if you wish, for you have power over these matters, over which as it happens I have no power. (3) If then the accuser, Odysseus, made his accusation through good will toward Greece, either clearly knowing that I was betraying Greece to the barbarians or imagining somehow that this was the case, he would be best of men. For this would of course[6] be true of one who saves his homeland, his parents, and all Greece, and in addition punishes a wrongdoer. But if he has put together this allegation out of envy or conspiracy or knavery, just as in the former case he would be the finest of men, so in this he would be the worst of men. (4) Where shall I start to speak about these matters? What shall I say first? To what part of the defense shall I turn my attention? For an unsupported allegation creates evident perplexity, and because of the perplexity it follows that I am at a loss in my speech, unless I discover something out of the truth itself and out of the present necessity, having met with teachers more dangerous than inventive. (5) Now I clearly know that my accuser accuses me without ⟨knowing⟩ the matter clearly; for I know in my heart clearly that I have done no such thing; and I do not know how anyone could know what did not happen. But in case he made the accusation thinking it to be so, I shall show you in two ways that he is not speaking the truth. For I could not if I wished, nor would I if I could, put my hand to such works as these.

(6) I come first to this argument, that I lack the capability of performing the action charged. There must have been some first beginning to the treason, and the beginning would have been speech, for before any future deeds it is necessary first for there to be discussions. But how could there be discussions unless there had been some meeting? And how could there have been a meeting unless the opponent

---

[6] Without the emendation of Stephanus-Blass, the meaning would be "of course not."

sent to me or ⟨someone⟩ went from me to him? For no message arrives in writing without a bearer. (7) But this can take place by speech. And suppose he is with me and I am with him—how does it take place? Who is with whom? Greek with barbarian. How do we listen and how talk to each other? By ourselves? But we do not know each other's language. With an interpreter then? A third person is added as a witness to things which need to be hidden. (8) But assume that this too has taken place, even though it has not. Next it was necessary to give and receive a pledge. What would the pledge be? An oath? Who was apt to trust me, the traitor? Perhaps there were hostages? Who? For instance, I might have given my brother (for I had no one else), and the barbarian might have given one of his sons; in this way the pledge would have been most secure to me from him and to him from me. But these things, if they happened, would have been clear to you all. (9) Someone will say that we made the contract for money, he giving it, I taking it. Was it for little? But it is not probable that a man would take a little money for a great service. For much money? Who was the go-between? How could one person bring it? Perhaps there were many? If many brought it, there would have been many witnesses of the plot, but if one brought it, what was brought would not have been anything much. (10) Did they bring it by day or by night? But the guards are many and closely placed and it is not possible to escape their notice. But by day? Certainly the light militates against such things. Well then. Did I go out and get it or did the opponent come bringing it? For both are impossible. If I had in fact taken it, how would I have hidden it both from those in the camp and from those outside it? Where would I have put it? How would I have protected it? If I made use of it, I would have been conspicuous; if I didn't, what advantage would I have gotten from it? (11) Still, assume that what did not happen has happened. We met, we talked, we reached an understanding, I took money from them, I was not detected after taking it, I hid it. It was then necessary to perform that for the sake of which these arrangements were made. Now this is still stranger than what has been discussed. For in doing it, I acted by myself or with others. But the action was not the work of one man. But was it with others? Who? Clearly my associates. Were they free men or slaves? My free associates are you. Who then among you was aware? Let him speak. How is it credible that I would use slaves? For they bring charges ⟨both⟩ in hopes of their freedom and out of necessity when hard pressed. (12) As for the action, how ⟨would⟩ it have taken place? Clearly enemy forces outnumbering you had to be brought in, which was impossible. How could I have brought them in? Through the gates? But it was not my job to shut or open them, but the commanders were in charge of these. But it was over the walls ⟨by⟩ a ladder? Wouldn't ⟨I have been seen?⟩ The whole place was full of guards. But it was through a hole made in the wall? It would then have been clear to all. Life under arms is carried on outdoors (for this is a camp!), in which ⟨everybody⟩ sees everything and everybody is seen by everybody. Altogether then and in every way it was impossible for me to do all these things.

(13) Consider among yourselves the following point as well. What reason was there to wish to do these things, assuming that I had a special capability? For no one wishes to run the greatest dangers without reward nor to be most wicked in the greatest wickedness. But what reason was there? (For again I revert to this point.) For the sake of rul⟨ing⟩? Over you or over the barbarians? But over you it would be impossible for me to rule, considering your numbers and nature and the fact that you have all manner of great resources: nobility of family, wealth of money, fame, strength of heart, the thrones of cities. (14) But over the ⟨barbarians⟩? Who is going to betray them? By means of what power shall I, a Greek, take over the barbarians, when I am one and they are many? Persuading or constraining them? For they would not wish to be persuaded and I would not be able to constrain. But possibly there are those willing to betray them to a willing receiver by giving money in return for the surrender? But both to believe and accept this is very foolish. For who would choose slavery instead of sovereignty, the worst instead of the best? (15) Someone might say that I ventured on this out of a desire for wealth and money. But I have a moderate amount of money, and I have no need for much. Those who spend much money need much,

not those who are continent of the pleasures of nature, but those who are slaves to pleasures and seek to acquire honors from wealth and show. None of this applies to me. I shall offer my past life as sure evidence that I am speaking the truth, and you be witnesses to the witness, for you are my companions and thus know these things. (16) Nor, moreover, would a man even moderately prudent put his hand to such work even for honor. Honors come from goodness, not from badness. How would there be honor for a man who is the betrayer of Greece? And in addition, as it happens, I am not without honor. For I am honored for the most honorable reason by the most honorable men, that is, by you for wisdom. (17) Nor, moreover, would anyone do these things for the sake of security. For the traitor is the enemy of all: the law, justice, the gods, the bulk of mankind. For he contravenes the law, negates justice, destroys the masses, and dishonors what is holy, and a man does not have security whose life ⟨is⟩ of this sort among the greatest dangers. (18) But was I anxious to assist friends or harm enemies? For someone might commit injustice for these reasons. But in my case everything was the opposite. I was harming my friends and helping foes. The action therefore involved no acquisition of goods, and there is no one who does wrong out of desire to suffer loss. (19) The remaining possibility is that I did it to escape some fear or labor or danger. But no one could say that these motives applied to me in any way. All men do all things in pursuit of these two goals: either seeking some profit or escaping some punishment, and whatever knavery is done for reasons other than these ⟨is apt to involve the doer in great evils. That I would most⟩[7] hurt myself in doing these things is not unclear. For in betraying Greece I was betraying myself, my parents, my friends, the dignity of my ancestors, the cults of my native land, the tombs of my family, and my great country of Greece. Those things which are all in all to all men, I would have entrusted to men who had been wronged.[8] (20) But consider the following as well. Would not my life have been

[7] The conjecture of Keil, which Diels approves in the *apparatus*.
[8] Perhaps "had done wrong"(?), Diels.

unlivable if I had done these things? Where must I have turned for help? To Greece? Shall I make amends to those who have been wronged? Who of those who suffered could keep his hands off me? Or must I remain among the barbarians? Abandoning everything important, deprived of the noblest honor, passing my life in shameful disgrace, throwing away the labors labored for virtue of my past life? And this of my own accord, although to fail through his own doing is most shameful for a man. (21) Moreover, not even among the barbarians would I be trusted. How could I be, if they knew that I had done something most untrustworthy, had betrayed my friends to my enemies? But life is not livable for a man who has lost the confidence of others. The man who loses his money ⟨or⟩ who falls from power or who is exiled from his country might get on his feet again, but he who throws away good faith would not any more acquire it. Therefore, that I would not ⟨if I could, nor could if I would⟩, betray Greece has been demonstrated by what has been said.

(22) I wish next to address the accuser. What in the world do you trust when, being what you are, you accuse such a one as me? It is worth examining the kind of man you are who says the kind of things you do, like the worthless attacking the worthless. Do you accuse me, knowing accurately what you say, or imagining it? If it is with knowledge, you know either from seeing or participating or learning from someone ⟨who was participating⟩. If then you saw, tell these judges ⟨the manner⟩, the place, the time, when, where, how you saw. If you participated, you are liable to the same accusations. And if you heard from someone who participated, who is he? Let him come forward; let him appear; let him bear witness. For if it is witnessed in this way, the accusation will be more credible, since as it is, neither of us is furnishing a witness. (23) You will say perhaps that it is equitable for you not to furnish witnesses of what you allege to have happened, but that I should furnish witnesses of what has not happened. But this is not equitable. For it is quite impossible for what has not happened to be testified to by witnesses, but on the subject of what has happened, not only is it not impossible, but it is even easy, and not only is it easy, but ⟨even necessary. But⟩ for you it was not possible, ⟨not⟩ only to

find witnesses, but even to find false witnesses, and for me it was possible to find neither of these. (24) Therefore, it is clear that you do not have knowledge of the things about which you make accusation. It follows that since you do ⟨not⟩ have knowledge, you have an opinion. Do you then, O most daring of all men, trusting in opinion, a most untrustworthy thing, not knowing the truth, dare to bring a capital charge against a man? Why do you share knowledge that he has done such a deed? But surely it is open to all men to have opinions on all subjects, and in this you are no wiser than others. But it is not right to trust those with an opinion instead of those who know, nor to think opinion more trustworthy than truth, but rather truth than opinion.

(25) You accused me through spoken words of two directly opposed things, wisdom and madness, which the same man cannot have. Where you say that I am artful and clever and resourceful, you accuse me of wisdom, and where you say that I was betraying Greece, you accuse me of madness. For it is madness to undertake tasks which are impossible, inexpedient, and shameful, which will harm his friends, help his enemies, and make his own life disgraceful and perilous. Yet how can one trust a man of the sort who in a single speech says to the same man the most inconsistent things about the same subjects? (26) I would like to ask you whether you think wise men are witless or intelligent. If witless, your speech is novel, but not true; if intelligent, surely it is not right for intelligent men to make the worst mistakes and to prefer evils to present goods. If therefore I am wise, I have not erred; if I have erred, I am not wise. Thus in both cases you would be wrong.

(27) I do not want to introduce in reply the many enormities, both old and new, which you have committed, though I could. For ⟨I wish⟩ to escape this charge by means of my own virtues, not by means of your vices. So much, therefore, to you.

(28) To you, O judges, I wish to say something invidious, but true about myself, not appropriate to one who has ⟨not⟩ been accused, but fitting to one who has been accused. For I am now undergoing scrutiny and furnishing an account of my past life. I therefore beg of you, if I

remind you of some of the fine things done by me, that no one be annoyed at what is said, but think it necessary for one who is dreadfully and falsely accused to say as well some true things among you who know them. This is the most pleasant for me. (29) First, then, and second and greatest, in every respect from beginning to end my past life has been blameless, free from all blame. No one could truthfully speak any imputation of evil to you about me. For not even the accuser himself has provided any evidence of what he has said. Thus his speech has the impact of abuse lacking proof. (30) I might say, and saying it I would not lie nor would I be refuted, that I am not only blameless but also a great benefactor of you and the Greeks and all mankind, not only of those now alive but ⟨also⟩ of those to come. For who else would have made human life well provided instead of destitute and adorned instead of unadorned, by inventing military equipment of the greatest advantage and written laws, the guardians of justice, and letters, the tool of memory, and measures and weights, the convenient standards of commercial exchange, and number, the guardian of items, and very powerful beacons and very swift messengers, and draughts, the harmless game of leisure? Why do I remind you of these? (31) For the purpose of making it clear ⟨on the one hand⟩ that it is to this sort of thing that I apply myself, and on the other giving an indication of the fact that I abstain from shameful and wicked deeds. For it is impossible for one applying himself to the latter to apply himself to this sort of thing. And I think it right not to be harmed myself by you if I myself have done you no harm. (32) Nor am I, because of other activities, deserving of ill treatment at the hands of younger or older men. For I am inoffensive to the older, not unhelpful to the younger, not envious of the fortunate, but merciful to the unfortunate; not heedless of poverty nor valuing wealth ahead of virtue, but virtue ahead of wealth; neither useless in council nor lazy in war, doing what is assigned to me, obeying those in command. To be sure, it is not for me to praise myself, but the present occasion requires me to make my defense in every possible way since I have been accused of these things.

(33) For the rest, my speech is to you and about you; when I have

said this I shall end my defense. Appeals to pity and entreaties and the intercession of friends are useful when a trial takes place before a mob, but among you, the first of the Greeks and men of repute, it is not right to persuade you with the help of friends or entreaties or appeals to pity, but it is right for me to escape this charge by means of the clearest justice, explaining the truth, not deceiving. (34) And it is necessary for you to avoid paying more attention to words than to actions, and not to prejudge the bases of the defense nor to think a short time affords wiser judgment than a long time nor to believe that slander is more reliable than firsthand knowledge. For in all matters good men must take great care against erring, and more so in matters irremediable than in those remediable. For these lie within the control of those who have exercised foresight, but are uncorrectable by those with hindsight. And it is a matter of this sort whenever men judge a man on a capital charge, which is now the case before you. (35) If then, by means of words, it were possible for the truth of actions to become free of doubt ⟨and⟩ clear to hearers, judgment would now be easy from what has been said. But since this is not the case, protect my body, wait for a longer while, and make your decision with truth. For your danger is great that by seeming unjust you lose one reputation and acquire another. To good men death is preferable to a shameful reputation. For one is the end of life, and the other is disease in life. (36) If you kill me unjustly, it will be evident to many, for I am ⟨not⟩ unknown, and your wickedness will be known and clear to all Greeks. And you, rather than the accuser, will have a responsibility for the injustice which will be clear to all. For the outcome of the trial rests with you. But greater error than this could not exist. If you give an unjust verdict, you will make a mistake, not only in regard to me and my parents, but by your action you will make yourselves responsible for a dreadful, godless, unjust, unlawful deed, having killed a man who is your fellow soldier, useful to you, a benefactor of Greece, Greeks killing Greek, though convicting him of no clear injustice nor credible fault.

(37) My side of the case is spoken and I rest. For to recapitulate briefly what has been spoken at length is logical before bad judges,

but it is not appropriate to think that Greeks who are first of the first do not pay attention and do not remember what has been said.

ART OF RHETORIC

Cf. Satyrus A 3; Diodorus Siculus A 4 (2); Scholia to Isocrates 13, 19; Sopater *Commentary on Hermogenes*, Rh.Gr. v 6ff. Walz.

12. Aristotle *Rhetoric* iii 18, 1419b3 Gorgias said that "the opposition's seriousness is to be demolished by laughter, and laughter by seriousness," in which statement he was correct.

13. Dionysius of Halicarnassus *On the Arrangement of Words* 12 p. 84 No orator or philosopher has up to this time defined the art of the "timely," not even Gorgias of Leontini, who first tried to write about it, nor did he write anything worth mentioning.

14. [To the *Art of Rhetoric* there probably belong also short models of defenses in the grand style like the *Helen* and the *Palamedes*.][9] Aristotle *On Sophistical Refutations* xxxiii 183b36 The educational method of those earning money by teaching controversial argumentation was like the system of Gorgias. For some assigned rhetorical speeches and others question-and-answer discussions to be learned by heart. Each thought that each other's arguments were for the most part encompassed in these. As a result, the teaching was quick but unscientific for those learning from them. For they thought they were teaching, although presenting, not art, but the results of art, just as if someone claimed to present a science to prevent feet from hurting and then did not teach shoemaking, nor where it was possible to get such things, but offered many kinds of shoes of all sorts. Cf. Plato *Phaedrus* 261b: [Phaedrus and Socrates are speaking] But most of what

---

[9] Diels here confuses rhetorical handbooks with collections of model speeches or parts of speeches. Cf. George Kennedy, *The Art of Persuasion in Greece* (Princeton, 1963), pp. 61–63.

is spoken and written under the rules of an art is related to lawsuits, but there is use of an art also in deliberative assemblies; more than that I have not heard. —— But surely then you have heard only of the *Arts of Speech* by Nestor and Odysseus which they composed when not busy at Troy, and you have been unaware of those by Palamedes? —— Why, indeed, I am unaware of those by Nestor, too, unless by somebody named Nestor you are disguising Gorgias, or by an Odysseus, Thrasymachus and Theodorus.

FROM UNIDENTIFIED WRITINGS

15. ARISTOTLE *Rhetoric* III 3, 1405b34 Frigidity in style occurs in four forms: in the use of compound words . . . also as Gorgias spoke of "begging-poet-flatterers" and "foresworn and well-sworn."

16. —— —— III 3, 1406b4 . . . and further the fourth form of frigidity is in the use of metaphor . . . for example, Gorgias "grass-pale (trembling)" and "bloodless matters." And "you shamefully sowed these and wretchedly reaped." For this is too poetically expressed.

17. —— —— III 17, 1418a32 In epideictic it is suitable to vary the speech with episodes of praise as Isocrates does. For he is always bringing in somebody. And what Gorgias said is the same, that he was "never at a loss for words." For if he speaks of Achilles he praises Peleus, then Aeacus, then the god, and similarly in the case of manliness, which does this or that or is of a certain sort.

18. —— *Politics* I 5, 1260a27 Those who itemize virtues, as Gorgias does, speak much better than those who so define [virtue in a general way].

19. PLATO *Meno* 71E [Meno is speaking with reference to Gorgias 71D] In the first place, if you want to know what is excellence in a man, that is easy, because excellence in a man is this, to be competent to perform public duties, and in doing them to help friends and harm enemies and to avoid suffering anything of the sort himself. And if you want to know the excellence of a woman, it is not difficult to describe, for she ought to manage her household well, keeping the contents safe and being obedient to her husband. There are distinct excellences for a child, female and male, and for an older man, of one sort if free, another if a slave.   72A And there are numerous other excellences so that there is no difficulty in saying what excellence is. For there is an excellence for each of us in each activity and in each time of life in regard to each action, and the same is true, I think, Socrates, of fault.

20. PLUTARCH *Cimon* 10   Gorgias of Leontini says that "Cimon acquired money to use it and used it to be honored."

21. ——— *How to Tell a Flatterer* 23 p. 64C   A friend will not, as Gorgias thought, "expect his friend to help him in just undertakings, but himself help the other also in many which are not just."

22. ——— *Bravery of Women* p. 242E   Gorgias seems to us in better taste when he demands that "a woman's fame rather than her form ought to be known to many."

23. ——— *On the Fame of the Athenians* 5 p. 348C   Tragedy bloomed and was celebrated, a marvelous sound and spectacle for the men of that time and one which by means of myth and suffering produced "a deception," as Gorgias says, "in which the deceiver is more justly esteemed than the nondeceiver and the deceived is wiser than the undeceived." The deceiver is more justly esteemed because he succeeds in what he intends, and the deceived is wiser, for a man that is not imperceptive is easily affected by the pleasure of words.

24. ——— *Table-Talk* VII 10, 2 p. 715E   Gorgias said that one of his [Aeschylus'] dramas was "filled with Ares," namely, the *Seven Against Thebes*. Cf. ARISTOPHANES *Frogs* 1021.

25. PROCLUS *Life of Homer* p. 26, 14 Wilamowitz Hellanicus [*FGrHist* 4 F 5b], Damastes [*FGrHist* 5 F 11], and Pherecydes [*FGrHist* 3 F 167] take his [Homer's] ancestry back to Orpheus. . . . Gorgias of Leontini takes him back to Musaeus.

26. ———— on HESIOD *Works and Days* 764 What Gorgias said is not quite the truth. He said that "existence is not manifest if it does not involve opinion, and opinion is unreliable if it does not involve existence."

27. SCHOLIA T on HOMER *Iliad* IV 250 [p. 154, 29 Maass] . . . and Gorgias' statement: "threats are mingled with entreaties and lamentations with prayers." [From the *Funeral Oration*?]

OF DOUBTFUL AUTHENTICITY

28. GRAECO-SYRIAN TEXTS trans. into German by Ryssel [*Rheinisches Museum*, LI (1896), p. 540, n. 34] *Gorgias* [? Syrian: *Gorgonias*] *said:* Outstanding beauty derived from some hidden quality is detected if judicious painters cannot paint it with their customary colors. For their extensive experience and their great exertion thereby exhibit a fine testimonial of how great the beauty is in its concealment. And when the separate steps of their work have been exhausted, by their silence in turn they give the crown of victory to the original. But how can the tongue express or the ear of a hearer perceive what no hand encompasses and no eye sees?

29. GNOMOLOGIUM VATICANUM 743 no. 166 [ed. Sternbach *Wiener Studien* x 36] Gorgias the rhetor said that those neglecting philosophy and devoting themselves to general studies were like the suitors who, though wanting Penelope, slept with her maids.

30. ———— 743 no. 167 [ed. Sternbach *Wiener Studien* x 37] Gorgias said that orators were like frogs: for the latter made their cry in water and the former before the waterclock.

31. SOPATER *Commentary on Hermogenes, Rh.Gr.* VIII 23 Walz   Gorgias, who says the sun is a red-hot stone. . . .

C. IMITATION

1. PLATO *Symposium* 194E–197E   [Speech of Agathon on Love, parody of the Gorgianic style of Agathon] Cf. 198C.   [Socrates is speaking] For the speech reminded me of Gorgias, so that I quite experienced what Homer says: I was afraid lest at the end of his speech Agathon might brandish the Gorgian head of clever speech at my speech and turn me into stone and make me dumb.   185C When Pausanias had paused (the sophists teach me [Apollodorus] to speak in this way like themselves), etc.

2. XENOPHON *Symposium* II 26   But if the slaves sprinkle us a little with their little cups, if I too may speak in Gorgianic phrases, etc.

83. LYCOPHRON

translated by WILLIAM O'NEILL

Lycophron was reputedly a sophist and an imitator of Gorgias. (Cf. W. Nestle, *Zeller-Nestle* I p. 1323 n. 3; M. Untersteiner, *The Sophists*, trans. K. Freeman [Oxford, 1954], pp. 339–40; E. Havelock, *The Liberal Temper in Greek Politics* [New Haven, 1957], pp. 373–74.)

1. ARISTOTLE *Metaphysics* VIII 6, 1045b10   Some speak of participation and are perplexed as to what is the cause of the participation, and what "to participate" means. Others speak of "communion," as when Lycophron says that "knowledge is a communion of knowing and of soul." ALEXANDER OF APHRODISIAS ad loc. But some speak of a communion of soul, as when Lycophron the sophist says that knowledge is a communion of knowing and of soul. But it would have been better and clearer if the writing had run somewhat like this: "that knowledge is of knowing a communion and of soul." For when asked what was the cause of the unity of knowledge and the soul, Lycophron replied: "the communion."

2. ARISTOTLE *Physics* I 2, 185b25   Even the more recent of the ancient thinkers [the Eleatics, Heraclitus] were troubled lest the same thing turn out for them, at the same time, one and many. So some, like Lycophron, removed the "is," while others changed the form of expression, to the effect not that man "is white" but "has been made white" . . . lest by the addition of the "is" they should make the one to be many. Cf. PLATO *Sophist* 251B; DAMASCIUS *On First Principles* 126 [II 2 Ruelle].[1]

---

[1] II p. 134 Chaignet.

3. —— *Politics* III 5, 1280b8 ... the community becomes an alliance, differing only in location from the other sorts of alliance, where the members live at a distance. And the law becomes a convention and, as Lycophron the sophist said, "a guarantor of mutual rights," but not such as to make the citizens good and just.

4. —— Fragments 91 Rose (Cf. STOBAEUS IV 29, 24.) What I mean is this: Is [good birth] something valuable and worthwhile or, as Lycophron the sophist wrote, something altogether worthless? Comparing it with other goods he asserts: "Now the nobility of good birth is obscure, and its grandeur a matter of words," on the grounds that preference for it looks to opinion, whereas in fact there is no difference between the ignoble and the well-born.

5. —— *Rhetoric* III 3, 1405b34 Insipid expressions occur in four cases: in compound words, as when Lycophron speaks of "the many-visaged sky of the mighty-peaked earth" and "the narrow-passaged promontory." [Here follows *DK* 82 B 15, Alcidamas fr. 10 Sauppe.] ... now this is one cause of dullness, and another is the use of strange expressions, as when Lycophron calls Xerxes "a monster of a man," and Sciron "a human destroyer." [Here follows Alcidamas fr. 14 *Orat.Att.* II 156a3.] [The Lycophron mentioned in *Rhetoric* III 9, 1410a18 is probably the Tyrant of Pherae.] Cf. Vahlen *Rheinisches Museum* XXI (1866) p. 143 = *Kleine Schriften* I 156.

6. —— *On Sophistical Refutations* XV 174b32 Sometimes also one should attempt points other than the one mentioned, taking it in a different sense, if one has no reply to make to the topic under discussion, as Lycophron did when it was proposed that he praise the lyre. ALEXANDER OF APHRODISIAS ad loc. [according to a false interpretation] ... or rather, when he was constrained by certain persons to praise the lyre, and then found himself at a loss for many words, he praised this tangible lyre for a little and then referred to the heavenly one; for there is in the heavens a constellation composed of many stars which is called the Lyre. On this subject he found many good things to say. Cf. ARISTOTLE *Rhetoric* II 24, 1401a15; III 17, 1418a29ff.

84. PRODICUS

translated by DOUGLAS J. STEWART

Prodicus was born on the tiny island of Ceos, near Athens. Because he appears in Plato's *Protagoras* as definitely younger than the dialogue's main speaker, it is calculated that his birth fell in the decade 470–460 B.C. He became an accomplished speaker and, no doubt because of this eminence, was frequently designated as ambassador from his small community to her large and powerful neighbor, Athens, where, too, he became popular and successful. Combining public service with personal profit, he employed his credit with his Athenian hosts to build up a thriving trade in lecturing and teaching for large fees while on his official visits. His most remarkable appearance in extant records is virtually a nonappearance: in the *Protagoras* Socrates reports that he tried in vain to get into the room where Prodicus was discoursing, still in bed, to a group of admirers who filled the room to overflowing (our fr. A 2 below). But the sophist was wrapped in bedclothes and his bass voice conspired with the acoustics of the room to obscure his words. Whether or not this is a symbolic epiphany designed by Plato to stigmatize the man as obscure and remote, it is undeniable that Plato's general estimation of him was very negative: Plato is particularly insistent upon Prodicus' avid pursuit of both pleasure and the financial means to achieve it, and upon his monomania for overly precise definitions. His second appearance, now out of bed in the *Protagoras* (our fr. A 13), is basically a parody of this specialty. Other, non-Platonic, sources do not necessarily support Plato: they give us rather an impression of a wide-ranging dilettante whose interests included ethics and physiology, cosmology and anthropology—and, of course, rhetoric, the chief preoccupation of all the sophists. It is not particularly clear that one should attempt a unified critique of a man possessing so many disparate and apparently bizarre interests. His preoccupation with semantics is clearly established. His ultimate authorship of the *Choice of Heracles*, as reported by Xenophon, is generally accepted and testifies to his interest in ethics. It is held to be a fragment of a major work, the *Horae* (perhaps "Seasons"), but there is no general agreement about its contents nor even about the real meaning of its title. He seems to have written other pieces including a treatise *On Nature*, to one or another of which one might attribute the other odd bits of information and speculation contained in our fragments. But prevailing opinion is that the real interests of all the sophists were rhetorical and educational (i.e., ultimately epistemological in a rough and pragmatic sense) and their reported views and writings on special questions in science, history, or politics are normally taken as mere methodological devices and stances bound up with their prime goal of teaching their pupils cultural and political adroitness. M. Untersteiner, *The Sophists*, trans. K. Freeman (Oxford, 1954), pp. 209–21, is the one serious modern attempt to interpret the remains we possess as parts of a unified system of cosmological, anthropological, and political thought. In the opinion of modern scholarship, the date and manner of Prodicus' death remain unknown; scholars universally reject the statement in our fr. A 1 that he, like Socrates, was executed at Athens upon conviction for corrupting the young.

A. LIFE AND TEACHINGS

1. SUIDAS   Prodicus, a Cean from the island of Ceos, of the town of Iulis, a natural philosopher and sophist, a contemporary of Democritus of Abdera and Gorgias, a student of Protagoras of Abdera. He was executed at Athens on a charge of corrupting the youth.[1] [From HESYCHIUS; a shorter version in SCHOLIA on PLATO *Republic* 600C.]

---

[1] The last statement is surely false; the Byzantine encyclopedist has Prodicus confused with Socrates.

1a. PHILOSTRATUS *Lives of the Sophists* I 12   Prodicus of Ceos had such a great name for wisdom that the son of Gryllus [Xenophon], when a prisoner in Boeotia, used to go hear him lecture after posting a bond for his return to custody. When on an embassy to Athens, he appeared before the council and showed himself an extremely capable man, though a bit hard to hear because of his low-pitched voice. He used to seek out nobly born youths and persons from rich families, and even employed go-betweens in this pursuit, for he was very fond of making money and addicted to his pleasures. And even Xenophon did not disdain to recount Prodicus' speech *The Choice of Heracles* which I mentioned at the beginning [of this catalog]. Of course, why should we dwell on the nature of Prodicus' eloquence, since Xenophon has done it at sufficient length himself?

2. PLATO *Protagoras* 315CD   And then I saw Tantalus;[2] for Prodicus of Ceos was also visiting—he was in a chamber which at one time Hipponicus had used as a storeroom. . . . Prodicus, it appeared, was still lying in bed, wrapped in skins and a great many covers. [Pausanias, Agathon, and others were also there.] E But from outside the room I was unable to hear what they were discussing, although I tried very hard to hear Prodicus, since he struck me as terribly wise and even 316A divinely gifted. But because of the deep pitch of his voice, a rumble was set going in the room that obscured what was being said.

3. ——— *Hippias Major* 282C   [Socrates is speaking] Our comrade Prodicus here has often in the past come to visit in a public capacity; but just recently, when he came here from Ceos on public business, he gained the greatest renown, both in speaking before the council and in giving private lectures—and he also earned some marvelous fees by tutoring young men.

3a. ——— *Theaetetus* 151B   But if, when these young men do not seem to be really pregnant, recognizing that they have no need of me

---

[2] Quoted from *Odyssey* XI 582. The point (according to Burnet) of the comparison is that Prodicus is ill, and his "physical wretchedness" reminds Socrates of Tantalus in Hades.

I willingly lend them my aid as a matchmaker, to speak on the side of the god,[3] and I can pretty well guess from whose companionship they would profit. And many of them I have sent to Prodicus, as well as to other wise and divinely gifted men.

4. ——— *Apology* 19E   Since this indeed seems to me a fine thing, that one should be able to teach men, as do Gorgias of Leontini and Prodicus of Ceos and Hippias of Elis. For, fellow citizens, each of these men can go into every one of the cities and persuade young men, who have the freedom to associate with whomever they please,   20A to leave their other companions and join their own circle, paying a fee for the chance to do so and thanking them into the bargain.

4a. XENOPHON *Symposium* IV 62   I know, he said, that you [Antisthenes] have played the pander between Callias here and the wise Prodicus, inasmuch as you saw that the former was in love with wisdom and the latter in need of cash.

4b. ATHENAEUS V 220B   His [Aeschines the Socratic's; fr. 16 p. 50 Krauss] *Callias* contains the discord between Callias and his father, as well as abuse of the sophists Prodicus and Anaxagoras. For he says that Prodicus was to blame for his pupil Theramenes, and the latter for Philoxenus the son of Eryxis and Ariphrades the brother of Arignotus the fiddler,[4] the point of his gibe being to delineate the nature of the teachers' instruction through an exposé of the students' corruption and enthusiasm for vice.

---

[3] "To speak on the side of the god," *syn theōi eipein:* to say what one says with the hope that the divine powers both excuse a bold manner of speaking and ratify what is said in its best sense. To say or do something "without the god," *aneu theou, theōn ater,* would be to risk its being misunderstood or failing to convey one's true meaning, especially if one is using language, as here, that may appear odd or unseemly.

[4] "Fiddler," *kitharoedos,* literally, a professional lyre-player. The instrument was considered perfectly respectable for men of good birth to play as amateurs (Achilles plays, *Iliad* IX 185–87), unlike the *aulos* or pipe, but *professional* musicians in historical times were *déclassés;* hence the slightly contemptuous English term rather than "lyrist" or something similar.

5. ARISTOPHANES *Clouds* 360ff.   [The Chorus of Clouds; see *Birds* 692] We would pay heed to no other space-thinker except Prodicus— because of his wisdom and wit—and you [Socrates]. . . .[5]   *Tagenistae* fr. 490 Kock   Either some book has corrupted this man, or Prodicus, or one of the word-spinners.[6]

6. SCHOLIUM on ARISTOPHANES *Clouds* 361   He [Prodicus] was also the teacher of Theramenes, who was called "Loose Boot."[7]

7. DIONYSIUS OF HALICARNASSUS *Isocrates* 1   He [Isocrates] was a hearer of Prodicus of Ceos and Gorgias of Leontini and Tisias of Syracuse—the men having at the time the greatest fame among the Greeks for wit[8]—and, as some report, of Theramenes the rhetor, who was put to death under the Thirty Tyrants for appearing to lean toward democratic policies.

8. AULUS GELLIUS *Attic Nights* XV 20, 4   [Euripides] attended the lectures of Anaxagoras the natural philosopher and of Prodicus the rhetor.

9. MARCELLINUS *Life of Thucydides* 36   For a short time, as Antyllus says, he [Thucydides] affected the balanced clauses and antithetical vocabulary employed by Gorgias of Leontini, which were at that time in vogue among the Greeks; and also the nice defining of words as propounded by Prodicus of Ceos.

---

[5] "Space-thinker," *meteorosophistes*, a comic coinage; literally, "one whose wits dwell on the higher atmosphere." To some, the sophists' speculations were as exotic as anything accompanying space exploration in our own day.

[6] *Tagenistae* = "The Broilers," produced perhaps 410 B.C. "Word-spinners" = *adolescheis*, literally "idle talkers."

[7] "Loose Boot" = *kothurnos*, the loose-fitting boot of tragic costume, which fit either foot, hence a suitable nickname for someone who easily changed his political loyalties (as his enemies saw it).

[8] "Wit" = *sophia*, a word we render as "wisdom" when a Plato or Aristotle or even Xenophon is talking, but must take down a notch or two for most other Greeks, who tended to use it in what was certainly its more usual connotation, professional ability or skill.

10. QUINTILIAN III 1, 12   Of these figures, the first who are said to have dealt with commonplaces were Protagoras and Gorgias; Prodicus, Hippias, the aforesaid Protagoras, and Thrasymachus, the first to touch on questions of emotion.[9]   SCHOLIUM on ARISTOPHANES *Birds* 692 "When once you learn from us what is correct concerning the heavens . . . you may tell Prodicus to disappear for good." [*DK* I A 12 follows.] Callimachus was incorrect in listing Prodicus among the rhetors; clearly, compared with these, he was a philosopher.

11. PLATO *Cratylus* 384B   [Socrates is speaking.] Knowledge about terms happens to be an important matter. If indeed I had heard Prodicus' fifty-drachma lecture, which he claimed would succeed in conveying a complete education in the matter to anyone who heard it, nothing would have kept you [Hermogenes] from learning the truth about the correct usage of words. But I didn't hear it, only the one-drachma performance.

12. ARISTOTLE *Rhetoric* III 14, 1415b12   And so, whenever the moment is appropriate, one should say: "Now, pay attention, for this matter is as much your concern as mine"—or: "I am about to tell you something more terrible—or 'more wonderful'—than you have ever heard before." This is the time, as Prodicus says, when your hearers are dozing, to throw in something from his "fifty-drachma" speech.[10] Cf. QUINTILIAN IV 1, 73.

13. On Synonyms: PLATO *Protagoras* 337A   As he finished speaking, Prodicus said, "It seems to me that you speak well, Critias. For those present at such conversations should be *impartial* hearers of both

---

[9] "Commonplaces" = *loci communes*, forms of forensic or political argument which are available to both sides in debate, and hence "common" to both parties. E.g., two political opponents might both appeal to patriotism or ancestral traditions or the national pride of their community to prove the merits of contradictory programs of action.

[10] See J. M. Schram, "Prodicus' 'Fifty-Drachma Show-Lecture' and the 'Mytilene Debate' of Thucydides," *Antioch Review*, XXV (1965), pp. 105–30.

speakers, but not *undecided*, for these are not the same thing: while one should hear both speakers *impartially*, one should not judge them to be *equal* [same word in Greek as "undecided" above], but rather assign greater credit to the wiser man, and less to the one who is less wise. And, Socrates and Protagoras, I myself think it right that you agree with each other to *debate* but not to *dispute*. в For friends debate with friends in a spirit of goodwill, but enemies and rivals dispute with one another. Thus our session here will pass most agreeably. And thus, too, you who are speaking will gain *esteem* from us hearers, but not *praise*, for esteem arises in the hearts of men without simulation, while praise is often merely verbal and quite at variance with the real opinion of the man who utters it. c Again, we the hearers would thus gain the greatest *satisfaction*, but not *pleasure*, for satisfaction attends the learning experience when we are exercising our understanding and our reason, while pleasure accompanies eating or some other enjoyable accommodation of the wants of the body." As he completed this discourse, Prodicus was greeted by the applause of many of the bystanders. Cf. A 19.

14. ———— ———— 340A [Spoken to Prodicus] Indeed, our explication of Simonides stands in need of your special talent, whereby you distinguish the meanings of "will" [*boulesthai*, "to take an interior decision"] and "desire" [*epithumein*, "to be eager for"] and show that they are not the same thing . . . 340B Do "becoming" [*genesthai*] and "being" [*einai*] seem to be the same thing or different? Different, by Zeus!, said Prodicus. 341B That which is "terrible" [*deinon*], he [Prodicus] says, is "evil" [*kakon*]. . . . What did Simonides mean by the term "difficult" [*chalepon*], Prodicus? He meant "evil."[11]

15. ———— *Meno* 75E What do you say the word "end" [*teleutēn*] means? I understand by it something like "limit" [*peras*] or "finality"

---

[11] On the whole discussion, see Leonard Woodbury, "Simonides on *Aretē*," *Transactions of the American Philological Association*, LXXXIV (1953), pp. 135–63.

[*eschaton*]; in fact, I say that all three terms mean the same thing, although Prodicus might disagree with me.

16. ———— *Euthydemus* 277Eff. First of all, as Prodicus says, one must learn the correct usage of words. Which indeed is what our two visitors here [Euthydemus and Dionysodorus] have just been demonstrating to you, namely, that you did not understand the meaning of the term "learning" [*manthanein*]. This term is used by men in two senses: first, of a situation wherein a person begins in simple ignorance of something and 278A thereupon proceeds to gain knowledge of it; but second, it is used of the case wherein a person already having knowledge of something uses that knowledge carefully to inquire into something that is being said or done. More frequently, men call this latter situation "understanding" [*synienai*] rather than learning, but sometimes also "learning."

17. ———— *Laches* 197B But I think that the terms "fearless" and "brave" are not the same thing. In my opinion few men share in "bravery" [*andreias*] and forethought, while many possess "boldness" [*thrasytētos*], that daring and fearlessness which is really a failure to think ahead. Cf. 197D: Don't answer him, Laches. For you seem not to have noticed that he has that piece of wisdom from our friend Damon, and Damon is a close follower of Prodicus, who of all the sophists seems to be most accomplished in making fine distinctions between terms.

18. ———— *Charmides* 163B Tell me, I said, do you say that "doing" [*poiein*] and "making" [*prattein*] are the same thing? No, indeed, he said, nor that "working" [*ergazesthai*] and "doing" mean the same thing. I understand this from Hesiod, who said that "work" [*ergon*] is no shame [*Works and Days* 311 Rzach]. Do you think, if he said that the kinds of activities you were just mentioning were examples of "making" and "working," that he meant that there is no shame in making shoes or selling pickles or serving in a brothel? It is hardly right to think so, Socrates, and I contend that he saw a distinction between mere "doing" [*poiēsin*] and "making" or "working" [*praxeōs kai ergasias*] c and felt that a job [*poiēma*, "a thing done"] is sometimes an occasion for shame, when it is unaccompanied by distinctive excellence, but that a work is never a shame. Tasks done with an accompaniment of excellence and to some good end he called "works," and he called such enterprises "workings" or "makings." Cf. D: Indeed, I have heard Prodicus making such distinctions about terms ten thousand times.

19. ARISTOTLE *Topics* II 6, 112b22 Then again, there is the case where someone has claimed that an accidental characteristic of a thing is different from itself, just because its name is different, as Prodicus did, distinguishing three forms of pleasure: "joy" [*chara*], "delight" [*terpsis*], and "good cheer" [*euphrosyne*]; but all these are just different names for the same thing, "pleasure." ALEXANDER OF APHRODISIAS ad. loc. 181, 2 Prodicus attempted to assign to every term its own peculiar significance, as the Stoics also do when they argue that joy is a movement [of the soul] in accordance with reason, while pleasure is a movement contrary to reason; that delight is a form of pleasure connected with the sense of hearing, and good cheer a form connected with speech. But this is the sort of thing said by men who love to lay down trivial laws, but have no care to say anything sensible.

20. PLATO *Phaedrus* 267B [After *DK* 82 A 25] Hearing me say this, Prodicus laughed and declared that he alone had discovered the real art of discourse, to wit: one must employ neither long nor short speeches, but speeches of just the proper length.

B. FRAGMENTS

THE *HORAI* [SEASONS] OF PRODICUS

1. SCHOLIUM ON ARISTOPHANES *Clouds* 361 There is extant a book of Prodicus entitled *Horai*, in which he portrayed Heracles interviewed in turn by Virtue and Vice, each soliciting him to elect the manner of life represented by herself, with Heracles ultimately choosing the hardships offered by the former over the fleeting pleasures promised by Vice. PLATO *Symposium* 177B . Or, if you wish, consider the excellent sophists, who wrote works praising—in systematic fashion—the virtues of Heracles and others, especially the most worthy Prodicus. Cf. *Protagoras* 340D.

2. XENOPHON *Memorabilia* II 1, 21   And the wise Prodicus also expresses himself in this manner in his composition on Heracles, which he recited to large audiences. As I recall it, the story went this way. "Heracles," he said, "when he was growing from childhood into man's estate, at that time of life when young men are beginning to make their own decisions and thus to show whether they are embarked on the path of virtue or that of vice, went off to ponder in seclusion which path he should choose.   (22) And there appeared to approach him two tall female figures. One had a noble address and a bearing untouched by servility, with skin fair and pure, her glance circumspect, her person modest, dressed in white. The other's figure bespoke softness and luxury, her countenance showing the exaggerated whites and reds induced by cosmetics, her carriage unnaturally lofty and stilted, her eyes darting about restlessly, and wearing a costume such as made her physical ripeness easy to estimate. She paid a great deal of attention to herself, and kept watch to see if she was noticed by others, and often even looked back at her own shadow.   (23) As they approached Heracles, the former continued at her same pace, but the latter, anxious to reach him first, barged ahead and accosted Heracles thus: 'I see, Heracles, that you are undecided about the course of your life. If you should accept my friendship and follow me, I shall show you the path of greatest enjoyment and ease, and you will not fail to experience every last pleasure, while living quite free from trouble.   (24) First of all, you will have no thought for wars or woes, and your only concern will be to decide which delicious food or drink you may look for, what sights and sounds you might enjoy, or what pleasures of smell or touch will please you, what amorous connections will satisfy you most, how you will sleep most contentedly, and—in short—how you will gain all these good things with the least effort. (25) But if you have any suspicion that the supply of my gifts might fail, have no fear that I would ever subject you to the necessity of physical or mental struggle to obtain your desires. Rather, you will enjoy the use of what other men produce, and never know what it is to restrain yourself from exploiting whatever you can. For, truly, I grant to my associates absolute rights to please their fancy from every source whatsoever.' (26) When she had said this, Heracles asked, 'Lady, what is your name?' She replied, 'I am known to my friends as Happiness, although those with a bilious temper hate me and call me Vice.' (27) At that point the second woman approached and addressed Heracles: 'I too propose my suit to you, Heracles, with some knowledge of your parentage as well as your character as it took shape through the course of your upbringing. Whence in fact I anticipate that if you should take the path to me you will achieve honorable and wondrous deeds, and that you will come to think me still more admirable and estimable because of the excellence you attain. But I shall not deceive you with overtures promising pleasures, rather I shall truthfully disclose to you the face of reality as the gods themselves have constituted it. (28) The gods give no real benefits or honors to men without struggle and perseverance: to obtain the gods' favor you must serve them; to achieve the love of friends you must do well by them; to win the honors of a community you must become its benefactor; to gain the admiration you might crave from all Greece you must attempt to serve Greece well; to get abundant fruit from the earth one must cultivate it; to earn wealth from livestock one must learn to care for them; to prosper in war, to gain the power to succor friends and best one's enemies, one must study the techniques of warfare from its masters and exercise oneself in their proper employment—and finally, if you should wish to enjoy physical vigor, it is to the mind that the body must learn subjection, and discipline itself with hard work and sweat.' (29) Vice interrupted at this point, as Prodicus tells it: 'Do you realize, Heracles, that this person is promising you a long and arduous journey to reach her satisfactions? I, on the other hand, shall conduct you on the short and easy road to Happiness.' (30) And then Virtue spoke, 'Hussy! What good have you to offer?

Or what pleasure, you who will do nothing to gain even *that?* You who do not even wait for the urging of desire, before you rush to stuff yourself with enjoyments? You eat before hunger and drink before thirst. You drench your food in sauces to enjoy it the more; you scour the world for expensive wines and ices in the summertime in order to get some pleasure from what you drink. To sleep more comfortably you contrive all manner of luxurious bedding—indeed, you seek sleep not to refresh yourself from labors but just because you have nothing to do. You try to incite sexual lusts long before nature prompts them, plying every trick and using men as women. This is how you treat your devotees, debauching them by night and making them sleep away the most important part of the day. (31) Though you are immortal you have been denied the company of the gods, and you gain no honor among decent men either. And that which is most pleasant of all— praise of yourself—you *never* experience; nor do you ever contemplate the most beautiful of all sights, a fair work of your own doing. Who would believe your invitation? Who would grant any request of yours, and who in possession of his senses would become a member of your company? Flabby young men and stupid old ones: those who have passed through youth lazy and shiftless, and pass into old age pained and feeble, those ashamed of what they have done and burdened by what they should do, those who scamper after pleasures in youth and thus must fend off woes in old age. (32) I, on the other hand, am a companion of the gods as well as of upright men; no great deeds are done, in heaven or on earth, except through me. I am honored more highly than all else both among gods and those men who have virtue; I am the favorite spirit of the skilled, the faithful guardian of house-holders, the ready helper of servingmen, the active promoter of the works of peace and a strong ally in the toils of war, and the best possible sharer of friendship. (33) My friends enjoy a pleasant and untroubled diet, because they leave food and drink alone until they really desire them; their sleep is sweeter than that of the lazy, and they do not grumble when they miss it nor neglect their responsibilities to get it. Young men enjoy the praise of their elders and the latter relish the respect of the young. They take pleasure both in the memory of past deeds and the performance of present tasks. On my account they are befriended by the gods, beloved by their friends, and celebrated in their communities. And when their appointed end comes, they do not lie forgotten and unhonored: their glory flourishes forever in the memory of the race and its poetry. All these things are yours to possess, Heracles, son of noble parents, if you undertake to work diligently for the most genuine form of happiness.' " (34) In some such fashion as this, Prodicus related the instruction of Heracles by Virtue. Of course his performance was a masterpiece of stylistic elegance compared with that I managed just now.

ON NATURE

3. GALEN *On the Elements* I 9 [I 487 Kühn; 54, 21 Helmreich; cf. *DK* 24 A 2] CICERO *On the orator* III 32, 128 Why should I mention Prodicus of Ceos, Thrasymachus of Chalcedon, or Protagoras of Abdera, all of whom in their time wrote and spoke on the subject of natural philosophy? Cf. A 5 and A 10 above.

4. GALEN *On the Physical Faculties* II 9 [III 195 Helmreich; cf. xv 325 Kühn] Prodicus said in his work *On the Nature of Man*, "Phlegm is a portion of the humors that has been subject to heat and as it were 'overcooked'. " He got at this by deriving the words from the verb "to burn" [*pephlechthai*], since he had a special meaning for terms, although he acknowledged the thing itself in the same way as other people. The man's hairsplitting attention to terms is well enough attested in Plato. [See A 13 ff.] On the other hand, that which all men call phlegm, being white in color, he called *blenna* ["mucus"], which, being cold and damp humor, is found in greatest quantity in the aged and in those who have suffered frostbite, and no one in his senses would call these anything but cold and damp. Cf. *DK* 44 A 27 and 68 A 159.

FROM UNIDENTIFIED WRITINGS

5. PHILODEMUS *On Piety* cols. 9, 7 pp. 75-76 Gomperz, *Herkulanische Studien,* II (Leipzig, 1866) Persaeus appears in reality to be an atheist or at least an agnostic; in his *On the Gods* he says that Prodicus was not unpersuasive in writing that nourishment and useful articles were first acknowledged and honored as gods, and later that persons who first invented shelters or found new means of obtaining food or hit upon useful techniques were called names like Demeter, Dionysus, and the like.[12] Cf. MINUCIUS FELIX *Octavius* 21, 2 CICERO *On the nature of the gods* I 37, 118 But what of this? Prodicus of Ceos, the man who said that those things which benefit human life are what are called gods—what has he left us of religion? 15, 38 Persaeus . . . says that they are held to be gods who have discovered some significant alleviation of life's daily wants; moreover, even that these useful things or protecting devices themselves are called by divine names. [See also HECATAEUS OF ABDERA, *DK* 73 B 7.] SEXTUS *Against the Schoolmasters* IX 18 [See also DEMOCRITUS, *DK* 68 A 75.] Prodicus of Ceos says, "The ancients considered that the sun, the moon, and rivers and springs and anything else that helped sustain life were gods, because of their usefulness; for instance, the Egyptians considered the Nile a god." And thus bread has come to be called Demeter, and wine Dionysus, water Poseidon, fire Hephaestus, and so on with everything that is useful to man. (51) Those who are called in derision atheists[13] say that there is no god at all, such as Euhemerus . . . and Diagoras of Melos and Prodicus of Ceos and Theodorus. . . . (52) Prodicus says

---

[12] Philodemus' work is known only from a papyrus found at Herculaneum in very tattered condition. It is largely reconstructed (including a misspelling in our passage) from reports to the same general effect by Cicero, Galen, and Themistius (see note 15, p. 84). On Persaeus, a very minor figure in the history of Stoicism, see *RE* (1937), XIX 1, esp. col. 928ff.

[13] "Atheist" = *atheos*, literally, "godless," nearly always had a derogatory sense in antiquity, implying that a person was not only unable to believe in the existence of the gods but that this itself was a sign of the gods' hatred of him! Thus atheists disliked the term *atheos*. This Sextus implies with the word *epiklēthentes* ("nicknamed," "called in derision").

that anything which benefits life is assumed to be a god, such as sun and moon and rivers and springs and grassland and everything of that sort. THEMISTIUS *Orations* 30 p. 422 Dindorf . . . we are already near to the mystical rites and we shall blend the wisdom of Prodicus into our discourse. He derived all of mankind's sacrifices and mysteries and cults from the fair works of tillage, since it is his opinion both that the idea[14] of the gods comes to men in this way, and thus * * * he guarantees every act of piety.[15]

6. PLATO *Euthydemus* 305C   These men are the sort, Crito, who Prodicus says "are on the boundary between philosophy and politics," but in fact they think they are the wisest of all men. . . . D They think they are wise indeed, that is clear: for they are moderately philosophical as well as moderately political.

7. STOBAEUS IV 20, 65   From Prodicus: that desire doubled is love, and love doubled is madness.

DOUBTFUL

8. [PLATO] *Eryxias* 397D   A wise man, Prodicus of Ceos, was addressing this very point a little while ago in the Lyceum, but he seemed to his hearers to be talking so pointlessly that he was unable to persuade a soul that what he said was so. . . . E For a youngster had asked him in what sense he thought it was good to be wealthy and in

---

[14] "Idea" = *ennoian*; Diels's reading of MS *eunoian* = "goodwill."

[15] Themistius is evidently a bit confused here. If the other authorities quoted in B 5 are correct, then Prodicus could hardly be called a friend of religion and a supporter of (even a rationalized) cult practice. Of course, the other "authorities" are themselves interpreting Prodicus' words in terms of a theological controversy that was far more clearly drawn in their own day than it was in his. Most likely, Prodicus contented himself with the outright anthropological observations on the possible origins of cult and left it at that. See M. Untersteiner, *The Sophists*, trans. K. Freeman (Oxford, 1954), pp. 209–11.

what sense bad. And he answered, much as you have just done, that wealth was a good for men of honor who know how to use it properly, but an evil for the disreputable who do not know how to use it. And the same is true, he maintained, in the case of everything else: the things themselves will be good or bad in correspondence to the natures of those who make use of them.

9. —— *Axiochus* 366B [Socrates is speaking] You are not giving trustworthy testimony about me, Axiochus, for you think, just like the populace of Athens, because I have an intense curiosity about things that I am learned in some respect or other. Indeed, I would give much just to know a few common things—no chance of my understanding sublime thoughts. c These things which I have been saying are just chance echoes from the words of Prodicus, which I purchased from time to time for a half-drachma, or two drachmas, or even four—for the man would teach no one for nothing and used to repeat constantly the tag of Epicharmus, "One hand washes another: give in order to get." Not long ago, in a speech he delivered at the house of Callias, son of Hipponicus, he said such things about life that I was ready to resign from mine forthwith and, Axiochus, my soul ached to die.

FALSE

10. PLUTARCH *On Health* 8 p. 126D Prodicus, it seemed, handled the question smartly, when he said that fire is the best spice.

11. GALEN *On Medical Methods* x 474 Kühn And indeed, milk is best if one sucks it directly from the teat, as Euryphon and Herodotus and Prodicus think.

85. THRASYMACHUS

translated by FRANCIS E. SPARSHOTT

Nothing is known of Thrasymachus' life and works beyond what may be gathered from the material translated here. He came from Chalcedon in Bithynia (A 1), where he died, or at least had a memorial (A 8). Dionysius (A 3) thinks he was born later than Lysias, whose birth he assigns to 459 B.C. (*Lysias* 6). He was well known as an orator before 427 (B 4), and alive after the beginning of Archelaus' reign in 413 (B2). Aristotle's putting him earlier than Theodorus (A 2) is no help, since the latter's dates are unknown. The relevance of inferences from Plato's *Republic* (A 10, B 6a) depends on the extent to which Platonic dialogues are taken to be historical documents.

Materials for a critical list of Thrasymachus' works are lacking. The list given in Suidas may be complete (A 1). *Long Textbook* (B 3), *Introductions* (B 4), *Plaints* (B 5), *Knock-Down Arguments* (B 7), and *Exemplary Speeches* (cf. A 13) may be alternative titles for works mentioned in Suidas, or for parts of them.[1] Cicero's suggestion that he wrote *On Nature* (A 9) lacks any substantiation and seems unlikely.

A. LIFE AND TEACHINGS

1. SUIDAS   Thrasymachus of Chalcedon; sophist; from the Chalcedon in Bithynia. First demonstrated the use of period and clause, and introduced the current style of rhetoric. Student [?] of the philosopher Plato and the orator Isocrates. Wrote *Deliberative Speeches*, *Textbook on Rhetoric*, *Trivia*, *Subjects for Speeches*.

---

[1] For some possible equations, see F. Blass, *Attische Beredsamkeit*, 2d ed., I, 249.

2. ARISTOTLE *On Sophistical Refutations* XXXIV 183b29   But the people with big names nowadays have taken up the running (as it were) from many men who made the subject grow by advancing it piecemeal: Tisias after the pioneers, Thrasymachus after Tisias, Theodorus after him. Many men have made many partial contributions. . . .

3. DIONYSIUS OF HALICARNASSUS *Lysias* 6   Besides these I find a truly remarkable excellence in Lysias. Theophrastus [*On Diction* fr. 3 Schmidt] says that Thrasymachus was its originator, but I think it was Lysias, who in my judgment has the priority over him in chronology as well—granting that both of them were in their prime at the same time. . . . What is this excellence I speak of? The diction that condenses the thought and expresses it distinctly, a diction which is wholly appropriate and indeed essential to forensic speeches and to every genuine contest.

4. ARISTOPHANES *Banqueters* [produced in 427] fr. 198, 5ff. [From GALEN *Glossary of Hippocratic Terminology,* Introduction XIX 66 Kühn, dialogue between son and father]

—— Well, you will be tripped up by time, maybe.

—— That "tripped up" comes from the orators.

—— What will be the upshot of these things you say?

—— That "be the upshot" comes from Alcibiades.

—— Why do you keep making insinuations and speaking ill of men strenuous in good behavior?

—— O God! O Thrasymachus! Which advocate uses that piece of hairsplitting?

5. ARISTOTLE *Rhetoric* III 11, 1413a7   . . . and to call Niceratus "a Philoctetes bitten by Pratys," an image that Thrasymachus used when he saw Niceratus still unkempt and unwashed after his defeat by Pratys in a recitation contest.

6. ——— ——— II 23, 1400b19 ... as Conon called Thrasybulus a "daring counselor," and Herodicus told Thrasymachus, "You are always a daring fighter," and Polus, "You are always coltish."[2]

7. JUVENAL VII 203 Many have repented of their vain and sterile chair, as the death of Tharsymachus [?] proves.[3] SCHOLIAST Said of an orator in Athens who hanged himself.

8. ATHENAEUS X 454F Neoptolemus of Paros says in his *Epitaphs from Chalcedon* that the following epitaph is inscribed on the memorial to the sophist Thrasymachus: "Name: theta, rho, alpha, sigma, upsilon, mu, alpha, chi, omicron, sigma. Birthplace: Chalcedon. Profession: wisdom."

9. CICERO *On the orator* III 32, 128 [Prodicus, Thrasymachus, Protagoras; see *DK* 84 B 3] each of whom both spoke and wrote a great deal at that time about the nature of the physical world.

10. PLATO *Republic* I 336B Even while we were talking, Thrasymachus repeatedly started to break into the argument, but was promptly suppressed by his neighbors, who wanted to hear the argument out. But as we broke off with these words of mine, he held his peace no longer, but gathered himself like a wild beast and went for us as if to tear us apart. Polemarchus and I took fright and stampeded. Thrasymachus addressed himself to the company at large: "What nonsense is this, Socrates," he said, "that has gotten into you?" etc. Cf. 338C [B 6a].

11. ARISTOTLE *Rhetoric* III 8, 1409a2 There remains the paean, which people have used since Thrasymachus' day without being able to define it.

---

[2] These are elementary puns: the literal meanings of "Thrasybulus," "Thrasymachus," and "Polus" are "daring counselor," "daring fighter," and "colt," respectively.

[3] W. V. Clausen (OCT) confirms that *Tharsimachi* is in fact the reading of the best MS. Whatever his name, there is nothing to connect this Athenian with our Thrasymachus, who is invariably described as "of Chalcedon." The chair mentioned is, of course, a professorial chair.

12. CICERO *Orator* 13, 40 Isocrates, . . . who thought Thrasymachus and Gorgias (who nevertheless, were the first, according to tradition, to have submitted words to a more or less methodical arrangement) were chopped up into tiny phrases, whereas Thucydides was a bit abrupt and not plump enough (so to speak), was the first to begin padding thoughts with words and filling them out with gentler rhythms.

13. DIONYSIUS OF HALICARNASSUS *Isaeus* 20 Of those who made a profession of accurate expression and devoted their energies to argumentative oratory, among whom were Antiphon of Rhamnus, Thrasymachus of Chalcedon, Polycrates of Athens, the Critias who led the Thirty, and the Zoilus who left the writings against Homer, . . . Thrasymachus was clean-cut and precise, formidable in invention and in giving his meaning distinct and striking expression; but his works are all technical or showpieces, and no forensic [or political] oration of his has survived. One might say the same about Critias and Zoilus, too, except insofar as they differ from one another in their stylistic traits.

14. SUIDAS Vestinus, called "Julius," sophist. *Epitome* of Pamphilus' *Glossary* in 95 Books; *Select Vocabulary from the Works of Demosthenes; Selections from Thucydides, Isaeus, Thrasymachus (the Orator) and Other Orators.*

B. FRAGMENTS

⟨THE CONSTITUTION⟩

1. DIONYSIUS OF HALICARNASSUS *Demosthenes* 3 [p. 132, 3 Radermacher-Usener] The third kind of diction was the mixed, an amalgam of the two already mentioned [viz., the "severe" and the "simple"]. I cannot say whether the first to make it up and cast it into its present form was Thrasymachus of Chalcedon, as Theophrastus supposes [*On Diction* fr. 4 Schmidt], or someone else; but those who took it over, developed it, and brought it close to perfection were Isocrates of Athens among the orators and Plato the Socratic among the philosophers. Aside from Demosthenes, it would be impossible to find anyone who either cultivated more zealously the essentials and practical requirements of writing than these men, or gave a better demonstration of fine writing and ornamental devices. Anyway, Thrasymachus' own diction, if it really was one of the sources of the intermediate manner, would seem to deserve commendation on the score of its intentions alone: it is a good sort of mixture, and has adopted just what was serviceable in the other two. However, this example, from one of his political speeches, will show that he did not wield a power equal to his purposes:

"I wish, Athenians, that I had belonged to that ancient time when silence sufficed for young people, since the state of affairs did not force them to make speeches and the older men were managing the city properly. But since our fortune has reserved us for this later time, in which we submit to ⟨the government of⟩ our city ⟨by others⟩ but ⟨bear⟩ its misfortunes ourselves, and of these the greatest are the work neither of gods nor of chance but of the administration, one really has to speak. That man is either lacking in feeling or outstanding in patience who will continue to present himself for mistreatment at the hands of anyone who likes and will himself endure the blame for the treachery and cowardice of others. The time gone by is enough for us: instead of peace, we are at war; danger ⟨has brought us⟩ to such a pass that we cling to the day that is ending and dread that which is to come; instead of comradeship, we have fallen into mutual enmity and turbulence. Other people are rendered violent and contentious by the abundance of their good fortune; but we were calm when we were fortunate, and in misfortune, which tends to calm other people down, we have gone wild.

"Why should anyone put off speaking ⟨what⟩ is in his mind, if ⟨it has fallen⟩ to him to be injured by the present situation and he thinks he is on to something that will put an end to such things?

"I shall begin by showing that in speaking against each other those of our politicians, and others too, who are at odds with each other, have undergone what inevitably happens to people who try to win without thinking. They think they are saying the opposite to each other, and fail to realize that they are pursuing the same policies and that their opponents' arguments are included in their own. Just consider, right from the start, what each of them is after. To begin with, our ancestral constitution troubles them, though it is very easy to understand and is what all our citizens have most in common. But surely, whenever anything is beyond the scope of our own judgment, we must abide by what our elders have said; and whatever the old-timers saw for themselves, we must learn of from those who beheld it. . . ."

Well, that was the sort of language Thrasymachus used, between the two of them, well blended, and a handy starting point for both manners.

FOR THE LARISAEANS

2. CLEMENT *Miscellanies* VI 16 [II 435, 16 Stählin]   And while Euripides says in the *Telephus* [produced in 438], "Shall we who are Greeks be slaves to foreigners?" [fr. 719 Nauck (2d ed.)], Thrasymachus says in his speech for the Larisaeans, "Shall we be slaves to Archelaus; we who are Greeks, to a foreigner?"

LONG TEXTBOOK

3. SCHOLIAST ON ARISTOPHANES *Birds* 880   Thrasymachus, too, says the same as Theopompus [on the inclusion of the Chians in the Athenian prayer at the onset of the Peloponnesian War[4]], in his *Long Textbook*.

Besides the *Subjects for Speeches* [see above A 1] the following fragments cited under specific titles also belong to the *Textbook:*

4. ATHENAEUS X 416A   Thrasymachus of Chalcedon says in one of his *Introductions* that when Timocreon stayed with the Great King on a

[4] *FGrHist* 115 F 104.

visit, he put away a lot of food. When the King asked him what he could achieve after that, he said he would knock out more Persians than one could count. And next day he did score many victories, one after the other; and after that he shadowboxed. When asked for his reasons, he said that that was how many punches he had left over for anyone who came forward.

5. ARISTOTLE *Rhetoric* III 1, 1404a13   But some people have made a start on the subject [i.e., dramatization] in a small way, such as Thrasymachus in his *Plaints*.

6. PLATO *Phaedrus* 267C Cf. *DK* 80 A 26.   It is the Might of Chalcedon who seems to me to have systematically mastered tearful and moving speeches on old age and poverty. D And he was a great one for enraging many, as he said, and charming the enraged again by his spells; and champion at slandering and dispelling slanders from whatever source.   HERMIAS ad loc. p. 239, 18 Couvreur   The Chalcedonian, i.e., Thrasymachus, taught as follows: one must arouse the juryman to sorrow and solicit his pity, bewailing one's age, poverty, children, and the like.

6a. PLATO *Republic* I 338C   [Thrasymachus] says that the just is nothing other than the interest of the stronger.

7. PLUTARCH *Table-Talk* I 2–3 p. 616D   [In placing one's guests at table] one must have Aristotle's *Topics* [III 1ff.] or Thrasymachus' *Knock-Down Arguments* ready, as if one were preparing a theme on Comparisons—and thus get nothing useful done, but import hollow fame from the marketplace and theaters into our parties.

7a. PHILODEMUS *Rhetoric* II 49 [Supplement, ed. Sudhaus (Leipzig, 1895) pp. 42ff.]   Metrodorus [fr. 20ff., A. Körte, *Jahrb. f. cl. Phil.*, Supplement 17 (1880) 548] seems to make it clear enough in his first book *On Poems* that the rhetoric of the sophists has the status of an Art. . . . speak adequately ⟨in public⟩ about what is useful to the public, without

having learned the *Art* of Thrasymachus or of any of the rest of them.
. . . Thrasymachus and many others who have the reputation of possessing such techniques of political or rhetorical speaking,[5] but have
achieved nothing in those fields of which they claim to possess the
techniques.[6]

FROM AN UNSPECIFIED WORK

8. Hermias on Plato *Phaedrus* p. 239, 21 Couvreur [on "strength"
at 267c; see B 6]   In one of his own writings, he [Thrasymachus]
wrote something to this effect: that the gods take no notice of human
affairs, or they would not have left out justice, which is the greatest of
goods among men. For we see that men make no use of it.

---

[5] The *DK* text omits τέχνας after ῥητορικῶν, presumably by mistake.

[6] The indication of lacunae throughout this fragment in the *DK* text is irrecon-
cilable with the indications of either of the authorities cited. I have indicated the
only place where the reading is rendered significantly doubtful by a lacuna recognized by *DK*: for "speak in public" (ἐ[ν π]λήθε[ι) Körte reads "speak the truth"
(τἀ]ληθὲ[ς).

86. HIPPIAS

translated by DAVID GALLOP

Hippias' dates cannot be fixed exactly. The setting of Plato's *Protagoras*, in which he figures prominently (C 1), appears to be shortly before the Peloponnesian War. At *Hippias Major* 282E (A 7), he represents himself as "much younger" than Protagoras. He may therefore be regarded as a contemporary of Socrates, in middle life in about 430 B.C. He was evidently an important figure in Elis and made a great name for himself on diplomatic missions and lecture tours throughout Greece. The two dialogues bearing his name in the Platonic corpus portray him as a conceited polymath, claiming great learning in mathematics, astronomy, music, linguistic studies, literature, handicrafts, and mnemonics, given to oratorical displays and edifying moral homilies. The same impression is conveyed by other sources. Few if any of his own words have survived. Writings ascribed to him include a *Trojan Dialogue* (A 2, A 9; B 5), an *Elegy* (B 1), and a *List of Olympic Victors* (B 3). He is mentioned by Proclus (B 21) as the codiscoverer of the curve known as the quadratrix, which was used for the trisection of rectilinear angles and for the squaring of the circle.

A. LIFE AND TEACHINGS

1. SUIDAS Hippias of Elis, son of Diopeithes, sophist and philosopher, pupil of Hegesidamus, who defined the end as self-sufficiency. He wrote many things.

2. PHILOSTRATUS *Lives of the Sophists* I II, I   Hippias of Elis, the sophist, had such powers of memory, even in old age, that after hearing as many as fifty names only once, he could repeat them from memory in the order in which he had heard them. He introduced into his discourses geometry, astronomy, music, and rhythms. (2) He also discussed painting and sculpture. (3) These things he did in other places; but in Lacedaemon he went through genealogies and the foundings of cities[1] and their achievements, a theme that the Lacedaemonians enjoyed, because of their ambition to rule. (4) There is also extant his *Trojan Dialogue* [B 5], which includes a speech: Nestor at the fall of Troy counsels Achilles' son, Neoptolemus, as to the pursuits which a man should follow to gain a good reputation. (5) Although he represented Elis in a great many Greek cities, in no place did he destroy his reputation for public speaking and discussion, but he amassed great wealth, and was registered in the communities of large and small cities. (6) For the sake of making money he even went to Inycus, the tiny community of Sicilians, whom Plato makes fun of ⟨in⟩ the *Gorgias*.[2] (7) Becoming famous, for the rest of his life he enchanted Greece at Olympia with his varied and carefully prepared speeches. His interpreting was not defective, but full and natural, seldom resorting to poetic expressions.

3. [PLUTARCH] *Lives of the Ten Orators* p. 838A There was also born to him [Isocrates] in his old age, a child Aphareus, who was conceived by Plathanē, daughter of Hippias the orator, and who was the youngest of her three children. p. 839B As a young man he did not marry, but in old age he had a mistress named Lagiskē ... and later he married Plathanē, daughter of the orator Hippias. She had three children, of whom, as has been said, Aphareus was his. HARPOCRATION Aphareus. He was the son of Hippias, although thought to be the son of Isocrates. ZOSIMUS *Life of Isocrates* p. 253, 4 Westermarck He married a certain Plathanē, offspring of Hippias the orator.

4. PLATO *Apology* 19E It seems to me a fine thing, if one can teach men, as do Gorgias of Leontini, Prodicus of Ceos, and Hippias of Elis. Cf. *DK* 84 A 4.

[1] Reading καὶ πόλεων ἀποικίας.
[2] Perhaps at 493A.

5. ATHENAEUS V 218C Plato in the *Protagoras* [cf. C 1] introduces Hippias of Elis also, in the company of some of his fellow citizens, who could probably not have stayed in Athens safely before the one-year truce was concluded in the archonship of Isarchus, in the month of Elaphebolion [423 B.C.; see THUCYDIDES IV 117–18]. Cf. *DK* 80 A 11.

5a. XENOPHON *Symposium* IV 62 [See above *DK* 84 A 4a.] I know, he said, that you [Antisthenes] introduced Callias here to the wise Prodicus, . . . I know too that you introduced him to Hippias of Elis from whom he learnt the art of memorizing also.

6. PLATO *Hippias Major* 281A [Socrates, Hippias] Hippias, the fair and wise, how long it is since you put in to see us at Athens! —— I have not had time, Socrates. For when Elis needs to transact any business with one of the cities, she always approaches me first among her citizens, and chooses me to represent her, since she regards me as the ablest judge and interpreter B of the pronouncements of each city. So I have often represented her in other cities, but most often, and on the most numerous and important matters, in Lacedaemon. So much for your question why I do not come often to these parts.

7. —— —— 282DE [Hippias is speaking] Once when I went to Sicily, while Protagoras [see *DK* 80 A 9] was visiting there, when he was already famous and an older man, I myself, though far younger, made more than a hundred and fifty minas in a very short time. In one tiny place, Inycus, I made more than twenty. I returned home, took it to my father and gave it to him, much to his surprise and astonishment and that of the other citizens. And I should think that I have made more money than any other pair of sophists you care to mention. [For his dress, see *DK* 82 A 9.]

8. —— *Hippias Minor* 363C [Hippias] I should be acting strangely, Eudicus, I, who always go up from my home at Elis to the congress of the Greeks at Olympia at the time of the festival, D and also submit myself at the sacred precinct to speak on whatever subject anyone may choose from those I have prepared for a display, and to answer whatever question anyone may wish to ask, if I were now to run away from the questioning of Socrates. . . .   364A For never, since I began to compete at Olympia, have I met anyone superior to myself in anything.

9. ——— *Hippias Major* 286A [Hippias] By Zeus, Socrates, I recently made a great reputation there, discoursing on noble pursuits that a young man should follow. For I have a beautifully composed lecture on the subject, well arranged in its wording and in other ways. The preface and opening of my lecture run something like this [cf. A 2 (4)]: the story tells of Neoptolemus, at the fall of Troy, B asking Nestor what sort of noble pursuits a young man should follow to achieve a great reputation. After that comes a speech from Nestor, recommending to him a great many excellent and customary practices. I delivered this speech there [in Sparta], and I shall give it here [in Athens] in two days' time, in the school of Pheidostratus, along with many other things worth hearing. I have been asked by Eudicus, the son of Apemantus.

10. ——— *Hippias Minor* 364C [Hippias] For I say that Homer made Achilles the best man of those who went to Troy, Nestor the wisest, and Odysseus the wiliest.

11. ——— *Hippias Major* 285B [Socrates and Hippias] By the gods, Hippias, what kind of things do they [the Spartans] praise you for, and enjoy hearing? Obviously, it must be the things of which you have the finest knowledge, c things to do with the stars and properties of the heavenly bodies? —— By no means. They cannot abide those subjects at all. —— Well, do they like hearing about geometry? —— Not at all. Most of them hardly even know how to count.[3] ——Then they could scarcely bear to hear you discoursing on arithmetic. —— Indeed not, by Zeus. —— But what of those matters in

---

[3] Reading $\dot{\alpha}\rho\iota\theta\mu\epsilon\hat{\iota}\nu$.

which you can draw distinctions with greater precision than any man, D the force of letters, syllables, rhythms, and harmonies? —— Harmonies and letters indeed, my friend. —— Well then, what can it be that they do like to hear from you, and for which they praise you? Tell me yourself, since I cannot discover it. —— They like hearing, Socrates, about genealogies of heroes and men and the founding of cities, about how they were originally established, and, in short, the whole study of antiquity. E So I have been obliged to learn by heart and prepare all that sort of thing for their sake. —— By Zeus, Hippias, you are fortunate that the Lacedaemonians do not enjoy someone's going through the list of our own rulers, from Solon onwards; otherwise you would have trouble learning them by heart. —— Why should I, Socrates? I only have to hear fifty names once and I can repeat them from memory. —— True, I did not recall that you possess the art of memorizing. So I can understand how natural it is that 286A the Lacedaemonians should like you for your wide knowledge, and that they should use you, as children use old women, to tell them enjoyable stories.

12. —— *Hippias Minor* 368B   You most certainly are the wisest of all men in the greatest number of skills, as I once heard you proclaim, when you were recounting your great and enviable wisdom at the bankers' tables in the marketplace. You said that you had once visited Olympia, with all the clothing you wore on your body made by yourself. First, the ring you wore (you began with that) was your own work, C for you knew how to engrave rings; and another seal was also your work, and there was a skin-scraper and an oil-flask that you had made yourself. Then you said that you had yourself made the sandals you had on, and that you had woven your own cloak and tunic. And what struck everyone as the most remarkable thing and proof of the greatest wisdom was your saying that the girdle you wore around your tunic was like the Persian girdles of the costliest kind, and that you had woven this yourself. Besides this, you said that you had brought with you poems, epics, tragedies D and dithyrambs, and many prose writings variously composed; and that you had come with

a knowledge surpassing others in the arts which I just mentioned and in rhythms, harmonies, and in the correctness of letters, and a great many other things besides, as I seem to recall. And yet it seems that I forgot your art of memorizing, which you regard as your most brilliant achievement. Cf. *DK* 80 A 26.

13. ATHENAEUS XI 506F   In the *Menexenus* not only Hippias of Elis is mocked, but also Antiphon of Rhamnus and the musician Lamprus.[4]

14. XENOPHON *Memorabilia* IV 4, 5   I know that he [Socrates] once had the following discussion with Hippias of Elis also, about justice. Hippias, who had arrived in Athens after a long absence, encountered Socrates conversing with some others. He was saying how strange it was that if you wanted someone taught shoemaking, or woodwork, or metalwork, or horsemanship, you would be in no doubt where to send him for instruction. It was said there was no shortage of teachers, even if you wanted to produce justice in a horse or an ox. Yet if you wished to learn justice yourself, or to have your son or servant taught, you would not know where to go for a teacher.   (6) Hearing this, Hippias said, as if to make fun of him, "Are you still saying the same old things, Socrates, that I heard you saying long ago?" Socrates replied, "Not only do I go on saying the same things, Hippias, but—stranger still—I say them on the same subjects. You, I daresay, with your wide learning, never say the same things on the same subjects." "Naturally," said Hippias, "I always try to say something new."   (7) "About the things you know," said Socrates, "such as how many letters there are in 'Socrates' and how you spell it? Do you first say one thing but later try to say something else? Or on numbers, should someone ask you if twice five are ten, would you not give the same answer now as you did before?" "On those matters, Socrates," said Hippias, "like yourself, I always say the same things. But on justice I am absolutely certain that I

---

[4] Antiphon and Lamprus are mentioned at *Menexenus* 236A, but Hippias is not mentioned there nor elsewhere in the dialogue.

now have something to say that neither you nor anyone else could dispute."

15. TERTULLIAN *Apology* 46 [In a catalog of the sins of pagan philosophers] Hippias was killed while organizing a plot against the state.

16. AMMIANUS MARCELLINUS XVI 5, 8 If then it is true, as various writers record, that Cyrus the king, Simonides the lyric poet, and Hippias of Elis, acutest of the sophists, had powers of memory that they had acquired by drinking certain potions. . . . Cf. A 5a, A 11, A 12.

B. FRAGMENTS

ELEGY OF HIPPIAS

1. PAUSANIAS V 25, 4 [On the loss of the Messenian boys' chorus on the crossing to Rhegium] On that occasion the Messenians mourned the loss of the boys, and among other works carried out in their honor they dedicated bronze statues at Olympia, including the trainer of the chorus and the flute-player. The original inscription declared that the dedications were made by the Messenians on the strait; but at a later date Hippias the Wise, as he was called by the Greeks, composed elegiac verses upon them; the statues are the work of Calon of Elis. Cf. 27, 8.

NOMENCLATURE OF TRIBES

2. [*FHG* 6 F 1 1 156, 34] SCHOLIA on APOLLONIUS RHODIUS III 1179 [preceding *DK* 2 B 1] Hippias of Elis says in his *Nomenclature of Tribes* that a certain tribe was called *Spartoi*, and Atrometus says the same thing.

RECORD OF OLYMPIC VICTORS

3. PLUTARCH *Numa* 1   It is difficult to fix chronology accurately, especially when it is derived from the *List of Olympic Victors*, which Hippias of Elis is said to have published late, lacking any reliable starting point for his work.

COLLECTION

4. ATHENAEUS XIII 608F   Among women famous for their beauty was Thargelia of Miletus, who was married fourteen times, and who was of great beauty in appearance, as well as wise, according to Hippias the sophist, in his work entitled *Collection*. HESYCHIUS Thargelia: "Thargelia is of Milesian descent, fair in looks, and wise in other respects, so that she controlled cities and rulers. Hence she was married to numerous eminent men."

TROJAN (DIALOGUE)

5. PLATO *Hippias Major* 286A [A 9] Cf. *DK* A 2.

FROM UNCERTAIN WORKS

6. CLEMENT *Miscellanies* VI 15 [II 434, 19 Stählin]   On the other side, we have the witness of the sophist Hippias of Elis, who made the same statement regarding the question before me. We may adduce his evidence to the following effect: "Some of these things may have been said by Orpheus, some by Musaeus briefly in various places, some by Hesiod and Homer, some by other poets, others in prose works of Greek and non-Greek writers; but by putting together the most significant and kindred material from all these sources, I shall make this piece both new and varied."

7. DIOGENES LAERTIUS I 24 [Concerning Thales' teaching on the soul of the universe; *DK* 11 A 1]   Aristotle and Hippias say that he [Thales] ascribed soul even to inanimate things, arguing from the magnet and from amber. Cf. ARISTOTLE *de Anima* I 2, 405a19.

8. EUSTATHIUS *Paraphrase of Dionysius Periegetes* 270   Hippias derives the names of the continents [viz., Asia and Europe] from Asia and Europa, the daughters of Oceanus.

9. HYPOTHESIS to SOPHOCLES *Oedipus Rex* v [SCHOLIA II 12, 11 Dindorf]   The poets since Homer have adopted a distinctive usage in referring to the kings before the Trojan War as "tyrants." For this term was passed on to the Greeks at some late period in the time of Archilochus, as the sophist Hippias says. Homer, at least, calls Echetus, who was the most lawless of all of them, not a "tyrant" but a "king": "to King Echetus, bane of mortals" [*Odyssey* XVIII 85]. It is said that the word "tyrant" is derived from the name "Tyrrhenians," for some of these were dangerous for their robbery.

10. PHRYNICHUS *Extract* p. 312 Lobeck   They say that Hippias and a writer named Ion used the term "deposit." We shall speak of a "trust deposit,"[5] following the usage of Plato, Thucydides, and Demosthenes.

11. PLUTARCH *Lycurgus* 23   Hippias the sophist says that Lycurgus himself was of a most warlike disposition and experienced in many campaigns. . . .

12. PROCLUS *On Euclid* p. 65, 11   Friedlein [See *DK* 14 A 6a.] After him [Thales], Mamercus, brother of the poet Stesichorus, is mentioned as having been consumed with zeal for geometry, and Hippias of Elis has recorded that it was in geometry that he gained his reputation.

---

[5] The contrast is between the terms *parathēkē* and *parakatathēkē*.

13. SCHOLIA on ARATUS 172 p. 369, 27 Maass [following *DK* 2 B 18] Hippias and Pherecydes [*FGrHist* 3 F 90 I 84, 33] seven [i.e., they say that the Hyades are seven in number].

14. SCHOLIA on PINDAR *Pythian* 4, 288   Pindar in the *Hymns* [fr. 49 Schroeder] says that she [the stepmother of Phrixus] was Demodice, but Hippias says that her name was Gorgopis.

15. ——— *Nemean* 7, 53   And, third, [Ephyra] at Elis, of whom Hippias makes mention.

16. STOBAEUS III 38, 32   From Plutarch's ⟨*On*⟩ *Slander:* "Hippias says that there are two kinds of envy: one kind is just, when one begrudges bad men the honor given them; the other kind is unjust, when one begrudges it to good men. The envious have double the distress of others; for they are vexed not only, as others are, by their own ills but also by others' goods."

17. ——— III 42, 10   From Plutarch's ⟨*On*⟩ *Slander:* "Hippias says that slander is a terrible thing; he calls it this, because the law provides no redress against slanderers, as it does against thieves. Yet slanderers are thieves of one's best possession, namely friendship. Hence violence, wicked as it is, is more just than slander, in that it is not concealed."

18. *Life of Homer* [Roman] p. 30, 27 Wilamowitz   Hippias again, and Ephorus [say that Homer came from] Cumae.

19. PETROGRAD PAPYRUS no. 13 col. 2, 11 [ed. Jernstedt, *Journal des Unterrichtsmin* (Russian), Oct. 1901, p. 51]   "Of Hippias"; title not preserved.

DOUBTFUL

20. ARISTOTLE *Poetics* 25, 1461a21   [One must solve the difficulty by paying regard] to the accentuation, as Hippias of Thasos solved the problems of "we grant him" and "the part of which decays in the rain." *On Sophistical Refutations* IV 166b1   It is not easy to base an argument upon accentuation in unwritten discussions, but in written ones and in poetry it is easier. Thus some critics emend Homer, to meet the charge that his expression τὸ μὲν οὐ καταπύθεται ὄμβρῳ [*Iliad* XXIII 328] is extraordinary. They solve the difficulty by accentuation, pronouncing the ου more sharply. And the passage about Agamemnon's dream they explain by saying that Zeus did not himself say "*we grant* him the fulfillment of his prayer" [B 15], but that he instructed the dream *to grant* this.

21. PROCLUS *On Euclid* p. 272, 3 Friedlein   Nicomedes trisected all rectilinear angles by means of conchoid lines, whose peculiar character he himself discovered, and whose genesis, structure, and properties he handed on. Others have done the same thing by means of the quadratrices of Hippias and Nicomedes, and they too have used mixed lines, the quadratrices.

C. IMITATION

1. PLATO *Protagoras* 337C   After Prodicus, the wise Hippias spoke: "Gentlemen present," he said, "I regard all of you as kinsmen, relatives, and fellow citizens,   D by nature, if not by convention: for by nature like is kin to like, whereas convention is a tyrant over men, and constrains them against nature in many ways. Hence, for you who know the nature of things, and who are the wisest of the Greeks, and for that very reason have assembled at the very shrine of wisdom in Greece, at the largest and finest house in this very city, it were a disgrace E to behave in no way worthy of this reputation, but to quarrel with one another like the meanest of men. I therefore request and counsel you, Protagoras and Socrates, to accept us as your mediators and agree 338A upon a compromise. You, Socrates, should not adopt a mode of discussion that insists on precision with excessive brevity, if this is unacceptable to Protagoras, but should let go and relax the reins of your discourse, so that it may appear more dignified and graceful to us.[6] Nor, on the other hand, should Protagoras unfurl full sail and give it to the wind, launching into an ocean of words, so that he loses sight of land. Rather, you should both of you strike a middle course. Do this, take my advice, and choose an umpire, chairman, or president, B who will preserve a proper length in the speeches of both of you.

[6] Reading ἡμῖν.

87. ANTIPHON

translated by J. S. MORRISON

CONTENTS

Contents

The Antiphon with whom we are concerned was an Athenian of the parish of Rhamnus and a contemporary of Socrates, with whom Xenophon portrays him in conversation (A 8). He is said to have been a little younger than Gorgias (A 3 [9]), by whom his oratorical style was undoubtedly influenced. He was a pioneer at Athens of the art of speaking, both teaching rhetoric (A 7) and writing books about it (XXXI–XXXII). One of the latter seems to be the collection of specimen speeches of prosecution and defense in each of the three types of homicide recognized under Athenian law, which is extant under the name of the *Tetralogies* (II–IV). Three actual forensic speeches of his survive (I, V, VI); and fragments are preserved of seventeen others, as well as of two speeches before the Athenian Assembly (IX–XXV, VII, VIII), and an indeterminate work called *Invective against Alcibiades* (XXX). His interest in *logoi*, words, speaking, and debate is to be compared with the activity of Socrates and the older visiting public teachers, Protagoras, Gorgias, Prodicus, and Thrasymachus. Like Socrates, Protagoras, Gorgias, and Prodicus, he was also interested at some time in the problem of knowledge and in the nature of the physical world, as appears from the remaining fragments of his two books *On Truth* (XXVI). To his work *On Concord* fourteen fragments are definitely attributed by the authors who preserve them; and we attribute to it a further fifteen fragments which appear to be concerned with problems of education, psychology, and sociology. The *Politikos* (XXVIII) seems to have dealt with similar general topics. In a book *On the Interpretation of Dreams* (XXIX) he seems to have exercised in a subject of much contemporary interest that trait of cleverness for which he was always noted. Again like Socrates, Antiphon was the butt of the comic writers. They picked on his ingenuity as a pleader, his money-making propensity (A 4 [13], 5 [7], 6 [7]), and his psychological ideas. It seems likely that the story, apparently deriving from Caecilius, of his Pain-and-Grief clinic at Corinth at which he advertised treatment by means of *logoi* was an invention of the comic stage analogous to Socrates' Thinking-Shop. As a politician (A 11) he was active in organizing the movement which led to the modified democracy of the Four Hundred in 412 B.C., and on its collapse stood his trial for treasonable dealings with the enemy. In spite of a famous speech in his own defense, he was condemned and put to death in 411. His epitaph was well written by Thucydides (A 11 [2]).

Pseudo-Plutarch (A 3 [9]) says that he was born at the time of the Persian wars (i.e., 479 B.C.) and was a little younger than Gorgias. Gorgias is said by Philostratus to have impressed the Athenians when he was getting on in years (cf. *DK* 82 A 1 [3]), that is to say, presumably on his diplomatic mission to Athens in 427. He would have been fifty-six or fifty-seven in 427, which seems about right. We may then accept the date of 479 for Antiphon's birth and suppose him to have been sixty-eight at the time of his death in 411. The name Nestor which he was given was, we are told, specifically connected with his persuasiveness (A 1 [2] for ref.), but he would perhaps not have been given it unless he was also getting on in years. The *Tetralogies* and the *Prosecution for poisoning* have been dated in the earliest period of his life on grounds of style and usage. The *Murder of Herodes* is dated about 424 and the *Chorus-boy* just before his death.

In the first century B.C., Caecilius of Calacte wrote a work on Antiphon which appears to be the source of our main secondary authorities, pseudo-Plutarch (A 3), Photius (A 4), and Philostratus (A 6). These accounts confuse Antiphon of Rhamnus with two other near-contemporary Antiphons, the son of Lysonidas and the tragic poet. Philostratus, writing the *Lives of the Sophists*, makes mention of Antiphon's nonrhetorical works; pseudo-Plutarch, writing the *Lives of the Ten Orators*, followed by Photius, makes no mention of them, as is natural. Didymus, also in the first century B.C., gave a critical account of Antiphon in which he appears to have distinguished two public teachers (*sophistai*) of that name from other Antiphons (presumably the two mentioned above). Didymus, in positing two *sophistai*, seems to have argued that the difference of genre (*eidos*) between the forensic and political speeches on the one hand and the *Truth*, *Concord*, and *Politikos* on the other (which latter he is satisfied were written by the "so-called diviner and interpreter of dreams") requires the conclusion that there were two different authors, not one only as had previously been thought. Hermogenes, who writes in the second century A.D. and reports Didymus' argument, declares that, although he is in two minds because of the marked difference of style between the two kinds of work, yet he is not convinced by Didymus' argument "owing to the remarks of Plato and others," for in his opinion the style of the *Truth* is Thucydidean while that of the speeches is not. Hermogenes appears then to be taking Plato *Menexenus* 236A (A 7 [1]) as referring to Thucydides as Antiphon's pupil and thus making a connection between Antiphon the teacher of rhetoric and Thucydides. In Hermogenes' opinion the connection lies between the author of the *Truth*, which he was presumably able to read, and Thucydides. Galen, writing like Hermogenes in the second century A.D., also appears not to distinguish between the orator and the author of the *Truth*. The distinction, of which there is no trace before Didymus, is quite arbitrary and appears to have been already rejected while the works on which it was based still survived. The reasons for maintaining it now are quite insubstantial.

The argument from style is unconvincing, since we should expect differences in the style of a writer whose work included speeches and treatises and was spread over a considerable period of time. The views put forward in the papyrus fragments of the *Truth* are indeed radical, but not necessarily to be associated with ultrademocratic opinions any more than with the critics of Athenian democratic society in the late fifth century. In any case Antiphon would probably have regarded himself, not as an antidemocrat, but as a reformer of democracy. If the critical attitude to contemporary views of *dikaion*, "justice," in the same fragments seem contrary to the extremely conventional views of law expressed in the speeches, there is no reason to think that the composer of a speech for a client to deliver before an Athenian jury would feel it necessary or desirable to credit his client with anything more than the most conventional attitude to law and religion, whether or not he held such an attitude himself. Nor are the opinions of the *Concord* on education, psychology, and sociology really at variance with the criticisms of the *Truth*. Much has been made of the so-called inconsistencies between the *Truth* and the speeches on the one hand and the *Concord* on the other,[1] but there is nothing which rules out a single author.

Antiphon, put together again, is in himself a striking figure, a man whose talents might well have been, as Thucydides says they were, both admired and feared by his contemporaries. He illustrates the wide range of indigenous intellectual activity at Athens before and at the outset of the Peloponnesian War, and more than any other person enables its map to be drawn. He also offers a striking contrast and comparison with Socrates, with whom he shared that intellectual climate, as he shared the fate of trial and death at the hands of an Athenian jury.

---

[1] E.g., S. Luria, *Eos*, LIII (1963), pp. 63–67, and E. Bignone, *Studi sul pensiero antico* (Naples, 1938), pp. 161–74. For a more extended argument against partition, see J. S. Morrison in *Proceedings of the Cambridge Philological Society* (1961), pp. 49–58.

CONCORDANCE

between the numbers in the A and B sections in Diels-Kranz and the numbers in the A and B sections in this edition

Diels-Kranz		This Edition		Diels-Kranz		This Edition	
A	1	A	1 (1) and (3)	B	21	B	89
	2		2		22		93
	3		8		23		94
	4		13		24, 24a		96, 95
	5		9		25		97
	6		3 (18), 6 (5)		26		98
	7		12 (1)		27		99
	8		12 (2)		28		100
	9		12 (3)		29		101
					30		102
B	1	B	67		31		103
	2		70		32		104
	3		71		33		106
	4		72		34		107
	5		73		35		108
	6		74		36		109
	7		75		37		110
	8		76		38		111
	9		77		39		112
	10		78		40		113
	11		79		41		114
	12		80		42		115
	13		81		43		116
	14		82		44, 44a		90–92,
	15		83				XXVII A 6 (11–12)
	16		84		45		120
	17		85		46		121
	18		86		47		122
	19		87		48		135
	20		88		49		123

Concordance

Diels-Kranz	This Edition	Diels-Kranz	This Edition
B 50	B 129	B 83	B 170
51	130	84	171
52	131	85	172
53, 53a	132, 133	86	173
54	134	87	174
55	126	88	175
56	127	89	176
57	128	90	177
58	124	91	178
59	125	92	179
60	117	93	180
61	118	93a	181
62	119	93b	182
63	136	94	183
64	137	95	184
65	138	96	185
66	139	97	186
67, 67a	140, 141	98	187
68	142	99	188
69	143	100	189
70	144	101	190
71	145	102	191
72	146	103	192
73	147	104	193
74	148	105	194
75	149	106, 106a	195, 196
76	150	107	197
77	151	108	198
78	152	109	199
79	153	110	200
80	154	111	201
81, 81a	155, 156	112	202
82	169	113	203

Diels-Kranz	This Edition	Diels-Kranz	This Edition
B 114	B 204	B 117	B 206
115	205	118	See note *ad fin.*
116	50		

A. LIFE AND WRITINGS

1. GENERAL BIOGRAPHY AND CRITICISM 1–6 *Suidae Lexicon* ed. Adler (= SUIDAS) 1 245 21–28 *A*

(1) [*DK* A 1] Antiphon, an Athenian, a diviner and writer of verses and public teacher (*sophistēs*). He was given the nickname of Speech-cook.

(2) Antiphon, son of Sophilus, an Athenian, by parish Rhamnusian. No teacher of him is known. Nevertheless, he started the forensic kind of speech after Gorgias. He is said actually to be the teacher of Thucydides. Cf. A 2 (5), A 5 (9).   [He is said to be a pupil of Thucydides at A 3 (7) and A 4 (8).] He was given the nickname of Nestor. Cf. A 3 (6), A 4 (12), A 5 (5), A 6 (5).

(3) [*DK* A 1] Antiphon, an Athenian, an interpreter of dreams. He wrote a book about the interpretation of dreams [A 12; B 152–56].

2. [*DK* A 2] Hermogenes *On Kinds* [*of Literary Composition*] B 399, 18 Rabe.[2]

(1) Discussion of Antiphon must be prefaced by the reminder that, as Didymus the grammarian and several others have remarked, and as inquiry reveals, there lived a number of Antiphons and two professional teachers whom we must consider.   (2) One of these two is the rhetorician to whom are attributed the forensic speeches and public addresses and others of this type.   (3) The other is the so-called diviner and interpreter of dreams to whom are said to belong the books *On the Truth* [B 67–116] and the book *On Concord* [B 117–45][3] and the *Politikos*

---

[2] Hermogenes, who wrote in the 2d century A.D., uses an account of Antiphon written by Didymus in the 1st century B.C.

[3] In the MSS, "and the public addresses" appears again here. Editors delete.

[B 146–51]. (4) I myself am in two minds. The difference of genre among these works convinces me that there were two Antiphons. For really there is a great discrepancy between the books of the *Truth* and the others, but the remarks of Plato [*Menexenus* 236A] and other authors remove this conviction. (5) For I am told by many that Thucydides was the pupil of Antiphon of Rhamnus [cf. A 1 (2)]; and while I know that it is to the Rhamnusian that the forensic speeches belong, I am also aware that Thucydides is very different from him [cf. A 10 (6)] and does employ a kind of literary composition which is common to the books of the *Truth*. (6) And so I am not convinced by Didymus' argument. (7) At the same time, whether there was one Antiphon employing two such different styles or two in fact, each practicing a different style, we must consider each separately. For there is, as I have said, a great gap separating them. (8) The Antiphon who was a Rhamnusian, accordingly, whose forensic speeches are preserved, while showing political flair in the clarity and practical nature and, in other respects, expressive quality of his style, all of which result in persuasiveness, nevertheless shows those qualities to a lesser degree than the other [nine] orators, for he is, of course, the first to have pursued this kind of speaking and is the absolute inventor and originator of the political genre. He is chronologically the eldest of all the ten orators. He employs grand language to no small degree, but yet in a rather fine way this grand language is worked into the context of the speech and does not seem out of place as in the case of Hypereides, nor, as in the case of Aeschines, is his language sophistically elaborated, although his style is often high-flown. Yet he takes care not to let it satiate the reader. Nevertheless, his style is rather forbidding, and clever at the same time. (9) The other Antiphon, on the other hand, to whom belongs the book *On Truth*, is not a bit the politician, but is grand and pompous, particularly in his way of dealing with every matter by categorical assertions, characteristic of a style which is dignified and aiming at grandeur. His diction is lofty and rugged, almost harsh, and employs amplifications without achieving clarity, with the result that he confuses the argument and is generally obscure. But he is at the same time painstaking in his composition and takes delight in the even

balancing of clauses. I should not, however, say that the author has
expressive character or a practical quality; nor would I allow him
cleverness, except of a superficial kind which is not really cleverness at
all. Critias, too, is close to this style. For this reason we will talk about
Critias immediately after him.

3. [PLUTARCH] *Lives of the Ten Orators* 832B–834B[4]
(1) Antiphon was son of Sophilus and, by deme, Rhamnusian.
(2) He was his father's pupil [cf. A 4 (7), A 5 (3), A 6 (4)]; (now his
father was a teacher to whom people say that Alcibiades went to school
when he was still a child) and acquired speaking ability, as some think,
from his own natural bent. Avoiding active politics, he formed a school.
[Cf. A 7.]   (3) He argued with Socrates over words, not disputatiously,
but wishing to convince his opponent, as Xenophon reported in the
Memorabilia. [See A 4 (9), A 8, A 9.]   (4) He also composed on behalf
of those Athenians who asked him certain speeches for suits in the
courts, being the first to turn to this employment according to some
authorities. [Cf. A 4 (10).]   (5) At any rate, no forensic speech is recorded
of his predecessors, nor indeed of his contemporaries, because it was
not yet customary to write speeches, neither of Themistocles nor of
Aristides nor of Pericles, although the circumstances of the time provided many opportunities and demands for such speeches. It was not,
furthermore, through lack of ability that they failed to compose them,
as is plain from what is said in the historians about each of the afore-
mentioned statesmen. But all those whom, going as far back as possible,
we can record as employed on speeches of this kind can be found to
have had contact with Antiphon late in his life, i.e., Alcibiades, Critias,
Lysias, Archinus.   (6) He first published manuals of rhetoric, being a
man of sagacity, which was why he was called Nestor.   (7) Caecilius,
in the treatise about him, is evidence that he was a pupil of the historian
Thucydides, in consideration of the praise Antiphon receives in his

---

[4] The author uses Caccilius of Calacte, 1st century B.C., who wrote a work on
Antiphon and also a work on the Ten Orators. See S. F. Bonner, *Literary Treatises
of Dionysius of Halicarnassus* (1939), p. 9, n. 4.

history.[5]   (8) In his speeches he is precise, persuasive, and ingenious in developing a theme, and has a professional touch when he is in a difficulty. He takes unexpected lines of argument and tries to turn the speech in the direction of what is customary and related to experience, aiming particularly at what has a good appearance.   (9) He was born at the time of the Persian war and of the sophist Gorgias, being a little younger than he; and his life lasted until the overthrow of the democracy by the Four Hundred, in which he seems to have had a hand. (10) He was trierarch of two ships, served as a general, and was victorious in many engagements; he brought over to their side important allies; he armed those of military age [cf. B 48] and manned sixty *triereis*; he was ambassador on a number of occasions on their behalf [and] in particular to Sparta when Eetioneia was fortified.   (11) But when the Four Hundred were overthrown, he was indicted with Archeptolemus, one of the Four Hundred, and condemned. He suffered the penalty of treason and was cast out of the city unburied, and, together with his descendants, was posted as an outlaw.   (12) and (13) [refer, like the greater part of (10), to Antiphon the son of Lysonidas; cf. XENOPHON *Hellenica* II 3, 40 as the writer himself notes].   (14) [refers to Antiphon the tragedian].   (15) Sixty works are extant under the name of the orator, twenty-five of which Caecilius says are spurious. (16) He is lampooned for love of money by Plato [the comic poet] in the *Peisander*.   (17) [refers to Antiphon the tragic poet, see A 13]. (18) [*DK* A 6] [He is said to have composed tragedies by himself and in collaboration with Dionysius the tyrant. While still engaged in poetry] he composed a manual for the avoidance of troubles, on the analogy of the treatment of the sick by doctors; and getting himself a room near the marketplace at Corinth he advertised that he had the power of curing those that were in trouble by means of speech; and discovering the causes of their sickness by inquiry he consoled the sick;[6] but

---

[5] Photius (A 4 [8]) and Tryphon (A 10 [5]) confirm the statement of Caecilius, but the Genos (A 5 [9]), the Suda (A 1 [2]) and Hermogenes (A 2 [5]) say that Antiphon was the *teacher* of Thucydides.

[6] Cf. A 4 (15), A 5 (6), A 6 (6). Antiphon's establishment looks like Socrates' "Thinking-shop," and, like it, seems to be a creation of the comic writers.

thinking that the profession was beneath his dignity he turned to rhetoric. (19) There are some who attribute the book of Glaucus of Rhegium about poets [*FHG* II 23] to Antiphon. (20) The speech about Herodes [B V] is particularly praised, and also the one against Erasistratus about the peacocks [B XX], and the one about the indictment which he wrote on his own behalf [B IX], and the one against Demosthenes the general for illegal conduct [B X]. (21) He also wrote a speech against Hippocrates the general[7] and secured a conviction in an undefended suit. (22) There follows the decree passed in Theopompus' archonship [411 B.C.], when the Four Hundred were dissolved, according to which it was decreed that Antiphon should be tried. It is quoted by Caecilius. (23) "The Council decreed, on the twenty-first day of the prytany, Demonicus of Alopece was secretary, Philostratus of Pallene was president, Andron [cf. B 32] proposed: concerning the men whom the generals denounce as having acted as envoys to Sparta to the detriment of the city, and having sailed on an enemy ship from the camp, and having proceeded by land through Deceleia, Archeptolemus, Onomacles, and Antiphon, that they be arrested and delivered to the court for punishment. The generals are to produce them, assisted in addition by whomsoever the generals may choose from the Council up to the number of ten, so that judgment may be delivered upon them in person. The Thesmothetae are to summon them tomorrow, and when the summonses have been returned to court they are to bring them into court for trial on a charge of treason. The chosen assistant prosecutors and the generals and anyone else who wishes shall prosecute them. Whomsoever the court condemns shall suffer whatever the law of treason lays down." (24) To the decree is appended the sentence: "Archeptolemus the son of Hippodamus of Agryle in person, Antiphon the son of Sophilus of Rhamnus in person, stand convicted of treason. For these two the penalty is to be handed over to the Eleven and for their property to be confiscated, a tithe being reserved for the Goddess, their houses to be demolished and marks to be set up on the sites with the inscription 'the property of the traitors Archeptolemus

---

[7] Some MSS read "doctor"; see A 4 (17) and B XXI.

and Antiphon,' the demarchs to make a declaration of their property, no one to be allowed to bury Archeptolemus and Antiphon at Athens or in land under Athenian sovereignty, and Archeptolemus and Antiphon to be deprived of citizen rights and their children both bastard and born in wedlock, and if anyone adopts one of the children of Archeptolemus and Antiphon, the adopter to be deprived of citizen rights. All this to be written on a bronze *stēlē* and to be set up in the place where the decrees relating to Phrynichus are."

4. PHOTIUS *Bibliotheca* cod. 259 p. 485b9[8] (1) Various works of Antiphon were read. His writings have the quality of precision, persuasiveness, and cleverness of invention. He also displays a professional touch when in difficulties and takes unexpected lines in argument. His speeches show an inclination to customary behavior and common experience, aiming particularly at what is fair-seeming.   (2) But the Sicilian Greek writer Caecilius says that he does not use artificial forms of speech, but that his thoughts are expressed in a straightforward and unaffected manner.

(3) He adds that he neither aims at nor employs an ingenious turn of speech or a deliberate change from the normal, but that he leads his hearer in the desired direction by means of the actual sentiments themselves and their natural logical sequence.   (4) For the ancient orators [unlike Antiphon] thought it sufficient if they could think of arguments and give them verbal expression in an uncommon manner. Their whole concern was with style and its adornments, firstly so that it should be significant and elegant, then that its composition should be harmonious. The result, he says, of this practice was an increasing difference between their style and that of the ordinary man.   (5) After remarking that the diction of Antiphon lacks contrived sentiments, as if correcting himself he says, "I do not mean that no figure of speech is to be found in Antiphon, there are examples in his writings of rhetorical question, deliberate omission, etc. What I mean is that he does not use them in a studied or regular manner, but on occasions when the very nature of the sequence of thought would lead to an

---

[8] The author uses Caecilius of Calacte, 1st century B.C.

abnormal expression, as can be observed even in ordinary speech. So when one says that the writings of Antiphon lack figures of speech, it is not to be thought that they are absolutely without such figures (which is impossible), but that there is no systematic, continual, and powerful use of figures observable in them." (6) Sixty of his writings are extant, twenty-five of which Caecilius says are spurious, so that thirty-five remain genuine. (7) He is said to have been pupil to his own father, who was a teacher. Cf. A 3 (2), A 5 (3), A 6 (4). (8) Caecilius says that the orator was the pupil of Thucydides the historian. Cf. A 3 (7) and note. (9) There is a tradition that he disputed with Socrates the philosopher himself, aiming not at scoring a point but trying to convince him. (10) Also that he first composed speeches for suits in the lawcourts. For no one of his predecessors seems to have entered into this kind of competition, nor can one find a forensic speech written before Antiphon. (11) There is a tradition that he first composed manuals of rhetoric, being a man of ready intelligence. (12) For this reason he got the nickname of Nestor. (13) Plato [the comic poet] in the *Peisander* lampoons him for love of money. (14) [refers to Antiphon the tragic poet; see A 13]. (15) [They say that while he was early in his life engaged in poetry] he discovered an "Art of Avoiding Troubles," and that he built a little room near the agora at Corinth and put up a notice to the effect that he could cure people in trouble by means of speeches. And in fact he used to discover the cause of the trouble by inquiry and give consolation. (16) But thinking that this occupation hardly fitted his ambition, he turned to rhetoric. (17) He also composed a speech against Hippocrates [the general; see A 3 (21): B XXI] and won an undefended suit. (18) He was at the height of his career at the time of the Persian invasion,[9] his birth being a little before that of the sophist Gorgias. (19) His life extended to the overthrow of the democracy by the Four Hundred, in which he was charged with having shared. (20) So after the overthrow of the Four Hundred he was brought to trial and convicted, and

---

[9] See A 3 (9), A 5 (2); the statement here is impossible. But if born in 480 he would have been 69 at the time of his death in 411.

being subjected to the penalty of treason he was cast out of the city unburied and lost his rights as a citizen, not himself alone but his descendants as well. (21) Lysias gives a different account, saying instead that he was put to death by the Four Hundred. (22) [There follows the story of the tragic poet's death at the court of Dionysius of Syracuse.]

5. GENOS OF ANTIPHON [prefaced to his speeches in the MSS] (1) Antiphon was the son of Sophilus and of the tribe Aiantis, by deme Rhamnusian. (2) Born at the time of the Persian war [i.e., 480], he was about the same age as Gorgias the sophist. (3) He first went to school with his father, who taught writing, and as he grew older he worked out the art of speaking. (4) To natural aptitude he added experience from practice, was no one's pupil, since there was not yet at that time any composer of speeches or of rhetorical manuals or a professor at the head of a school, but he was acquainted with the books of his predecessors and in particular with those of the poets, (5) and attained such a degree of cleverness that he was called Nestor, because he gave so much pleasure in speaking. (6) Shunning political life as a young man, he set up house at Corinth near the marketplace for the reception of pupils, and put up a notice saying that he comforted those in trouble. (7) Then, since he was fond of money and did not make much from this occupation, he [began to write tragedies. He gave up this as well and] turned to rhetoric, (8) and, collecting a school at Athens, he disputed with Socrates about the art of refutation. (9) He had many pupils, among them Thucydides. (10) He became very powerful in the Peloponnesian War, and modified the democracy and set up the Four Hundred with Archeptolemus' faction. (11) He was indicted, convicted, and suffered the penalty of treason, and was thrown out of the city without burial. [There follows another version of his death, which refers to Antiphon the tragic poet.]

6. PHILOSTRATUS *Lives of the Sophists* I 15 Kayser (1) I do not know whether one should speak of Antiphon the Rhamnusian as a good or as a bad man. (2) His good points are as follows: he was very often

general and very often achieved victory. He secured the addition of
sixty manned *triereis* to the Athenian navy and had the reputation of
being the most capable man of his time in speech and understanding.
On account of these points he deserves praise from me and from others.
(3) The points on which he might be regarded as a bad man are the
following: he overthrew the democracy, enslaved the Athenian people,
early in his career was secretly pro-Spartan, later openly, and so let
loose on Athenian politics the horde of the Four Hundred tyrants.
(4) Some say that Antiphon invented the art of rhetoric which had
not previously existed, others that it had been invented before but he
developed it. Some say that he taught himself his wisdom, others that
he had it from his father, and that his father was Sophilus, a teacher of
rhetoric, who educated a number of the sons of leading men including
[Alcibiades], the son of Cleinias.[10]   (5) [*DK* A 6] Antiphon was
extremely persuasive and was given the name of Nestor because he
would persuade people in any subject he chose.   (6) He advertised
"Painless Lessons," claiming that no one could tell him a sorrow so
terrible that he could not remove it from the teller's mind.   (7) Comedy
lampooned Antiphon for his cleverness in pleading suits and for selling
at a high price, particularly to those who stood in jeopardy, speeches
composed to frustrate the course of justice.   (8) The nature of the case
is as follows: in other disciplines and crafts men respect those who
achieve eminence and admire good doctors more than bad ones and the
man who has greater skill in prophecy and in music, and the same is
true of craftsmanship and all trades; but in the case of rhetoric, although
they praise it, they are suspicious of it as mischief-making and money-
grubbing and designed to frustrate justice.   (9) It is not the majority
who form this judgment of the art of rhetoric but the most distinguished men of standing. At any rate, they call clever orators those who
have a good understanding and are good at expressing themselves,
giving the trick a scarcely fair-sounding name. Since this is the nature
of the case, it is not surprising, I think, that Antiphon became a theme

---

[10] That Antiphon's father was not a teacher of rhetoric but a teacher of writing
to boys is shown by Plutarch A 3 (2), and the Genos A 4 (5).

of comedy, which always picks on what is important. (10) [An account of the death of Antiphon the tragic poet at the court of Dionysius] (11) The majority of his writings are forensic speeches, in which cleverness and the whole art of rhetoric is displayed. (12) There are other sophistic writings but the most sophistic is the work *On Concord*, in which there are brilliant and profound maxims, diction elevated and embellished with poetical words and diffuse exposition like the smoothness of the plain.[11]

7. ANTIPHON AS TEACHER [See A 1 (2), A 2 (1), A 3 (2), A 4 (11), A 5 (3), A 5 (4).] (1) Plato *Menexenus* 236a [Socrates claims that Connus is his music teacher and Aspasia his teacher of rhetoric.] "It is not surprising that a man should be good at speaking after such an education. Even a man less well taught than I who had learnt his music from Lamprus and his rhetoric from Antiphon of Rhamnus, even he could nonetheless win credit by praising the Athenians before an audience of themselves." (2) Cicero *Brutus* 12, 47 Aristotle gave an account of the history of rhetoric beginning with Tisias and Corax and continuing with Gorgias, Antiphon of Rhamnus, and Lysias. He says that Antiphon wrote much the same sort of thing as Gorgias. That fertile writer Thucydides recorded that no one that he had heard had ever pleaded his own case on a capital charge better than Antiphon. (3) Galen *Glossary of Hippocratic Terminology*, Introduction xix 66 Kühn (after a mention of Aristophanes' *Banqueters*) "... the fact that each and every one of those concerned with speaking felt entitled to coin new words is shown by Antiphon too very clearly, insofar as he actually taught the best way of coining them [A 69]; it is shown too by Aristophanes himself in the same play in the following passage. ...." [A conversation follows between a son who has just acquired a city education and his father; the son keeps using new words, which are identified each time as borrowed from Lysistratus, the orators, Alcibiades, and Thrasymachus.] (4) Plutarch *On the Fame of the Athenians*

---

[11] The entry about Antiphon in *Eudociae Violarium* 108 (Flach p. 100) seems to be entirely derived from Philostratus.

5 p. 350c . . . those who teach the youths in the schools, Isocrateses and Antiphons and Isaeuses. (5) DIONYSIUS OF HALICARNASSUS *Against Ammaeus* 2 The schools of Theodorus, Thrasymachus, and Antiphon are to be reckoned with in the development of rhetorical instruction. (6) PHILODEMUS *Rhetoric* II p. 3 fr. 21 Sudhaus Corax [of Syracuse] and [Anti]phon of Athens.

8. [*DK* A 3] XENOPHON *Memorabilia* I 6 Cf. A 3 (3), A 4 (9), A 5 (8). (1) We should not be doing justice to [Socrates] if we omitted his conversation with Antiphon the sophist. For, on one occasion, wishing to draw away Socrates' disciples, he approached him in their presence and said: (2) "I thought, Socrates, that philosophers should be happier than other people, but you seem to me to get just the opposite out of philosophy. You live indeed in a fashion which no slave in his master's house would tolerate. Your food and drink is of the commonest kind, and the cloak you wear is not only common but the same summer and winter, and you are always without shoes or shirt. (3) What is more, you take no money, which gladdens the heart of the possessor and allows those that have it to live a freer and pleasanter life. In other professions, masters have pupils to show who are copies of themselves. If you are going to have this effect on your pupils, be assured that what you are master of is misery." Socrates' reply was as follows: (4) "You seem to me, Antiphon, to think that I have such a horrible existence that you would rather die, I am sure, than live like me. Let us consider, then, what you think disagreeable about my life. (5) Is it that, while those who take money have to produce what they take the money for, I who take none do not have to discourse with those I don't want to discourse with? Or do you regard my way of life as bad because I eat things that are less healthy than what you eat or less productive of strength? . . . (10) You seem to me, Antiphon, to think that happiness is luxury and expensive living, but I think that it is an attribute of God to want nothing [cf. B 78], and it is next to divine to want as little as possible: that the divine is best, and that what is next to the divine is the next best thing." (11) On another occasion, Antiphon, in conversation with Socrates, remarked: "I account you a fair man, Socrates, but wise, not at all. And you appear to me to realize this yourself, since you ask no fee for attendance with you. Yet if you thought your coat or house or any other of your possessions was worth something, far from giving it to anyone free, you would accept its exact worth and nothing less. (12) Clearly, then, if you thought attendance with you was worth anything, you would ask nothing less than what this too was worth. Fair, then, you may be, for not getting money on false pretenses, but not wise, for your wisdom is worth nothing." (13) To this Socrates replied: "Our theory is this, Antiphon. Good looks and wisdom may be exploited in a good as well as in a bad way. For example, if a man sells his good looks to a customer for money, the world scornfully calls him a prostitute. But we consider it moral and good if a man procures for himself as a friend someone whom he discerns to be a high-principled lover. So with wisdom. The world scornfully calls sophists those who sell their wisdom to a customer for money. But we consider it behavior befitting a citizen of high principles, to discern someone with good natural ability, teach him whatever good thing we may possess, and thus gain his friendship. (14) Indeed, Antiphon, as other people take pleasure in a good horse or dog or hawk, I myself to an even greater extent take pleasure in having good friends, and teach them whatever good thing I may possess myself, and put them in the company of others from whom I think they are likely to be helped on the way to a good education. Furthermore, I unroll and peruse in my friends' company the treasures of the wise men of old which they have written down and bequeathed to us, and we excerpt anything good we come upon. We consider ourselves amply rewarded if we win each others' friendship." To me as I heard this [Socrates] appeared to be a man of supernatural blessedness, and to be leading his hearers to a high standard of personal conduct. (15) On another occasion Antiphon asked him how he claimed to train others in public life, when he, in spite of his knowledge, did not enter politics himself. [Socrates] replied: "In which way do you think, Antiphon, I should practice politics more intensively: if I practiced the art by myself or if I were to take care that as many as possible were fitted to practice it?"

9. [*DK* A 5] Aristotle fr. 75 Rose in Diogenes Laertius ii 46   As Aristotle says in the third book of his treatise on the art of poetry, Antilochus of Lemnos and Antiphon the diviner argued contentiously with [Socrates], just as Cylon did with Pythagoras.[12]

10. ANTIPHON AS SPEECH WRITER [See A 1 (1), A 3 (4), A 4 (10); B 19; B XXXI and XXXII.]

(1) Diodorus Siculus in Clement *Miscellanies* i 79 [ii 51, 15 Stählin] Antiphon who first wrote a forensic speech for publication . . . and first pleaded a suit at law for a fee.

(2) Quintilian iii 1, 8–13   Antiphon, too, both was the very first to write a speech and, furthermore, himself composed a manual and is credited with an excellent speech on his own behalf.

(3) Ammianus Marcellinus xxx 4, 5   The famous Antiphon of Rhamnus, who, according to the ancient authorities, was the first to have accepted a fee for conducting a defense.

(4) Plato Comicus *Peisander* [shortly before 412 b.c.] A 3 (16) Antiphon composed for love of money. Cf. Philostratus *Lives of the Sophists* A 6 (8) where the love of money seems to be connected with taking fees for writing speeches. Cf. also Xenophon *Memorabilia* A 8 (3) and A 5 (7).

(5) [Tryphon] *Concerning Figures of Speech, Rh.Gr.* iii 201, 6   Thucydides practiced the austere style, and Antiphon his pupil.

(6) Dionysius of Halicarnassus *Demosthenes* 8   The main types of speaking were those of Gorgias, Lysias and Thrasymachus. Antiphon, Theodorus, Polycrates, etc., modeled their mode of speaking on these.

On the Arrangement of Words 10 The prose of Thucydides and Antiphon of Rhamnus is certainly well composed, but scarcely attractive.   (22) Antiphon offered the best example of the austere style.

Isaeus 20 [Antiphon of Rhamnus is named first among those who composed polished speeches and practiced the art of rhetoric in forensic debate.]

---

[12] This statement of Aristotle seems to have been deliberately contradicted in the source of A 3 (3), A 4 (9).

Art of Rhetoric XI 10 [Antiphon is classed among the forensic speakers.]

On Thucydides 51 Although there were many orators and philosophers at Athens during the Peloponnesian War none used the way of speaking of Thucydides, neither the orators of the schools of Andocides, Antiphon, and Lysias, nor the Socratics. . . .

11. ANTIPHON AS POLITICIAN [See A 8 (15).]

(1) ARISTOPHANES *Wasps* 1267–71 [422 B.C.] Amynias "is hungry just like Antiphon." Cf. *Birds* 1281–82 where being hungry is one of the symptoms of being pro-Spartan. *Wasps* 1301–2 [Antiphon listed with Hippyllus, Lycon, Lysistratus, and Thouphrastus as "Phrynichus' gang."]

(2) THUCYDIDES VIII 68 Yet the man who contrived every detail of the affair to this end and took the most trouble about it was Antiphon. He was one of the ablest Athenians of his time, achieving preeminence in intellectual power and in the expression of his thoughts. He did not come forward publicly nor involve himself in any contest if he could help it, but remained an object of suspicion to the multitude because of his reputation for cleverness. Nevertheless, if anyone was involved in a legal or political contest, his single assistance was of more value than anything, if anyone asked his advice. And when the democracy was overthrown and the Four Hundred broke up into factions, and he was ruined and badly treated by the public, of all the men up to my time who were brought to trial on the same charge he seems to me to have defended his life best. [90, 1 Antiphon is named with Phrynichus, Aristarchus and Peisander as among "the most influential" and 92, 2 Antiphon is sent to Sparta with Phrynichus.]

(3) PLUTARCH *Nicias* 6 Seeing that the people made use of the skills of those who were powerful speakers or excelled in intelligence but were always suspicious of and guarded against cleverness and curbed its pride and reputation, as was obvious from the condemnation of Pericles and the ostracism of Damon and the popular distrust of Antiphon of Rhamnus. . . .

(4) ARISTOTLE *Constitution of Athens* XXXII 2 In this way the oli-

garchy was established, those that particularly brought it about being Peisander and Antiphon and Theramenes, men of good breeding who had a reputation for intelligence and understanding.

(5) ———— *Eudemian Ethics* III 5, 1232b7 ... the high-minded man would take more account of the opinion of the one expert than that of the many ordinary men, as Antiphon said to Agathon when after Antiphon's conviction Agathon praised his defense.

(6) LYSIAS 12, 67 [403 B.C.] Theramenes, wishing to seem loyal to all of you, accused and put to death his closest friends, Antiphon and Archeptolemus. ...

12. ANTIPHON AS INTERPRETER OF DREAMS

(1) [*DK* A 7] LUCIAN *True Stories* II 33 [The island of dreams] and nearby are two temples, one of Deception and the other of Truth. There they have a sanctuary and prophetic seat where Antiphon the interpreter of dreams stands forth to give prophecy, receiving his commission from Sleep.

(2) [*DK* A 8] CLEMENT *Miscellanies* VII 24 [III 17, 18 Stählin] ... the story about Antiphon is amusing. A man took it as an omen when a sow ate her litter; but, noticing that the sow was thin with lack of food through the meanness of its owner, [Antiphon] declared: "Be of good cheer at the omen. In her hunger she might well have eaten your children."

(3) [*DK* A 9] GNOMOLOGIA VINDOBONENSIS 50 p. 14 Wachsmuth Antiphon, being asked what divination is, replied: "a wise man's guess." [The remainder refers to the tragic poet.]

13. [*DK* A 4] ATHENAEUS XV 673E [For Antiphon the tragic poet, cf. A 3 (17), A 4 (14), A 5 (7), A 6 (10), A 12 (3); and also HEGESANDER in ATHENAEUS XII 544D; ARISTOTLE *Eudemian Ethics* III 5, 1239a38; *Rhetoric* II 2, 1379b15; 6, 1385a11; 23, 1399b25; *Mechanics* 847a20] For after [Adrastus the Peripatetic] had published a treatise in five books on the matters investigated, as to their facts or style of narration, in Theophrastus' *On Characters*, and a sixth on points in Aristotle's *Nicomachean Ethics*, adding a long dissertation on Plexippus in Antiphon the tragic poet [*TGF* p. 792], and saying a good deal about Antiphon himself, [Hephaestion], I say, appropriated all these works and added a book *On the Antiphon Who Appears in the "Memorabilia of Xenophon,"* quite without any originality of his own.[13]

B. WRITINGS

(i) EXTANT SPEECHES

The text from which this translation is made is that of Blass-Thalheim (Teubner ed., 1966), except when it is stated to the contrary in the footnotes, where the more important textual points are also noted.

Editions: J. H. Thiel: *Antiphons Erste Tetralogie* (Groningen, 1932).
　　　　　A. Barigazzi: *Antifonte, Prima Orazione* (Florence, 1955).
　　　　　Id.: *Antifonte, Sesta Orazione* (Florence, 1955).
Translations: L. Gernet: *Antiphon,* Collection Budé (Paris, 1923).
　　　　　K. J. Maidment: *Minor Attic Orators,* I, *Loeb* ed. (Cambridge, Mass., 1941).
　　　　　K. Freeman: *The Murder of Herodes* (I and V) (London, 1946).
General: F. Solmsen: *Antiphonstudien* (Berlin, 1932).

I. Prosecution for poisoning against the stepmother

The comparative crudeness of its style indicates that this speech is earlier than V and VI. It probably belongs to the middle years of the fifth century. The name of the prosecutor for whom Antiphon wrote the speech is unknown.

[13] The implication is that Hephaestion, at the time of the Antonines, distinguished between Antiphon the tragic poet and Antiphon in Xenophon.

1–4 Appeal to the jury

(1) I am a young man, and as yet have had no experience of the courts. The case furthermore puts me in a terrible dilemma, men of the jury. I have to choose between not proceeding against my father's murderers, in the face of his express injunction to do so, on the one hand, and on the other of proceeding against them and finding myself inevitably on the opposite side of those to whom I should least of all be opposed, my brothers by my own father and my stepmother.

(2) The course of events and the defendants themselves leave me no option but to make them the object of the indictment, who would naturally be the dead man's avengers and the support of the prosecution. As it is, just the opposite of what is natural has occurred. It is these very men who are my adversaries at law and the murderers, as both I and the indictment allege.

(3) I have this request to make, men of the jury. If I shall demonstrate that the defendants' mother, by a deliberate and premeditated act, is the murderer of our father, and that she has been caught several times already, not on a single occasion only, in the act of contriving his death, I ask in the first place to act as champion of your own laws, which you received from heaven and from your ancestors and according to which you now, as they did, sit in judgment on the guilty, and in the second place to come to the aid of that dead man and, at the same time, of me, who am left an orphan. (4) You are my kinsmen, now that those who ought to have avenged the dead and been my support, these have become the dead man's murderers, and stand as my adversaries in this court. To whom then can a man turn for help, or where can he find refuge, unless it be with you and with justice?

5–13 The refusal of the defense to hand over the slaves for examination

(5) I wonder, indeed, what my brother has in mind in standing as adversary to me, and if he thinks that righteousness consists in this, in not betraying his mother. To my mind it is much more irreligious to neglect to avenge the dead, especially when he has died suddenly, by a premeditated plot, and she killed him by intention and with fore-

thought. (6) He will certainly declare that he knew well, of course, that his mother did not kill our father. But this declaration will not do, since it was open to him to know for sure, by means of the examination,[14] and he refused; although he was correspondingly eager for verification, where there was no chance of ascertaining the truth. Yet he ought to have been eager for the course which I challenged him to take, so that the facts of the case should be verified, (7) because then, if the slaves did not make any admissions, he would confidently have sustained his case against me on the basis of sound knowledge, and his mother would have been acquitted of this charge. But where he refused to submit to a test of the facts, how can he claim to have knowledge of matters whose truth he refused to ascertain? [By what token then is it likely that he would know the facts, men of the jury, when he did not in actual fact ascertain their truth?][15]

(8) Whatever is going to be his reply to my charge? The truth is that he knew perfectly well that he could expect no salvation for his mother from the examination of the slaves, but that he believed that her salvation lay in avoiding the examination, since he thought that the facts would thus be kept dark. How then can he have made an affidavit to the effect that he knew the facts well, if he refused to ascertain them beyond doubt, when I was willing to employ the fairest examination of this matter? (9) In the first place, I was agreeable to the examination of the defendants' slaves. These slaves were aware that, even on a previous occasion, this woman, the defendants' mother, was contriving death by poison for our father; and that he caught her in the act; and that she did not deny it, but asserted in excuse that she was not giving it him as poison but as a love-philter. (10) This, then, was the reason why I was agreeable that such an examination should be made of the facts, after I had composed a written memorandum of the charges I am bringing against this woman. I told the defendants to conduct the examination themselves, although in my presence, so that the slaves

[14] The word *basanos*, here translated "examination," certainly implies torture.

[15] This sentence, which appears here in the MSS, is transposed by Thalheim to follow the first sentence of § 6. It is, perhaps better, omitted as by Gernet and Maidment.

under my influence might not say what I put into their mouths. I was content if they merely used the questions I had written in the memorandum. And this, I said, was a fair indication that I was prosecuting my father's murderer correctly and legally. But if the slaves denied what was alleged, or their statements were contradictory, ⟨the examination⟩[16] would reveal what actually happened, since it will cause even those who are determined to tell lies to reveal the truth.

(11) Of course, I know well that if they had come to me as soon as they heard that I was prosecuting my father's murderer and had been willing to hand over the slaves in their possession, and I had been the one who refused to accept their evidence, they would have produced these facts as the most weighty proofs that they are not guilty of the murder. As things are, since in the first place I am willing myself to conduct the examination, and in the second place I am telling them to conduct it instead of me, it looks likely, to me at any rate, that these very facts are evidence that they are guilty of the murder, (12) [since if they were willing to submit the slaves to the examination and I did not accept them, they would have used this refusal of mine as a proof. So then let this refusal of theirs be a proof of my case, if, when I am willing to take a test of the matter, they refuse to allow one].[17] It is, in my opinion, a strange thing if they try to ask you not to convict them, while they were not prepared to be judges in their own suit by handing over their own slaves for examination. (13) In this respect, then, it is quite clear that they were trying to avoid the establishment of the true facts of the case, since they knew that what would be established would be to their own detriment, and so they wished to leave it hushed up and uninvestigated. But you, certainly, do not share that view, men of the jury, of that I am quite sure; you will make the matter plain. So far, then, so good: I will try to recount to you the truth of what happened; and may justice be my guide.

---

[16] These words are supplied in the Greek by Thalheim, Gernet, and Maidment.

[17] This clause is, perhaps rightly, omitted by Gernet as an explanation which has become part of the text.

14–20 Rehearsal of the "facts of the case"

(14) In our house there was a first-floor room which Philoneos, a man of high standing and a friend of our father's, used to occupy when he stayed in town. Philoneos had a concubine whom he was minded to place in a brothel. So [when] my brothers' mother [knew of this, she][18] made friends with her.   (15) Seeing that the girl was going to be ill-treated by Philoneos, she sent for her, and when she came told her that she too was being ill treated by our father. If the girl would agree, she said, she had the means to make Philoneos love her, and my father love herself. It was her idea, she said, but it was up to the girl to assist her.

(16) She asked the girl accordingly if she was prepared to help, and the girl, it appears, gave her immediate assent. The next thing that happened was that Philoneos had a sacrifice to make to Zeus Ctesias in Piraeus, while my father was contemplating a voyage to Naxos. So Philoneos thought it would be an excellent opportunity to make the same journey serve two purposes, for him to see off his close friend, my father, at Piraeus, and at the same time to make his sacrifice and to entertain my father to dinner afterwards.   (17) Philoneos' concubine came to help with the sacrifice. Now, when they had got to Piraeus, it appears that he made the sacrifice; and then it was, when the rite had been performed, that the girl planned to give them the poison, wondering should she do it before dinner or afterwards. After some deliberation she decided that it was best to give it after dinner, following closely the instructions of her Clytemnestra [the defendant's mother].[19]

(18) The rest of the details of the dinner would be a tale too long for you to listen to or for me to tell. I will try to give you an account of what happened as briefly as possible, and of how the poison was actually administered. It appears that when they had finished dinner, Philoneos, sacrificing and entertaining the other, my father on the point of sailing and enjoying dinner with his friend, the two were pouring libations and burning frankincense as an oblation for themselves,   (19) and Philoneos' concubine, while she was engaged in pouring the libation wine

---

[18] Omitted by Dobrée, Gernet, and Maidment.
[19] Omitted by Thalheim, Gernet, and Maidment.

into their cups as they prayed (a prayer which, I remind you, men of the jury, was not in fact to be fulfilled), added the poison. And, thinking that she was doing something for his good, she gave a larger dose to Philoneos, presumably in the belief that the more she gave him the more she was likely to inspire his love. She did not at this point realize that my stepmother had tricked her, not until she was caught up in the disaster. She gave a smaller dose to our father. (20) So those two unhappy men first poured away some of the wine in libation, holding in their very hands their own destroyer, and then tossed off their last potation. Philoneos died instantaneously, but our father fell into a sickness, from which he too died three weeks later. For these crimes the girl who acted as accomplice and carried out the deed has received her deserts, although she was in no way the cause[20] of what happened—she was broken on the wheel[21] and handed over to the public executioner, while the party who was the cause of the crime and actually premeditated it shall still receive her due, if you and heaven will.

21–31 The case for the prosecution

(21) Consider how much juster is the plea I make to you than the plea my brother makes. I bid you avenge to all eternity[22] the man who is dead and who has suffered wrong. He will ask nothing of you concerning the dead man, who deserves to receive at your hands pity and help and vengeance, having met an untimely death in a godless and ignominious manner at the hands of those who least of all should have brought it about. (22) On the contrary, he will make a plea on behalf of the murderess, a plea which is against human laws, against God's law, which cannot be fulfilled, cannot be heard either by heaven or by this court. He prays you not to avenge the crimes which she could not restrain herself from committing. But you are here to give

[20] The Greek word translated here (*aitia*) has also the meaning of guilty.

[21] I.e., as a slave was subjected to the examination in order to extort a confession.

[22] Gernet takes the words "to all eternity" with "suffered wrong," Maidment with "avenge."

comfort not to murderers but to the victims of premeditated crime, and to the victims of people at whose hands they least of all should die. It depends on you now to return this verdict aright, and what I bid you do is just this. (23) My brother will plead with you on behalf of his mother, who is alive and who did my father to death without scruple and without respect for heaven, arguing that she should not, if he makes his case, pay the penalty of the crimes she has committed. I ask you on behalf of my dead father to let her pay the penalty in full. You have assumed the name and role of jurymen for this very reason, that criminals should pay the penalty for their crimes.

(24) I am making this speech of prosecution to secure that she is punished for her crime, and that I shall avenge our father and your laws—in this matter you all should come to my aid if what I say is true. My brother's aim is the exact opposite of mine; he has appeared in her defense so that she who has disregarded the laws may escape the punishment for her crimes. (25) And yet is it more just that one who commits a premeditated murder should be punished or that he should not? And is the murdered man more to be pitied, or the murderer? The dead man, in my opinion, because for you to pity the murdered man would be juster and more righteous in the eyes of gods and men. Accordingly, I now claim that as she put him to death without pity or scruple, so she too should be put to death by you and by justice. (26) She ⟨killed him⟩[23] deliberately after planning his murder, and he died a violent and sudden death. Of course his death was violent, men of the jury. He was, was he not, intending to leave the country by sea, and was being entertained to dinner at the house of a friend. She sent the poison, gave instructions for its administration, and killed our father. In these circumstances how does she deserve mercy, or to receive consideration from you or from anyone else, who herself did not think that her own husband deserved pity? No, she put him to death unrighteously and ignominiously. (27) Thus, in general, mercy is more appropriate in accidental cases than in deliberate and premeditated crimes and wickedness. She put him to death without any respect or

[23] Supplied by Thalheim, Gernet, and Maidment.

fear for god, hero, or man. So, if she also is put to death by you and by justice, receiving from you no consideration nor mercy nor respect, her punishment would be most just.

(28) I am amazed at my brother's temerity, and the notion he has had to state under oath on his mother's behalf that he knows for certain that she did not do these things. For how, I ask, can a man know for certain things of which he was not an eyewitness. I do not suppose that those who plot the death of their nearest and dearest do their planning and make their preparations in front of witnesses. No, they do it as secretly as possible and in such a way that no one is likely to know. (29) Those against whom the plotting is done know nothing, until they are already caught up in the disaster and realize the doom that has overtaken them. At this moment, if they are able and can do so before they die, they call ⟨their⟩[24] kith and kin and tell them who are responsible for their death, and implore them to avenge the crime of which they are the victim. (30) This is just what my father implored me, then a boy, to do, when he was ill of his last unhappy illness. If the victims cannot do this, they write a message and call upon their house slaves as witnesses and reveal those responsible for their death. He revealed this knowledge to me, and laid this injunction on me, not on his own slaves, though I was still of tender years.

(31) My case is complete, and so is my attempt to succor the dead man and the law. It is up to you to consider in your own consciences what is to be done next, and to give a just verdict. The gods below, as well, I believe, have at heart the cause of those who have been wronged.

II. First Tetralogy

Being imaginary school speeches, the Tetralogies are naturally different in style from I, V, and VI. J. H. Thiel gives good reason, against Gernet and Solmsen, for believing them genuine. He regards them as the earliest of the orator's extant works by reason of the more

---

[24] Supplied by Thalheim, Gernet, and Maidment.

poetical language and the greater number of ionicisms they contain. Pollux certainly regarded them as by Antiphon. [See II (iii) n. 32.]

i. Prosecution in a case of murder: first speech

(1) Crimes which are contrived by ordinary people are not difficult to expose. But if the criminals are people of good natural ability, men of experience who have reached that age of maturity at which they are at the height of their mental powers, detection and exposure are difficult, (2) since, because of the great risk involved, they have spent much time in planning the means of carrying out the plot with safety, and they do not put it in hand until they can achieve complete security from suspicion. Realizing these facts, you must place great reliance on any kind of probability which you can infer. We who are prosecuting in this charge of murder are not pursuing the innocent and letting the guilty go free, (3) since we know[25] well that while the whole city is defiled by the murderer until he is caught, so the impiety becomes ours and the penalty of error on your part recoils on us if we are prosecuting wrongly. Thus, as the whole pollution devolves on us, we shall endeavor to demonstrate to you, as clearly as we can from the facts at our disposal, that the defendant killed the man.

(4) Professional criminals are not likely to have killed the man,[26] as no one would surrender an obvious and achieved advantage for which he had risked his life; and the victims were found[27] still wearing their cloaks. Nor again did anyone who was drunk kill him, since the murderer in that case would be known to his fellow guests. Nor would the victim have been killed because of a dispute, since people would[28] not

---

[25] The Greek word here translated, $o\tilde{\iota}\delta\alpha\mu\epsilon\nu$, is in place of the usual Attic $\tilde{\iota}\sigma\mu\epsilon\nu$. J. H. Thiel rightly explains it as a simple "*Analogiebildung*" which may have been current in the common speech beside $\tilde{\iota}\sigma\mu\epsilon\nu$. He does not think it necessary to infer that the usage is a borrowing from the Ionian dialect. The oddness might be indicated by translating "ken," but this would not imply Thiel's explanation.

[26] Added in the Aldine edition to fill an obvious gap in the MS.

[27] "Would have been found," MS.

[28] The text of Dobrée, Gernet, and Maidment, which inserts $\check{\alpha}\nu$.

become involved in a dispute in the middle of the night or in a deserted spot. Nor was it a case of a man aiming at someone else and killing the victim, since in that case his attendant would not have been killed too. (5) In the absence of any suspicion ⟨to the contrary⟩,[29] the manner of death itself suggests that he died by premeditation. Who is more likely to attack him than one who had already suffered great injuries and expected to suffer still more? Such a man is the defendant. He has been an old enemy of his and has launched many serious charges against him, but has failed to secure conviction. (6) Again, he has himself been prosecuted in more serious and more numerous suits, but has never yet been acquitted, and has thus lost a good part of his possessions. On the last occasion he was sued by the dead man for two talents on a charge of embezzlement of sacred monies. Realizing his own guilt, and having felt the weight of the other man's power, as well as bearing a grudge for the previous convictions, he is likely to have devised the plot, no less likely to have killed the man, to protect himself against his hostility. (7) The desire for revenge, no doubt, made him reckless of the dangers, while fear of the evils threatening him made him panic and do the deed with the greater passion. His hope was that by doing this he would be both undetected in the murder and acquitted in the suit, (8) since no one would continue the proceedings and the suit would be dismissed in default of a prosecutor. But if he were convicted here, he reckoned that he would suffer less in reputation if he paid the penalty after exacting vengeance than if he were ruined by the suit and, like a coward, did nothing in retaliation. He knew well that he would be convicted in the suit, since otherwise he would not have thought that the present trial was the safer course.

(9) The motives which drove him to crime are those which I have mentioned. If there were many witnesses, we would produce them one and all. Since one attendant was present, those who heard him will give evidence. He was taken up still conscious, and on being questioned by us said that the only one of the assailants whom he recognized was the defendant. Convicted both by circumstantial evidence and by the

---

[29] Text of Pahle and Gernet, which inserts ἄλλης.

evidence of eyewitnesses, he could not in any way be acquitted by you on grounds either of justice or of expediency. (10) It would prove impossible to convict anyone of premeditated crime, if a conviction cannot be obtained on the evidence either of eyewitnesses or of circumstance. It is also inexpedient for you that the defendant, in a state of pollution and impurity, should enter the sanctuaries of the gods and stain their sanctity, and join innocent people at table and so infect them. Such conduct often leads to sterility and to the frustration of courses of action. (11) Regarding it then as a matter of our own interest to take vengeance, and visiting on the defendant his own transgressions, you must ensure his suffering and the city's purification.

ii. Defense: first speech

(1) I do not think I should be wrong in thinking that I am the unluckiest man in the world. In general, men who are in trouble, if they are the victims of bad weather, get a respite when the weather improves; or if they fall sick, recover when the illness leaves them. Or if any other disaster befall them, they get the benefit of the opposite when it comes about in due course. (2) But in my case the man was the destroyer of my household when he was alive; and now that he is dead, even if I am acquitted, he has succeeded in giving me enough pains and troubles. I am indeed afflicted by misfortune to such a degree that it is not sufficient for me to show myself righteous and law-abiding to escape destruction. Unless I discover and convict the criminal whom the dead man's avengers have been unable to detect, I must myself fall under suspicion as a murderer and be convicted and condemned to a dreadful death. (3) According to their showing, it is difficult to convict me, and so I must be clever; but also according to their showing, the things which I actually did show plainly that I am the doer of the deed, and so I must be stupid. Indeed, if on grounds of probability you suspect me because of the intensity of my hostility, it is still more probable that before I did the deed I should foresee the present suspicion falling upon me; and if I knew that someone else was making a plot against him I would rather try to prevent it than by doing the deed

myself deliberately incur certain suspicion;[30] since if the deed itself pointed to me, I was finished; and if it did not, I knew well that this suspicion would fall upon me.   (4) I am therefore in a miserable situation, since I must not only make a defense, but detect the murderers as well. Nevertheless, I must do my best to accomplish this added task, since necessity, it seems, is the sharpest goad. My only method of proof is to employ the evidence which permits the prosecution to allege that everyone else is innocent while the manner of death itself brands me as the murderer, since the crime will be seen to be mine, if they appear guiltless, and similarly, if suspicion falls on them, I shall rightly appear innocent.

(5) It is not, as the prosecution alleges, improbable, but probable, that a man wandering about in the middle of the night should be killed for his clothes, since the fact that he was not stripped is no evidence. If the criminals had not the time to strip him but made off in panic at people's approach, they would have showed, not madness, but good sense, in preferring their skins to their loot.   (6) On the other hand, it may be that he was not killed for his clothes, but had caught sight of other people committing some crime and been killed by them to prevent him becoming an informer of this crime. But is it not probable that those who hated him not much less than I did, and there were many of these, killed him rather than I? They could see plainly that suspicion would fall on me, and I knew well that I would be held in suspicion on their account.

(7) Further, what is the value of the attendant's testimony? It was not probable that he would recognize the killer in the panic of the moment. What is probable is that he would assent to the persuasion of his masters. When slaves are not as a rule held trustworthy in the witness-box—otherwise we should not subject them to the examination—how is it fair to destroy me on the evidence of this one?   (8) But if anyone thinks that probability has the weight of proven truth against me, let them on the other hand consider by the same token that it was

[30] Text of the MS, as Gernet and Maidment. Thalheim emends to $\dot{\alpha}\tau\nu\chi\dot{\iota}\alpha\varsigma$, "misfortunes."

more plausible that I should wait for a safe opportunity for the plot and not be present when the deed was done, rather than that he should identify me as he was being cut down. (9) I will now make another point. I must have been out of my senses not to think that the danger I am now in was, not less, but many times greater, than the danger from the charge which was hanging over me. Indeed, while I knew that if I was convicted on the charge I would lose my possessions, I would not stand to lose citizenship or life; but so long as I survived and remained alive I would not have come to the worst plight, if my friends got up a collection for me. On the other hand, if I am now convicted and put to death, I shall leave shame and pollution to my children; or if I go into exile, I shall go begging in a foreign land, an old man without a city.

(10) In conclusion, while the charges which are brought against me are all baseless, I am entitled much rather to be acquitted by you, if it seems probable (but is not actually the case) that I killed the man. In the first place, I was defending myself against what clearly were great injustices. Otherwise I should not have seemed a likely murderer. And in the second place you would do best to convict the men who actually killed him, not those who had reason to do so.

(11) Acquitted of the charge in every particular, it is not I who pollute the sanctity of the gods by entering their precincts, nor do I act unrighteously by persuading you to acquit me. Those who prosecute me who am guiltless, but let the guilty go free—these are the cause of sterility; and in persuading you to be lacking in reverence towards the gods, they deserve themselves to suffer everything which they say I deserve to suffer. (12) These then, who deserve this treatment, you must consider unworthy of trust, and recognize me on the basis of my past record as neither a plotter nor as covetous of what does not belong to me, but, quite the contrary, as one who has made many large subventions to the state, as a trierarch often, as an outstanding *choregus*, as a frequent contributor to the necessities of friends, as a large provider of sureties for many, as one who has acquired his wealth, not by litigation, but by hard work, a maker of sacrifices, and a law-abiding citizen. This is the sort of man I am, and you must not

convict me of any godless or shameful crime. (13) If I was being prosecuted by a living man, I would not merely be making my defense on my own behalf; but I should have shown up as scoundrels the man himself and those who, while assisting him, are actually seeking to feather their own nests at my expense—the true reason for the prosecution. But, out of respect rather for propriety than for justice, I shall omit this, and ask you, men of the jury, who decide and control matters of life and death, to pity my misfortune and bring a remedy for it, and not, by joining in these men's attack upon me, to look on passively while I am unjustly and unrighteously put to death by them.

iii. Prosecution: second speech

(1) The defendant does outrage to Misfortune herself when he puts her forward as a pretext for his criminal acts, in an attempt to disguise his own bloodguiltiness. Nor does he deserve your pity, since he has involved his victim in a disaster he never bargained for, while deliberately hazarding his own safety. In my earlier speech I demonstrated that he killed the man. I shall now try testing[31] his defense[32] and showing that it does not hold.

(2) If the murderers saw people approaching and then left the victims, making good their escape before stripping them, then those who fell in with them, even if they found the master dead, would have found the slave still conscious, as he was picked up and gave evidence;[33] and after making inquiry they would have reported the criminals to us and the defendant would not have been accused. Alternatively, if other people were seen by the victims committing some similar crime and had killed them so as not to be identified, the other crime would have been published[34] at the same time as their murder, and suspicion

---

[31] Thiel observes that the construction of the Greek here is common in Herodotus but rare in Attic prose.

[32] The word used here in the Greek, ἀπελογήθη, is quoted by Pollux II 119 as from Antiphon.

[33] This clause is omitted by Thalheim, but retained by Gernet and Maidment.

[34] I.e., by the *archon basileus*. Cf. Thiel ad loc.

would have fallen on those others.   (3) But I do not see how those who ran less danger would have been more likely to attack him than those who were in more anxiety. Fear and injustice were sufficient to overcome prudence in the latter; but, for the former, the danger and the shame were greater than the profit, even if they had planned to do the deed, and were sufficient to bring the passionate part of their character[35] to its senses.

(4) The defense is wrong in saying that the testimony of the attendant is untrustworthy, since in giving evidence of this kind slaves are not examined, but are given their freedom. But when they deny a theft or conspire with their masters to hide the truth, then we expect them to speak the truth only on examination.

(5) Nor is it more likely that the defendant should be absent than that he should be present at the scene of the crime. If he was absent, in the first place, he was going to run the same risks as if he were present, since each of his accomplices would, if caught, confirm that he was the instigator of the attack; and, in the second place, he was less likely to get the business done, since none of his accomplices who were present would have dispatched the business as eagerly as he.   (6) I will make the point that he believed that the danger which was hanging over him from the lawsuit was much greater, not less, than the danger he incurs here. Let us, for the sake of argument, suppose that he has an equal chance of conviction and acquittal in both prosecutions. He had no hope that the suit would not be proceeded with, at any rate while the victim was alive, since the latter would never listen to his plea. In this case, on the other hand, he never thought that he would be brought to court, since he believed that his act of murder would be undetected. (7) In claiming that you could not think him guilty because the suspicion fell so obviously on him, he argues falsely, since, if the suspicion was sufficient to deter him, in spite of his being involved in the greatest

---

[35] τὸ θυμούμενον τῆς γνώμης. This use of the neuter of adjectives and participles is common in Thucydides (cf. II 59, 3; VII 60, 1) and Gorgias (cf. DK 82 B 6, τὸ φρόνιμον τῆς γνώμης). For γνώμη as the whole character, including the irrational aspects, compare below fr. 158. Γνώμη is, on the other hand, opposed to ὄργη, "passion," in V (69) and (72).

legal perils, from making an attack, no one at all would have plotted against the victim. Everyone of those who were in less peril, fearing suspicion more than peril, would have been less likely than the defendant to attack the victim.

(8) Contributions to the treasury and *chorēgiai* are an excellent sign of personal prosperity, but of his innocence they are evidence to the contrary. It was in his anxiety lest he should lose his prosperity that he killed the man. Such is the probable though dreadful conclusion; and, in saying that not those who probably, but those who actually, kill are murderers, he is quite right as far as actual murderers are concerned, provided that it is clear to us who are the men who actually killed the victim. But where the men who actually killed the man have not been detected, we must rest on the findings of probability and declare that he and no one else is the murderer of the victim. Crimes of this sort, we must remember, are committed in secret, not before witnesses.

(9) Since the conclusion arising from his own defense is that the defendant is plainly guilty of the murder, he asks nothing else from you than to be allowed to devolve his own pollution onto yourselves. We ask you nothing, but we do declare to you that if he is not proved guilty, neither from circumstantial nor from direct evidence, there is no longer any possibility of convicting people who are the subject of prosecution. How could you justly acquit him, when you have plain knowledge of how the murder was committed, when you see clearly the tracks of suspicion leading to him, and when the attendant has given testimony of a trustworthy nature? (10) If you acquit the defendant unjustly, the dead man will not cry to us for vengeance, but on your conscience he will lie heavy. (11) In this knowledge come to the dead man's aid, take vengeance on the murderer, purify the city of the guilt of blood. Thus you will do three good things: you will diminish the number of murderers and plotters, you will increase the number of those who live god-fearing lives, and you yourselves are released from the taint which the defendant brings upon you.

iv. Defense: second speech

(1) See, here I am, of my own volition,[36] placing myself in the hands of that Misfortune whom the prosecution says I blame unfairly, and in the power of these men's malice. I am indeed afraid of the enormity of this charge, but at the same time I have confidence in your good sense and in the true account of my actions. If I am prevented by them from bewailing to you even my present misfortunes, I am at a loss to know to what other means of safety I am to have recourse. (2) The accusation they make against me is most novel, if novel rather than evil is the word I am to use. Pretending to be prosecutors and avengers of murder, they speak in defense of everyone who might genuinely fall under suspicion, and as a result are unable to find the actual killer. So they say that I am the murderer. Acting as they do in the opposite fashion to that which is enjoined upon them, they plainly are more anxious to do away with me unjustly than to take vengeance on the murderer. (3) All I ought to do is to make my defense against the evidence of the attendant. I am no informer or crime detective, but a man prosecuted and engaged in making his defense. However, I must speak outside my brief to demonstrate that they are conspiring against me and that I myself am free from suspicion.

(4) Nay, the misfortune with which they reproach me I am asking you to change to good fortune. I claim that you should acquit me and make me blessed, instead of condemning me and making me the object of your pity.

The prosecution alleges that it is more likely that anyone who came across the victims as they were being attacked would clearly recognize the murderers and report the affair to the victims' household rather than make off and disappear. (5) But in my opinion no man is so bold and courageous that when he comes across expiring corpses in the middle of the night he would not turn round and run rather than put his own life in danger by looking for the criminals. On the assumption that these bystanders did what was likely rather than what was not, the men who killed the victims for their clothes could not reasonably be

---

[36] As opposed to the behavior of the defendant at IV (iv) 1. Cf. V (13).

acquitted; and that lets me out of suspicion. (6) Whether or not there were public announcements of other criminals at work at the same time as these men were being murdered is not to be known. If there was an announcement and it went unnoticed, it is not beyond belief that he was killed by these professional criminals.

(7) Why must the evidence of the servant be regarded as more trustworthy than that of free men? The latter are punished by loss of rights and they are fined, if they are found not to have told the truth. But the slave who was not subjected to scrutiny of examination, in what court will he be punished? Or what scrutiny will there be? With the prospect of giving evidence without fear of reprisal, I should not be surprised if he has been persuaded by his masters, who are my enemies, into giving false testimony against me. I, on the other hand, would suffer a fate which would cry to heaven if I were destroyed by you because of false testimony.

(8) The prosecution alleges that it is less credible that I should not have been present at the murder than that I should have been present. I shall demonstrate from fact, not from probability, that I was not present. All my male and female slaves have been surrendered by me for examination. If on this evidence I am shown not to have been sleeping at home on that night or to have gone anywhere, I freely admit that I am the murderer. The night was not an ordinary one. It was the Dipoleia[37] during which the man was killed.

(9) As concerns my comfortable circumstances, in fear for which the prosecution alleges that according to the rules of probability I killed him, the facts are just the reverse. It pays men who are in misfortune to take the law into their own hands. As a result of changes, their misfortune may be likely to turn into good fortune. But those who are comfortably off, it pays to remain as they are and thus preserve their present good fortune. As things change, people who before were well off become badly off.

(10) They pretend to use probabilities to convict me, but they assert that it is actually the case, not that it is probable, that I am the murderer,

---

[37] 14 Skirophorion (June–July).

although it has been demonstrated that these probabilities are in general on my side. In particular, the man whose evidence is against me has been shown to be unreliable, and no check is possible. I have shown that the clues are on my side, not on his;[38] and that the traces have been shown to lead, not to me, but to those whom they acquit. Since all the arguments of the prosecution have been shown to be baseless, there will not, if I am acquitted, be lacking grounds on which criminals will be convicted; but, if I am found guilty, no defense will be good enough to save anyone who is prosecuted.

(11) The prosecution is thus plainly outrageous. Yet, although they are seeking to put me to death unrighteously, they claim that their hands are clean, and assert that I am acting unrighteously, when all I am doing is asking you to act in a god-fearing way. I am innocent of all the charges made against me and call upon you, on my own behalf, to respect the piety of people who have committed no crimes. On behalf of the dead men reminding you of your duty to avenge, I urge you not to punish the guiltless and let the guilty go free, since, once I have been executed, no one will any longer seek for the guilty. (12) Bearing these things in mind, acquit me in a just and god-fearing manner, and do not recognize your mistake when later you repent. In matters of this kind repentance brings no remedy.[39]

III. Second Tetralogy

i. Prosecution: first speech

(1) When there is agreement on the facts, cases are predetermined either by the law or by the decrees of the Assembly, which together control the whole state. But if there is any dispute, the matter is submitted to you, men of the city, to decide. However, I do not think that the defendant will actually dispute with me, since my son, while training, was hit by a javelin through the ribs by this young man, and

[38] Text óf MSS τούτων, Thalheim.
[39] Cf. V (91) and Gorgias *Palamedes* 34 (*DK* 82 B 11a).

died immediately. I do not charge him with deliberate murder, but with unintentional manslaughter. (2) Yet, to me, manslaughter has constituted no less a disaster than murder. To the dead boy he has given no cause to rest uneasily, but to those that are alive he has.[40] Pity the childlessness of the parents, show sorrow for the untimely end of the dead boy, and banish the killer from those rites from which the law prescribes banishment. By so doing refuse to tolerate the pollution of the whole city by him.

ii. Defense: first speech

(1) It is clear to me now that sheer accidents and necessities compel men who are not litigious[41] to appear in court and men who are mild-tempered to take their courage in both hands and, in general, to speak and act out of character. In my case, unless I am much mistaken, I neither was, nor wished to be, such a person, but was compelled today by sheer accident, contrary to my usual behavior, to make my defense for actions of which I find it difficult to get an accurate account, and which I am still more at a loss to relate to you. (2) Under the pressure of harsh necessity I have myself had recourse to your compassion, men of the jury, and ask you, if I shall seem to speak to you with greater particularity than is usual, not to accept my defense with ill grace because of this fact and make your decision on the appearance rather than on the reality of the matter. The appearance of things is on the side of those who are able speakers, but the truth is on the side of those whose actions are just and done in the fear of God.[42]

(3) I believed that, if I educated my son in those pursuits which are most beneficial to the community, some good would ensue for both of us. But the outcome has been quite the opposite of what I expected. The young man, acting not with violence or intemperance, but practicing

[40] Gernet omits this sentence as "*une adjoinction maladroite*," but it seems a typical, if rather empty, rhetorical paradox.

[41] ἀπράγμονας. Cf. VI (1).

[42] Note the common 5th century contrast between appearance, *doxa*, and reality, *aletheia*.

the javelin with his classmates in the gymnasium, hit and killed no one
as far as the reality of what he did is concerned, but, by another's
mistake which affected himself, became accidentally involved in blame.

(4) If the javelin had reached the boy outside the range of its normal
trajectory and had wounded him, I should not be able to deny that
death was caused by us. But the boy ran into the path of the javelin and
placed his body in the way; while my son was prevented from reaching
the target, the other, running into the javelin's path, was hit and threw
upon us blame which was not really ours. (5) Since the boy was hit
because he ran in the way, the young man is not rightly accused. He
struck no one of those who were standing away from the target. If
it is clear that the boy was not hit because he stood where he was, but
only because he deliberately ran into the javelin's path, then he is
shown still more clearly to have died by his own error. If he had stood
still and had not got in the way, he would not have been hit. (6) Since,
you see, it is agreed by both sides that the killing was involuntary, by
establishing responsibility for the mistake, we are likely to reach a
clearer proof of responsibility for the death. It is indeed people who
through an error fail to act as they intend who are the cause of accidents, just as it is those who voluntarily achieve or experience something who are responsible for what results. (7) The young man, then,
made no mistake about anyone. He was engaged in practicing something which was prescribed, not forbidden; and he was using the
javelin in the javelin class, not in the exercise class. Nor did he miss the
target and shoot into the bystanders, thus hitting the boy. He did
everything exactly as he intended and nothing by mistake, but became
involved in the accident because he was prevented from hitting the
target. (8) The boy wanted to run in front, but failed to do it at the
moment when, if he had run in front, he would not have been hit, and
met with something he was not prepared for. By an unintentional
mistake which affected himself he was involved in an accident which
is his own affair. He brought his own punishment upon himself and
has paid for his mistake. But we, of course, did not rejoice in or approve of the outcome, but rather shared in the ensuing pain and grief.
The error, then, belongs to the boy; and the fatal action is not ours but

is attributable to the party who made the mistake, just as the result, falling upon the agent, acquits us of blame and has justly brought punishment on the agent at the moment of his error. (9) The law, too, acquits us, the law, on which he relies in prosecuting us for the boy's death, forbidding either justifiable or unjustifiable homicide. Since the mistake is the mistake of the dead boy himself, the young man here is acquitted of even unintentionally killing him, while the prosecutor himself does not even summon him for intentional killing. Thus he is acquitted of both charges, ⟨manslaughter⟩[43] and murder.[44] (10) We are acquitted by the truth of the events and by the law under which he is prosecuted, and our daily habits of life do not justify our involvement in a disaster like this. My son's fate will cry to heaven if he is held accountable for errors which are nothing to do with him; and I who am as innocent of guilt as he, though not more so, shall meet misfortunes many times greater. When he has been put to death, the rest of my life will be intolerable for me; made childless, I shall live on, but I shall seem to be in my grave.

(11) Have compassion then on this child whose misfortune was not due to his error, on me who am old and wretched and who am suddenly stricken with disaster; and do not condemn us to an evil fate by a verdict of guilty, but rather, like god-fearing men, acquit us. The dead boy is not unavenged for the disaster into which he fell, and justice does not require that we should share in[45] the consequences of the plaintiffs' mistakes. (12) Respect, therefore, the requirements of righteousness and justice in this matter and acquit us in a god-fearing and just manner. Do not involve two most wretched people, father and son, in untimely disasters.

iii. Prosecution: second speech

(1) That the circumstances of the case drive all the participants to speak and act out of character, the defendant seems to me to show by no mere figure of speech. Whereas, in the past, he was far from being

[43] Words supplied in Aldine edition. So Thalheim, Gernet, and Maidment.
[44] The construction of the Greek is Thucydidean; cf. I 95.
[45] This meaning of the Greek word $\sigma\upsilon\mu\varphi\acute{\epsilon}\rho\epsilon\iota\nu$ is common only in tragedy.

without conscience or restraint, now the very accident has forced him to say things which I never expected him to say. (2) I was perhaps very foolish, but I should not have supposed that he would reply. I would not, if I had thought so, have made one speech only, instead of two, and thus have deprived myself of half my opportunity for prosecution. If he was not so audacious, he would not have a twofold advantage over me by making one defense against one speech of prosecution and then making his accusations without my having an opportunity to answer. (3) With such an advantage over us in his speeches, he has a manifold greater advantage over us in his procedure; and then he importunes[46] you, quite without conscience, to accept his defense. Yet I who have committed no crime but have suffered dreadful misery, and now am suffering still more dreadful things than these, have recourse to your compassion in deed and by no figure of speech;[47] and I beseech you, who are the avengers of godless and the rewarders of god-fearing deeds, not to be persuaded by a wicked subtlety in words in matters which are quite clear, and thus treat the truth of certain actions as false. (4) His subtlety is devised for plausibility rather than truth, while the truth will be spoken with simplicity and will thus be less convincing. I believe in justice and accordingly despise the defense. Yet I distrust the harshness of fate; and I am afraid that I may not only be deprived of the benefit of my son, but also may see you condemn him as a suicide.[48] (5) The defendant has been so bold and shameless as to declare that the thrower of the javelin and the killer of the boy neither wounded nor killed him; that the boy, who never touched the javelin, nor had any idea of throwing it, missed the whole earth and all the people in it and struck the javelin through his own side. If I were prosecuting him for willful murder, I would seem to have a better

---

[46] Thalheim retains the rare adverb συχνῶς. Gernet does so too, translating "*d'un bout à l'autre*"; i.e., "lock, stock, and barrel." Maidment accepts Reiske's emendation εὐμενῶς, "kindly." There seems no reason for rejecting συχνῶς in Antiphon, but it must have the sense [asks] "often."

[47] The common contrast of *ergon* ("deed") and *logos* ("word"). Cf. V (84), VI (47).

[48] Antiphon's word here, αὐθέντης, is used to mean "murderer" in Herodotus and only here means "suicide."

case then he, ⟨who⟩[49] says that the young man neither threw the javelin nor killed the boy. (6) The boy was called at the critical moment by the instructor for whom[50] he had undertaken the job of recovering the javelins for the throwers; and, because of the thrower's lack of discipline, was struck by this young man's offensive weapon, and without acting wrongly to anyone died a pitiable death. The young man made an error about the time for recovery; he was not prevented from hitting the mark, but aimed at a target which was for me a wretched and bitter one. He did not kill the boy deliberately, but if the alternative is that he did not throw the javelin and did not kill the boy, then he did do it intentionally.

(7) They have killed the boy, as much unintentionally as intentionally. Yet they utterly deny having killed him,[51] nor do they admit that they are caught by the law forbidding justifiable or unjustifiable killing. But who threw the javelin? On whom does the killing rest? On the spectators or on the boys' attendants? Nobody accuses them of anything. His death is no mystery. It is, to me at any rate, as clear as daylight. I say that the law rightly lays down punishment for the killers. The man who kills someone unintentionally is liable to find himself in trouble which he did not intend, while the man who is destroyed is harmed just the same, whether it is intentional or unintentional, and gets no justice unless he is avenged. (8) The mischance of the accident provides no just grounds for acquittal. If the mischance happens by no act of God or divine intervention, the accident is just one of those mistakes which are liable to prove disastrous to those who commit them. If, on the other hand, religious impurity attaches to the doer because of his impiety, it is not just to frustrate the visitations of heaven. (9) The defense also mentioned that it is not proper that they who have led good lives should get ill-treatment. But should

[49] ὅς added in Aldine edition. So Thalheim, Gernet, and Maidment.

[50] ᾧ = emended text of Thalheim; ὅς is the reading of the MSS which is retained by Maidment; Gernet reads ὡς ὑποδέχοιτο.

[51] Emended text of Blass, as Gernet and Maidment: ἀποκτείναντες . . . ἀρνούμενοι.

we be getting proper treatment if, living a life no whit inferior to theirs, we are punished with death? When he says that he is innocent and claims that disasters fall on those who err and do not fall upon the innocent, he is arguing the prosecution's case. My son, who never did anything wrong to anyone, and died at the hand of this young man, would suffer injustice if he were not avenged. I, to a greater extent than he, am guiltless, and it will be outrageous if I do not get my due under the law.   (10) That he can be acquitted, on the arguments of the defense, neither of the mistake nor of the unintentional killing, but that both of these are attributable to them both, I shall demonstrate as follows. If the boy deserves to be treated as his own killer because he moved into the path of the javelin and did not stand still, neither is the young man clear of blame. He is only clear of it if the boy died with the young man doing nothing, instead of throwing. The death occurred through the agency of both of them, but the boy, making a mistake to his own hurt, has punished himself to a greater extent than the mistake warranted, since he has lost his life. The young man, on the other hand, who aided him and was his accomplice in an error committed on an innocent party—how is it right that he should get off without penalty? (11) The young man is a sharer in the killing, as the actual speech of the defendants shows; and you cannot justly or conscientiously acquit him. Neither would we who have been destroyed by his error, if we are condemned as suicides, get treatment from you which was pleasing to heaven, displeasing rather. Nor, if those who had caused death to us were not barred from the customary rites, would it be less an impiety than acquitting the godless. Since all the impurity is likely to recoil onto your heads, you must take great care. If you condemn him and bar him from the rites from which the law debars killers, you will be free from the charges;   (12) but if you acquit him you are liable to them. So, for the sake of righteousness and for the sake of the laws, take him away and punish him; and on your own account do not take a share in his pollution, while on account of us, the parents, whom his action has placed living in the tomb, make our troubles at any rate appear the lighter.

iv. Defense: second speech

(1) It is probable that my opponent, in his preoccupation with his own speech of prosecution, did not understand my defense; but you must understand it, recognizing that we, the litigants on each side, no doubt because our judgment is colored by prejudice, naturally each think that what we say is just, recognizing, too, that your job is to make a conscientious assessment of the facts, since it is from what is said that the truth of the matter must be deduced.   (2) For my part, if I have said anything which is false, I agree that even what I have correctly stated is reasonably to be assailed;[52] if, on the other hand, my arguments have been true, but subtle and sophisticated, it is not I who have made them, but those whose conduct they describe, who should bear the brunt of the disfavor they arouse.

(3) I want you first of all to understand that a man is not a murderer if someone says that he has killed another, but if he is proved a murderer. The prosecutor, while admitting that the occurrence took place as we describe it, takes issue about the killer, who cannot be determined otherwise than on the basis of what took place.   (4) He indignantly complains that the boy is slandered, if he is declared to be a suicide when he neither threw the javelin nor had an intention to do so, and makes no reply to the defense's arguments. I do not say that the boy threw the javelin or hit himself, but that by coming within range of the javelin he was destroyed, not by the young man but by himself. He was not killed standing where he was.[53] As this running across was the cause of death, if he had run across at the instructor's bidding, it would be the instructor who was the cause of his death, but if he went within range of his own accord, then he was responsible for his own destruction. (5) I do not want to proceed to any other point until I have made this point still clearer: to which of the two the causative action be-

---

[52] ἄδικα εἶναι can hardly be right, as Gernet, after Hüttner, sees, although Thalheim and Maidment accept the text. If the words are to be emended, δίκαια (or οὐκ ἄδικα) εἶναι would seem to be preferable to Bohlmann's ἄξια.

[53] Thalheim accepts the insertion of ἄν proposed by Franke, who compares § 5 of the first speech of defense, "He would not have been killed if he had stayed where he was."

longed. The young man did not miss his target any more than anyone else among his training class; nor did he do, through his own mistake, any of the things charged against him. The boy's action, on the other hand, was not the same as that of his fellow spectators. He ran into the path of the javelin, and thus is clearly shown to have become involved, by his own error, in accidents which those who stood where they were escaped. The thrower indeed would have been in no error if no one had run into the range of the missile; and the boy would not have been hit if he had stood with the spectators.

(6) I shall demonstrate that the young man is no more concerned in the death than any of his fellow javelin-throwers. If the boy died through my son's javelin-throw, all his training class would be participants in the blame. They did not fail to hit him because they did not throw, but because he did not come into the range of their javelins. The young man made no greater mistake than these, and, like them, would not have hit the boy if he had been standing where he was, with the spectators.   (7) Again, it is not only the mistake which is the boy's, but the lack of proper precautions too, since if he saw no one running across, how could the young man have taken precautions not to hit anyone? But the boy saw the javelin-throwers and could easily have taken the precaution of not running across. He had the alternative of standing still.   (8) The law which they cite deserves praise, since it rightly and justly punishes those who kill unintentionally with penalties they had no intention of incurring. But the young man has made no error, and he would not fairly be punished on account of the boy who was the one to err; it is enough for the latter to bear the consequences of his own mistakes. The boy, on the other hand, destroyed by his own mistakes, simultaneously made the mistake and was punished by his own motion. Since the killer has been punished, the death is not unavenged.

(9) Since the killer has indeed had his punishment, you will have a weight on your consciences, not if you acquit, but if you condemn us. The boy bears the brunt of his own mistakes himself and will leave to no one any supplication for vengeance. But if the young man, who is clear of blame, is destroyed, he will be the greater load on the conscience

of those who condemn him. If the boy is declared a suicide as a result of what is said, it is not we the speakers who are responsible for his conviction, but the way the thing happened. If the examination correctly proves the boy to have been a suicide, the law which acquits you of blame places the responsibility where it lies. Do not you then cast us into disasters which we do not deserve; nor do you, by helping them in their misfortunes, take a decision contrary to heaven's will. No, act according to conscience and right; and, bearing in mind that the accident occurred because the boy ran into the path of the javelin, acquit us. We are not to blame for his death.

IV. THIRD TETRALOGY

i. Prosecution: first speech

(1) It is rightly prescribed that, in murder trials, the jury should take the greatest pains that the prosecution and the presentation of evidence should be just, and that they should neither let the guilty go free nor bring the innocent to trial. (2) For when[54] God desired to make humankind and created our first ancestors, he provided earth and sea to feed and ⟨preserve⟩[55] them, so that we should not die before the term of old age through lack of the necessities of life. Whoever, then, unlawfully kills one of those whom God has found worthy of such provision, he is guilty of sin against the gods and throws the principles of human society into confusion. (3) The dead man, deprived of the gifts of God, naturally leaves behind as God's punishment the hostility of avenging spirits, which those who judge or bear witness contrary to what is just, joining the doer of the deed in his impiety, bring on to their own households—a pollution which does not belong to them. (4) If we, the avengers of the dead, prosecute the innocent out of some malice, we shall, since we are not avenging the dead, be haunted by terrible avenging spirits, the suppliant souls of the dead; and if

---

[54] ὅτε γὰρ ⟨ὁ⟩ θεός, Thalheim; accepted by Maidment.

[55] ⟨σωτῆρας⟩, Thalheim; accepted by Maidment.

we unjustly put to death the guiltless, we are liable to the penalties for murder; and if we persuade you to act lawlessly, we too become responsible for your error. (5) This is what I fear; and so I bring the sinner before you, while I stand clear of reproach. Taking due account of what has just been said, do you accordingly attend to the legal verdict and pass upon the criminal a sentence fitting the crime. In so doing you will render the whole city clear of pollution. (6) If the defendant killed the man involuntarily he would be deserving of your clemency. In fact, he was drunk, he behaved with violence and lack of self-control against an old man, beating and throttling him until he was dead. Thus, for killing him, he is liable to the penalties for murder; and, as breaking all the customs concerned with respect for the elderly, he deserves not to be exempt from any of the punishments normal for such people. (7) The law, accordingly, is correct in handing him over to you for punishment. You have heard the witnesses who were present when he was behaving drunkenly. Requiting the lawlessness of the crime and punishing the violence in proportion to the outcome, you in turn must take away the life of the man who planned the deed.

ii. Defense: first speech

(1) I am not surprised that the prosecution's case was short. The matter at issue for them is not to avoid some harm, but to fail to put me to death unjustly out of malice. I think I may reasonably be angry that they were prepared to put the matter, in which the victim had himself to thank more than me, on the level of the most serious charges. He was the aggressor and was drunk, facing a man much more in control of himself. As a result, he not only brought death upon himself, but also this charge against me. (2) I consider that these men's charges against me show respect for the laws neither of God nor of man. He struck the first blow, and if I had defended myself with either steel or stone or wood, I would not even thus have been[56] at fault, since those who begin a fight are liable to get in return not the same

---

[56] Thalheim accepts Blass's insertion of $\ddot{\alpha}\nu$.

treatment, but something on a larger scale than they gave. Receiving blows from his fists and giving with mine as good as I got, how was I at fault? (3) Well and good. "But," he will say, "the law which prevents either justifiable or unjustifiable killing shows that you are liable to the penalties for murder, since the man died." But I say, for the second and third time, that I did not kill him. If the man had died on the spot from my blows, he would have died at my hands, albeit justifiably. Those who have begun a fight are liable to get in return not the same treatment but something on a larger scale. (4) In the event, he was handed over to a bad doctor many days later; and because of the doctor's bad treatment, not because of his bruises, he eventually died. Although other doctors warned him that if he took this particular treatment he would die, he was destroyed by your advice though he was curable, and has thereby cast a terrible charge upon me. (5) The very law under which I am being prosecuted does actually acquit me, since it lays down that the party acting with malice aforethought is the murderer. Now how could I have acted with malice aforethought more than he so acted against me? I paid him back in his own coin and gave as good as I got, so it is clear that my malice was matched by his. (6) If anyone thinks that death occurred because of the blows he received, and accordingly that I am the murderer, let him reflect, on the other hand, that the blows which were struck were the result of aggression; and declare that he is the cause of death, not me, since I never would have been defending myself if he had not been hitting me. Acquitted thus by the ⟨law and by the fact that he is the⟩ aggressor,[57] I am by no means his murderer. The dead man, if he died by misfortune, was himself to blame. He was unfortunate in hitting the first blow; and if he died by some lack of good sense, it was his own lack of good sense by which he has been destroyed. He was out of his mind when he hit me.

(7) I have demonstrated that I am accused unjustly. I want to demonstrate that those who accuse me are themselves answerable to all the charges they bring against me. In charging me with murder, who am innocent of blame, and in trying to deprive me of the life which God

---

[57] Reiske's addition, accepted by Thalheim, Gernet, and Maidment.

gave me, they are sinning against God. In unjustly plotting my death, they are overthrowing society and becoming my murderers. In persuading you to kill me in ungodly fashion, they themselves are actually murderers of your righteousness.

(8) May heaven, then, lay on them the punishment they deserve. You, on the other hand, must consider your own interest and be prepared to acquit, rather than condemn, me, since if I am unjustly acquitted, getting off because you have not been correctly instructed, I shall arouse the dead man's spirit of vengeance against the faulty instructor, not against you. But if I am wrongly condemned by you, I shall cause the wrath of the avenging spirit to be wreaked on you, not on him. In this realization allow the impiety to recoil upon them, clear yourself of the blame, and acquit me in a god-fearing and just manner, since in this way all of us in the city would best be clear of guilt.

iii. Prosecution: second speech

(1) After the defendant's shocking conduct I am not surprised that his speech was no less shocking; and I pardon your readiness, in your desire to discover the details of what happened, to put up with hearing such things, which deserve indeed to be rejected out of hand. Admitting that he struck the blows from which the man died, he denies that he was himself the murderer of the dead man, but claims, though he is perfectly alive, that the avengers of the dead man are his own murderers. I want to demonstrate that the remainder of the defense is in the same style.

(2) His first point is that, even if the man did die of the blows, he did not kill him, on the ground that the aggressor is to blame for what occurred, and is so condemned by the law; and the aggressor was the dead man. Now you must realize in the first place that it is more probable that younger men should be aggressors and should behave drunkenly, rather than older men, younger men being prone to self-indulgence through pride of birth, the fullness of their physical strength, and their inexperience of wine, while older men tend to greater sobriety through their experience of the effects of drink, the

weakness of their time of life, and their nervousness in the face of young men's strength. (3) The deed itself indicates that the victim defended himself, not with the same means, but with the plain opposite. The young man killed him by employing the fully developed strength of his hands; but the other feebly defended himself against the stronger and died without leaving a trace of the means with which he made his defense. If the defendant killed him with his fists and not with a sword, he is all the more a murderer insofar as fists are a more suitable weapon for him than the sword. (4) He had the temerity to say that the one who struck the first blow, but did not kill, was really more a killer than the man who did actually kill him, since by his account the aggressor was the contriver of the murder. I say quite the opposite of this. If the hands are the instruments by which we each of us carry out our plans, the man who hit without killing was the contriver of the blow alone, whereas he who struck the blow and killed the man was the contriver of the murder. The man died as a result of what the defendant did by premeditation. The striker had bad luck, the receiver of the blow had disaster. For the victim, who died as a result of what the other did, died not as a result of his own, but as a result of the striker's, mistake. The one achieved more than he was intending and, by his own mistake, killed a man he was not intending to kill.

(5) When the defendant alleges that the man died because of the doctor, I am surprised that he says[58] that he perished because of our advice that he should be put in the doctor's care, since, if we had not committed him to the doctor, the prosecutor would certainly have said that he died through lack of medical care. Consequently, even if he died because of the doctor (and he did not so die), the doctor is not his murderer it seems, since the law acquits him; but since we put him in the doctor's care because of the blows which he received, how could anyone else than the man who made it necessary for us to employ the doctor be his murderer?

(6) The conclusion is that, although on every count he is plainly

---

[58] Omitting the negative which the MSS read and Gernet accepts. Thalheim and Maidment omit it.

proved to have killed the man, the boldness and shamelessness of the man is such that he is not content to make his defense of his own sin. No, he alleges that we who are seeking expiation for this pollution are acting against divine and human laws. The defendant, after committing such crimes, is quite in character in making these allegations and others still more dreadful. The prosecution, on the other hand, clearly demonstrating the manner of death and showing that the blow from which the victim died is admitted and that the law attributes the responsibility for death to the striker of the blow, beseeches you, in requital for what has happened, to appease by his death the wrath of the avenging spirits, and thus render the whole city clear of the pollution.

iv. Defense: second speech

(1) The defendant has withdrawn,[59] not admitting his guilt, but fearing the vigor of the prosecution. For us, his friends, it is more in keeping with our duty to defend him living than dead. He would be pleading his case best if he were doing it himself. But since the course he has taken seemed to him less risky, we, who would feel the greatest sorrow if we were deprived of him, must make his defense for him.

(2) It seems to me that the crime lies at the door of the aggressor. The prosecution says that my client was the aggressor on grounds which are not probable. If violence is the natural property of the young, and self-control of the old, in the same way as seeing is the natural property of the eyes and hearing of the ears, there would be no need for you to give a verdict, since their age would condemn the young. But the fact is that many young men are self-controlled and many old men are drunk, and both provide no more evidence for the prosecution than for the defense. (3) Since evidence is available to both parties, we, in fact, have the advantage in all this, since the witnesses declare that the dead man began the fight. Since the dead man began the fight, my client is acquitted of blame in all the other things with which he is charged. If the striker, through his blow, made it necessary for your

---

[59] Cf. II (iv) 1 and V (13).

client to be put in the care of the doctor, and therefore is a murderer, more than the actual killer, the first striker becomes the murderer, since he made it necessary for the man who defended himself to hit back and for the man who was then struck to go to the doctor. It will be, a shocking state of affairs if the defendant is to be convicted of murder in place of the killer, though he did not kill, and in place of the aggressor, although he was not the first to strike. (4) Nor is the defendant any more likely than the prosecutor to be the one who contrived the murder, since, if the first striker had intended to strike but not to kill, while the man who was defending himself had intended to kill, the latter would be the one who contrived it. As things are, the man who defended himself meant to strike but not to kill; he did not, however, achieve his purpose, striking with an effect he did not intend. (5) He contrived the blow. But how could he have contrived the death, since he hit the man involuntarily? Error is also more natural to the first striker than to the man who is defending himself, since the defendant, seeking to give as good as he got, made a mistake under the compulsion of the other man, while the victim, since the blows he gave and received were the result of his own lack of self-control, deserves to bear the burden of his own and the other's mistake.

(6) Again, I will demonstrate that the defendant retaliated not more strongly, but less adequately,[60] than his sufferings justified, since the other, throughout, acted with drunken violence and did not defend himself. The defendant, in his efforts to avoid hurt to himself and to push the other away, suffered involuntarily what he did suffer. With regard to his actions in trying to escape what was being inflicted on him, he defended himself against the aggressor less strongly than the occasion warranted and initiated no attack. (7) If he was stronger of arm, and gave more vigorously than he got, even this does not justify his conviction by you, since it is upon the aggressor that the greater penalties are everywhere laid, while no penalty is ever prescribed for the man who defends himself. (8) The point about not killing either

---

[60] In this paragraph there are three non-Attic adverbs, κρεισσόνως, ὑποδεεστέρως, and ἐλασσόνως. The third occurs in Hippocrates' *On Regimen* and the second in Thucydides.

justifiably or unjustifiably has already been met, since it was not because of the blows but because of the doctor that the man died, as the witnesses confirm. The accident is the responsibility of the first striker, not of the man who defends himself, since the man who did and suffered everything involuntarily was involved in the other's accident, while the man who did everything voluntarily, bringing the accident upon himself by his own actions, failed through his own misfortune.

(9) It has been demonstrated that the defendant is answerable to none of the charges. It is possible, however, to regard the action and misfortune of the two men as something they have in common, and to recognize, as a result of what has been said, that the defendant has an equal claim to acquittal as to conviction. But on this view of the matter, too, he is more deserving of acquittal than of conviction. The prosecution cannot justly secure a conviction unless it shows clearly that he is the injured party; and it is shocking for the defendant to be convicted unless the charges against him can be proved beyond reasonable doubt. (10) Thus, since in every respect our client is cleared of the accusations, on his behalf we enjoin upon you the more righteous alternative, not to kill the innocent in your attempt to punish the murderer. The spirit[61] of the dead man is just the same the avenger of the guilty, and if my client is godlessly destroyed he makes double the wrath of the avenging spirits against those who killed him. With fear of this in your hearts, regard it as your task to clear the innocent of the charge, and relying on time to bring to light the polluted man, leave it to the next of kin to take vengeance. In this way you would act in the most just and god-fearing manner.

V. On the murder of Herodes

A speech written by Antiphon for a defendant, Helos of Mytilene. As Maidment says, the setting of the speech suggests a date not much earlier or much later than 415 B.C. At § 76, note 77, 418 B.C. is suggested as the earliest date.

[61] The passage is corrupt and is so marked by Gernet and Maidment. Thalheim's emendation ἀλιτήριος is translated.

1–7 Plea to the jury

(1) I would like, men of the jury, to have at my disposal an ability in speaking and an experience of the courts to match my plight and the adversities I have been through. But, in fact, of these last I have had more than my fitting share, while in speaking I am more ill equipped than I can afford to be. (2) When indeed I had to put up with physical suffering as an outcome of this quite inappropriate charge, then experience helped me not at all, while now, when I ought to win my safety by means of the truth, telling what actually occurred, at this point my case is weakened by my inability to speak. (3) There have already been many cases where people, through inability to speak, have failed to win credence with a true story and have perished, truth and all, because they have not succeeded in making their true story plain. There have also been many cases where people with the ability to speak have gained credence with a false story and have been acquitted through that very lie. It is therefore essential, when a man is inexperienced in pleading, for him to pay more attention to the words of the prosecutor than to the actual facts and the truth of the matters in question. (4) So then, men of the jury—and I shall not ask you what most pleaders ask, viz., for a hearing, because they have no confidence in themselves and have already condemned you as unjust; since before honest men, of course, even without a special plea it is to be expected that the defendant will be given a hearing, which the plaintiff certainly gets without having to ask for it—(5) so then I make this request of you, first, to forgive me any mistake in speaking and to regard the mistake as the result of inexperience rather than a mark of guilt; and secondly, if I am at all successful in speaking, to regard it as the result of the truth of my story rather than of cleverness, since it is as unfair that a bad choice of words should cause a man of good behavior to be put to death as it is that a good choice of words should lead to the acquittal of a criminal. A false word is an error of the tongue, but a false action is an error of the will. (6) It is, moreover, inevitable that a man who stands in peril of his life should make some mistake. He must inevitably consider not only what he is saying but also what the future holds—seeing that all things which are still in obscurity are

more at the mercy of chance than of foresight.[62] It is therefore inevitable that these should strike great dismay in the heart of the man in peril. (7) Indeed, I have noticed that even those who have much experience of pleading speak much worse than they could when they are in some peril. But when they are engaged in an affair without risks they are more successful. So my request, men of the jury, is in accordance with the law of God and man and conforms with what is just for both you and me. I will make my defense against the charges one by one.

8-19 Objection to the prosecution's procedure

(8) The first thing I want to tell you is that I have been brought into this court in a most illegal and arbitrary manner. I want to tell you this, not because I want to avoid a popular court, since I should happily entrust to you the verdict on my life, even if you had sworn no oath and were constituted as a court according to no particular law, because of my confidence that I have done no wrong in this matter and that you will know what is just. No, my aim is to exhibit these men's arbitrary and illegal conduct as an indication to you of other aspects of my case. (9) The first thing is that I am defendant on a charge of murder, although I have been indicted as a "malefactor," something which has never yet happened to anyone in this country. Furthermore, the prosecution itself is witness to the fact that I am not a "malefactor," and am not chargeable under the law relating to malefactors. For the law concerns thieves and robbers, and they have not shown that that has anything to do with me. Accordingly, at any rate as concerns this summary arrest and trial, they have offered you grounds for my legal and just acquittal. (10) Again, they make the point that murder is a gross malefaction, and I agree that it is, indeed one of the grossest, and so is temple robbery and treason. But in each of these cases there are separate laws. In my case the prosecution has, in the first place, put on the trial in the *agora*, the one place which is out-of-bounds to other men

[62] A very Thucydidean observation.

who are defendants in cases of murder. In the second place, they have made an assessment of damages, although a murderer must give life for life according to the law; and they have done this, not for my advantage, but for their own benefit; and in the assessment they have given the dead man less than his legal due. The reason for this you will recognize as the defense proceeds. (11) Secondly, there is a point of which I expect you are all aware. All courts sit out of doors in cases of murder, for the sole reason that this location prevents the jurors going into the same room with those whose hands are defiled, and the prosecutor in a murder-case from going under the same roof with the murderer. But you have acted clean contrary to other people's practice, both in breaking the law and in this point too. You are required to swear the most solemn and binding oath, perdition to yourself, to your family and your house if you are perjured, an oath declaring that you will not charge me with anything else than what pertains to the actual murder, viz., that I was the murderer, whereby even if I had committed many crimes I would not be condemned for anything else except that very crime, nor again if I had done many virtuous acts would I be acquitted because of these acts—(12) but all of this you omitted, inventing your own laws for yourself, and then, yourself unsworn, you are accusing me, while the witnesses who give evidence against me are unsworn too, although the law says that they must give evidence against me after swearing the same oath as yourself, with their hands on the sacrifice. Furthermore, you ask the jury to decide in a case of murder, trusting in unsworn witnesses, whom you yourself have rendered untrustworthy by transgressing the established laws. Indeed, you claim that your illegal procedure should have greater weight with them than the laws themselves.

(13) You reply that I would not have stayed in the country if I had been given my freedom, but would have disappeared abroad, as if you had forced me to come to the country against my will. Yet if it was of no consequence to me to lose my citizenship here, I should have had nothing to lose if I had refused to come when summoned and had let the case go by default; or, alternatively, I should have gone abroad after making my defense at the first hearing. Everyone has this possi-

bility open to him.[63] Yet on your own initiative you seek to deprive me alone of this right, which belongs to every other Greek, making your own law to this effect. (14)[64] And yet the laws which are established for such cases all, I think, would admit are the best and most righteous of laws. They certainly have the prime quality of being the most ancient in the land; and, in the second place, they are quite consistent in application, which is the greatest mark of good laws. For the passage of time and continuous use shows up defective qualities. You must not, accordingly, expect to discover from the speeches of the prosecution whether the laws are well framed or not, but rather from the laws whether the prosecution explains the matter correctly and legally or not. (15) The conclusion is that the laws of murder, at any rate, are excellently framed, and no one has ever had the temerity to alter them. You alone it seems have had the temerity to be a lawmaker, and that for the worse; and by transgressing their provisions you seek to put me to death. The very illegality of your conduct is, in fact, the most powerful witness on my side, since you know quite well that you would have found no one who would have testified against me once he had sworn an oath. (16) Furthermore, you did not show your confidence in your case by putting it to the arbitration of a court once and for all. On the contrary, you provided escape clauses, as if you had no confidence in the court here. The consequence is that there is no advantage to me in this court even if I am acquitted, since you can say that I was acquitted as a malefactor, but not on the charge of murder. If, on the other hand, you gain the verdict, you will claim my life, since I have been found guilty of murder. Now, I ask you, could there be a cleverer contrivance than this, if you get what you want by persuading this court once only, while, even if I get off on this one occasion, I am to be subjected to another peril.

(17) Again, men of the jury, I was kept in prison in the most illegal possible way, since, although I was ready to provide three sureties as the law requires, these men so contrived it that I could not secure bail.

---

[63] Cf. II (iv) 1 and IV (iv) 1.
[64] §§ 14–15, cf. VI (2).

No other alien who has ever been ready to provide sureties has been imprisoned. And yet this same law applies to the commissioners for malefactors. The result was that, although the relief is common to everyone else, in my case alone it failed to secure bail.[65] (18) The reason was that this procedure is convenient for them, in the first place that I should be in as unprepared a state as possible, unable to deal with my own case myself, secondly that I should be in a weak state of health, and that my friends would be more ready to perjure themselves on their side than bear true witness[66] on mine [because of my physical infirmity].[67] They also thereby involved me and my family in lifelong disgrace.

(19) In all these many particulars, therefore, I have been injured by your laws and your justice, and am thus brought to trial. Nevertheless, even in such a pass, I shall try to make clear my innocence, although it is indeed difficult to rebut in a moment lies and attacks of long standing, since it is not possible even to guard against what one did not expect.

20–24 The facts of the case: circumstances of Herodes' disappearance

(20) I set sail from Mytilene, men of the jury, on the same ship as the aforesaid Herodes, whom they say I killed. Our destination was Aenus; I was going to see my father, since that is where he happened to be at the time, and Herodes was going to hand over slaves to some Thracians. Our fellow passengers were the slaves which he had to release and the Thracians who were going to get them freed. I shall call witnesses to substantiate these facts for you.

(Witnesses)

(21) Such was the reason for the voyage in each case. We met a storm and were forced to put in at a place in Methymnaean territory,

---

[65] The text is corrupt. The translation is of Thalheim's emendation which Maidment accepts.

[66] Thalheim and Gernet omit, but Maidment retains, λέγειν.

[67] Dobrée and Gernet rightly omit these words, as an intrusive gloss. Thalheim and Maidment retain them.

where the ship was at anchor to which they allege he transshipped and met his death. Now first note these circumstances, if the death occurred by design rather than by chance. No proof has been adduced to show that I persuaded the man to be my fellow passenger. It is clear that he made the voyage on his own account and for his own private purposes. (22) Nor, again, do I appear to have made the voyage to Aenus without sufficient motive. Nor do we appear to have run in to this place for any preconceived purpose, but because we had to. Nor, again, when we anchored, did the transshipment to the other vessel take place with any contrivance or deceit. The ship we were sailing in was undecked, but the one to which we transshipped was decked. We did it because of the rain. I shall call witnesses to substantiate these facts for you.

(Witnesses)

(23) When we had transshipped to the other vessel, we began drinking. It was noticed that Herodes left the vessel and did not return on board. I definitely did not leave the vessel that night. The next day, when the man was not to be seen, no one looked for him more diligently than I; and if his absence concerned any of the others it certainly did me. On my initiative a messenger was sent to Mytilene, and his dispatch was my idea. (24) When no one else was prepared to go, either any of the sailors or any of Herodes' own attendants, I was ready to send my own attendant, though I would not, I suppose, have sent an informer against myself if I had known.[68] When Herodes was looked for in Mytilene and did not appear to be there or anywhere else, and the weather was fair for sailing, with the result that all the other vessels put out to sea, I went off to sea as well. I will provide you with witnesses of these events.

(Witnesses)

25–28 Conclusions to be drawn from the foregoing account

(25) These are the facts. Now consider the explanation which emerges from them as likely. In the first place, before I put out for Aenus,

---

[68] This messenger was presumably the slave who incriminated the speaker under examination. See below §§ 30 and 31.

when the man had disappeared, no one accused me, although they already knew that the messenger was being sent. If someone had, I never would have put out to sea. No; at the time the truth and the actual happening prevailed over these men's accusation; and I was still on the spot. But when I had gone off to sea, and these men had deliberately concocted their conspiracy against me, then did they lay the accusations. (26) Their story is that the man met his death on land, and that I hit him on the head with a stone, I who definitely never left the ship. They know this in detail, but they have no plausible story to show how the man disappeared, since plainly the killing is likely to have taken place near the harbor, on the one hand because the man was drunk and on the other because he left the vessel after dark. He would not, accordingly, have managed to control his limbs; nor is there any likely reason why anyone should take him far away at night. (27) But although the man was sought for two days both in the harbor area and outside, no eyewitness came forward, nor was any bloodstain or any other clue found. Well, then, I agree with the prosecution's story, although, of course, I have provided witnesses to show that I did not leave the vessel.[69] But suppose I did actually leave the vessel, it was still to a high degree unlikely that the man would have left no trace if he had been made away with, unless he had gone some distance away from the sea. (28) But they say that his body was thrown into the sea. From what vessel? The vessel must have come from the harbor itself. How then was it not discovered? Indeed, it is certainly likely that some trace would remain in a vessel on which a dead body had been taken and thrown overboard at night. But now they say they found traces in the ship in which he was drinking and from which he went ashore, the ship in which they themselves agree that the man did not meet his death. But as concerns the ship from which he was thrown overboard, they have found neither the ship itself nor any clue. I will produce witnesses to substantiate these facts for you.

(Witnesses)

[69] Thalheim, following Reiske, places a question mark here. The translation follows Gernet and Maidment, who print a colon.

29-30 The prosecution's inquiry

(29) When I had departed on my voyage to Aenus and the ship on which Herodes and I had had our drinking party had arrived in Mytilene, they first went on board and conducted an investigation; and when they found blood they said that the man had been killed there. But when this line of argument did not prosper, but the blood turned out to be sheep's blood, they abandoned this story and arrested and examined the men. (30) The man whom they then examined on the spot said nothing bad about me. But the man they examined many days later after keeping him with them for the intervening period—he was the one who was persuaded by them and who gave false testimony against me. I will produce witnesses for these statements.

(Witnesses)

31-41 The evidence of the first witness: the slave

(31) Testimony has been given before you that the man was examined after such a period of time. Pay attention to the kind of examination which was used. The slave, to whom probably they promised freedom and who would gain an end to his ill-treatment on these conditions, was probably persuaded by both considerations to lie against me, expecting to gain his freedom and wanting an immediate end to the examination. (32) I think you are well aware of this, that those who are examined are prepared to speak on the side of whichever party has the most power to examine, and that they say whatever is likely to please them. Their salvation lies in these very men's power, especially if the people they are lying against do not happen to be present. If I had given orders for him to be put to the rack as a liar, in this situation he might well have abandoned his lies against me. As things were, the examiners were also men who were conscious of their own interests. (33) The consequence was that, while he thought he had something to gain from telling lies against me, he stuck to his story, but when he realized that he was going to die, then indeed he told the truth and declared that it was at their instigation that he was telling lies against me.

(34) Though first he told lies under duress and only afterwards spoke the truth, neither line of conduct did him any good, since they took and killed him, the informer on whom they base their case for the prosecution, doing quite the opposite of the usual practice. Generally, people pay money to informers who are free men and free them if they are slaves. But these have rewarded their informer with death, although my friends forbade them to kill him before I arrived. (35) It is plain that they have no use for him alive, only for his evidence. Plainly, if he was alive, subjected to the same examination by me, the fellow would be vital evidence against them for a charge of criminal conspiracy. Dead, he will deprive me of an opportunity of reaching the truth, because he has been made away with, while I am being made away with because of words uttered by him and assumed to be true.[70] Please call the witnesses for these statements.

(Witnesses)

(36) In my view, they ought to have refuted me by producing the informer in person in court and have reduced the case to this issue. They ought not to have killed him, but to have produced him openly and challenged me to examine him. As it is, which, I ask you, of the two stories will they use? The one they first told, or the one they told later? And is it the truth when he stated that I had done the deed or when he denied it? (37) Indeed, if the matter is to be looked at from the point of view of verisimilitude, the later statements would seem to be the truer. When he lied, he lied to help himself, but when his lies brought him face to face with death,[71] he had the idea that he would be saved by speaking the truth. However, no one appeared to defend him for telling the truth (I did not happen to be there, I to whose aid the later, true, statements had come), while there were those who designed to do away with him so that the evidence of his former statements could never be corrected.

---

[70] An empty play on words.
[71] The text needs some small/emendation: Thalheim and Gernet insert δία. Maidment reads τῷ for τό. The sense remains the same.

(38) Generally, people who have information laid against them kidnap the informers and make away with them, but these men who arrested me and set the investigation on foot have actually made away with the informer who informed against me. If I had made away with the man or had not been prepared to surrender him to them or was obstructing the trial in any other way, the prosecution would have laid the greatest emphasis on just these points in favor of their case, and they would have been claimed by them as the most powerful proofs of my guilt. As it is, when they themselves obstructed the trial in this way, although my friends challenged them, it is surely only fair that these same points should be evidence against them, showing that they are not bringing a true accusation against me.

(39) They make the further allegation, that the fellow admitted under examination that he had been my accomplice in killing the man. I maintain that this is not what he said, but rather that he conveyed me and Herodes from the vessel, and that when Herodes had been killed by me he helped me take the body up, put it in the vessel, and throw it overboard. (40) Yet mark these points: first, that before he was put on the wheel, up to the time extreme pressure was applied, the fellow told the truth and held me innocent of the charge. It was only when he was put on the wheel, under extreme pressure, that he at last lied about me, wanting to be released from the examination. (41) When he ceased being examined he no longer said that I had done any of these things, but up to his last breath lamented that he and I had been unjustly made away with, not showing any consideration for me—why should he?—the man about whom he had given false testimony, but because he was compelled by the truth and because he wanted to emphasize that what he had said before was right.

42–52 The evidence of the second witness: the free man

(42) Then there was the second man, who was a passenger in the same ship, was present throughout, and was in my company. When subjected to the same examination, he agreed that the first and last statements of the other man were true. He held me innocent

throughout. He disagreed with the story told on the wheel, which the first man had told at the prompting of necessity rather than truth. The first man said that I had gone ashore and killed the man, and that he had helped me to take him up after he was dead, while the second definitely declared that I had never left the ship.

(43) Yet here I have an ally in probability. I would surely not be so foolish as to plan on my own to kill the man, so that no one should be my accomplice (for in accomplices lay my whole danger), but when the deed was done, then enlist witnesses and confidants. (44) Herodes was killed near the sea and the ships, according to their story. But in the course of meeting his death at the hand of a single man, did he neither cry out nor make anyone aware of it either on shore or aboard the ship? Again, at night noise carries much farther than by day, and on the shore much farther than in a town. And, again, the prosecution asserts that the man left the ship while the men on board were still awake. (45) A further point is that although he was killed on shore and was put aboard the ship, no trace or bloodstain appeared either on the shore or on the ship, in spite of the fact that he was killed after dark and put aboard ship after dark. Or do you think that a man engaged in such an affair can scrape away the traces on the ground and wash them off the ship, when such traces no one even in daylight would be able[72] to remove completely, when he is completely in control of himself and in no fear? I ask you, men of the jury, how is such a thing probable?

(46) There is one point which you must particularly bear in mind—and do not be angry with me if I tell you the same thing many times over. My peril is great, and my salvation depends on the correctness of your decision, while if you miss the truth, that is the end of me—so let no one remove this from your mind: viz., that they killed the informer; and it was they who took good care that he should not come into this court and that I should not have an opportunity of taking and examining him, (47) although this was to their advantage. As it is, they purchased him, and put him to death secretly on their own premises; they put the informer to death without any vote of the popular

---

[72] Thalheim, Gernet, and Maidment insert ἄν.

courts and when he was not the man's killer. The proper procedure for them was to keep him in custody or give him up to my friends on security or hand him over to your archons and have a vote taken about him. But, as it is, you, the prosecution, yourselves condemned him to death and executed him, although even the authorities may not do this, i.e., put anyone to death without a vote of the Athenian Assembly. You ask this court here to be judges of what he says, but you yourselves have constituted yourselves judges of what he did. (48) And yet not even slaves who kill their masters, if they are caught red-handed, not even these are put to death by their owners themselves, but they hand them over to the authorities according to your ancestral laws. Indeed, if it is permissible for a slave actually to appear as a witness in a case of murder against a free man and for a master, if he wishes, to go to court on behalf of a slave, and if the sentence is equally valid for the killer of a slave and for the killer of a free man, it was by the same token right and proper that he should have had a public trial and that he should not have been put to death without his case being heard by you. The conclusion I reach is that justice would be better served by your appearing for judgment in this court rather than that I should be appearing unjustly as defendant against your charge.

(49) I ask you, men of the jury, to consider on the basis of the stories of the two men who have been examined what is a just and fair conclusion. The slave made two statements. On one occasion he said that I had done the deed, and on another that I had not. The free man has up to now made no damaging statement about me, although he was subjected to the same examination. (50) The reason was partly that, although it was possible to persuade the former, it was not possible to persuade the latter by a promise of freedom; and partly that he was prepared to risk telling the truth, come what may. He too knew what was to his interest and that he would cease being racked as soon as he spoke what they wanted to hear. Which of the two is it reasonable to trust, the one who always told the same tale consistently, or the one who said one thing at one moment and denied it the next? Indeed, even without such examination, those who always tell the same tale about the same things are more to be believed than those who are inconsistent with them-

selves. (51.) Again, an equal part of the slave's statements favor each side, assertion for the prosecution, denial for the defense. A tie, moreover, favors the defendant rather than the prosecutor, if indeed it is the case that, when the number of the jurymen's votes is equal, the defendant gets the benefit rather than the prosecutor.

(52) Such then, men of the jury, was the result of the examination, on which the prosecution place such reliance that they say that they are certain that the man was killed by me. Yet, definitely, if I had anything on my conscience and if I had committed a crime like that, I would have made away with the two men, since it was in my power in the first place to take them off with me to Aenus, and in the second place to put them on the mainland and not leave behind as informers against myself men who were implicated in the crime.

53–56 The letter to Lycinus

(53) The prosecution say that they found a note in the ship, which I sent to Lycinus, telling him that I had killed the man. Yet why should I send a note, when the man who took the note was apparently aware of the fact? Two points arise from this: he, as a guilty party, was likely to be able to tell it in greater detail; and there was no need to keep the matter from him. People only commit messages to writing which must be kept from the messenger. (54) Alternatively, someone might be driven to write down a long message since it would be too long for the messenger to remember. But the matter was a short one to tell, viz., that the man was dead. Next, consider that the note conflicts with evidence of the slave under examination, and the slave conflicts with the note. For the slave under examination said that he killed the man, but the note when opened said that I was the killer. (55) Yet which of the two are we to believe? They did not find the note when they first searched the ship, only afterwards. On the first occasion the plot was not so fully elaborated. But when the first man who was examined said nothing against me, then they placed the note in the ship so that they might have this accusation to make against me. (56) But when the note was read and the man later to be examined gave evidence

which did not tally with the note, they could not now make away with what had been read out. If they had thought that they would persuade the man from the first to tell lies against me, they would never have contrived the evidence of the note. Please call the witnesses for these statements.

(Witnesses)

57–59 The question of motive

(57) What motives do you suppose I had for killing the man? There was no quarrel between him and me. They have the audacity to allege that I killed the man as a favor. Yet who ever did a thing like that to curry favor with another man? No one, I think. No, a man who is going to do a thing like that must have a powerful grievance in the first place, and premeditation must be manifest from many indications. But between Herodes and me there was no quarrel at all. (58) All right, "I was afraid for my own skin in case he should do the same to me, and it is from such motives that a man might be compelled to do this thing." But I had no feelings of this sort toward him. Well then, "I was going to get his money when I had killed him." But he had no money. (59) No, I might with truth more reasonably advance this motive for your prosecution, saying that you are trying to put me away for money, rather than you attribute it to me in respect of him. And you would much more justly be convicted of murder by my family for killing me, than I would be by you and his kith and kin. I can demonstrate your open premeditation against me, while you are trying to convict me on an obscure story.

60–63 The case against Lycinus

(60) While this is the answer I give you, that I myself had no motive for killing the man, I must also make a defense not only on behalf of myself but also, it appears, on behalf of Lycinus, since the charge against him is equally absurd. I declare to you, then, that Lycinus' relations with Herodes were the same as my own. He had no source from which

he could obtain money by killing him, nor was there any danger he would avoid if the man were dead. (61) The strongest piece of evidence that he did not want to make away with him is this: he could have brought him into court and great peril, and put him to death according to your laws, if he had any score to pay off; and by so doing he would have combined the exaction of his private debt with laying up a debt of gratitude with the city, if he had shown Herodes guilty. But this was not the course he chose to take; indeed, he did not even proceed against him, although peril at law was a more respectable [means of revenge].[73]

(Witnesses)

(62) No, he let him go on this occasion, but where risk was inevitable for both himself and me, on this occasion, then, he set a plot on foot, a plot in which, if he were to be caught, he will deprive me of my country and himself of those holy and sacred rites and all the other things which are greatest and of the highest value to man. Furthermore, even if Lycinus had the strongest desire for Herodes' death—and here I am proceeding to the prosecution's case—would I ever have been persuaded to do the deed instead of him, which he was not prepared to do with his own hands? (63) Was I ready to risk my life, and was he ready to compensate me for the risk with money? No, of course not. He had no money, whereas I had. On the contrary, he would probably have been more quickly persuaded by me than I by him, since he was not even able to secure his own release when he had passed the day appointed for the repayment of a debt of seven minas and was released by his friends. This, indeed, is the strongest indication of the relationship between Lycinus and me, that I did not treat him exactly as a friend, so as to do everything he wanted. It was not surely the case that I would not pay seven minas for him when he was in custody and disgrace, but that I would undertake the colossal task of killing a man on his behalf.

---

[73] There appears to be a lacuna in the MSS here.

64–73 Why should the defendant have to explain
how Herodes disappeared?

(64) I have demonstrated to the best of my ability that I am
not responsible for the deed myself and that Lycinus is not responsible either. But the prosecution make much of the point that
the victim has disappeared, and you perhaps would like to hear
about just this matter. If I must make a guess, my guess is as good as
yours. You are innocent of the crime and so am I. But if the truth is
to be discovered, let the prosecution inquire from some of those who
did the deed. They would best know about that.   (65) For me, who did
not do the deed, this is as far as I can go in my answer, that I did not
do it. But the man who did do it can easily give the facts, or if he does
not give them he can make a good guess. Criminals find an excuse for
their crime as soon as they have committed it. But the man who has not
committed the crime finds it difficult to hazard a guess about what is
obscure. Each of you, I believe, if he was asked something he did not
happen to know, would only say that he did not know. But if he was
asked to enlarge on his answer, I think he would be put to considerable
embarrassment.   (66) Do not, then, give me this embarrassment,
in which you would not feel at all comfortable yourselves. Nor, if I
make a good guess, regard my acquittal as depending on that. No, let
it be sufficient for me to demonstrate that I am guiltless of the deed.
My guiltlessness consists in this, not in discovering how Herodes
disappeared, but in there being nothing to connect me with his murder.
(67) I know from hearsay that on previous occasions it has happened
that victims and their killers have not been found. It would not have
been a good thing, if those who were with them were subject to accusation for their deaths. On previous occasions many who have been
accused of other crimes have perished before the matter has been cleared
up.   (68) For example, the murderers of your countryman Ephialtes
have not been discovered up to now. If, then, anyone were to have
asked his companions to make a guess as to who Ephialtes' murderers
were, on pain of being held guilty of murder, it would have been
distinctly unpleasant for them. Then those who killed Ephialtes did
not attempt to get rid of the body, or run the risk of discovery in the

process, although they say that, while having no accomplice in the murder, I had accomplices in getting rid of the body.

(69) Again, a short while ago, a slave scarcely twelve years old attempted to murder his master, and if the victim had not cried out and the boy been frightened, and instead of leaving the dagger in the wound and running away he had dared to remain, all those in the house would have been put to death. No one would have thought that the boy could have done such a thing. As it was, he was arrested and subsequently confessed. Then again, your own Hellenotamiae once were subject to an unfounded charge of embezzlement, as I am now, and all except one ⟨as it chanced⟩[74] were put to death, out of anger rather than deliberate policy, but afterwards the matter was cleared up. (70) This one survivor—his name was said to have been Sosias—had been condemned to death, but the sentence had not been carried out. In the meantime it was discovered how the money had been missing; and the man was released by the Assembly, although he had already been handed over to the Eleven, and the rest died in spite of their innocence. (71) I think that the older generation among you remember the actual case; the younger ones like me have heard the story. The moral is that it is a good thing to have the help of time in testing the truth of matters. This case, too, might become clear later on, ⟨the place⟩[75] and the manner of the man's death. Do not reach this truth later on after you have put me to death in spite of my innocence. No, be well advised beforehand, and do not act in anger and malice, since these are the worst counselors you will ever find. (72) It is quite impossible for a man under the influence of passion to judge a matter rightly, since passion destroys his very means of decision, his judgment. Day following day is a greater factor in changing passion into judgment and in finding the truth of what has occurred.

(73) You can be quite sure that I deserve to be pitied by you rather than to be punished. It is right and proper that criminals should be punished, and those who are unjustly put in peril should be pitied. Your power to save me with justice should prevail over my enemies' wish to

---

[74] Thalheim inserts ἔτυχον.
[75] Thalheim inserts ὅπου.

destroy me unjustly. If you hold your hand you can still do those terrible things they bid you do, but summary action is the complete contradiction of good counsel.

74–80 The speaker defends his father

(74) I must also make a defense on behalf of my father, although it would be much more reasonable that he, as my father, should speak in my defense. He is much too old to share in my affairs, and I am much too young to have a part in his. If, when my opponent was brought to court, I were to bear witness on matters which I did not know accurately but only had learnt by hearsay, he would think I had treated him outrageously. (75) As it is, in compelling me to put forward in my defense matters which I am much too young to know except by report, he thinks he is doing nothing outrageous. Yet, employing the best of my knowledge, I will not betray my father who has been unjustly slandered in this court. I may of course make a mistake. I may not recount to you with correctness things which he actually did quite correctly.[76] Nevertheless, the risk will be taken. (76) Before the revolt of Mytilene,[77] my father showed his goodwill towards you in concrete terms; but when the whole city revolted through bad counsels, and fell into error, he in company with the whole city was forced to fall into error too. Even then he was still in his own mind consistent in his attitude to you, but it was no longer possible for him to show the same goodwill to you as before. It was not easy for him to leave the city, since it held considerable hostages from him, his children and possessions, although it was quite impossible for him to feel confidence so long as he remained there. (77) However, when you punished the guilty among them, in whom my father was not numbered, and allowed

---

[76] Here, as in § 35 above, there is an empty play on words. Maidment's "I may describe but faultily a life which was without fault" does not seem to give the right sense and flatters the writer.

[77] The date of the revolt is 428 B.C. If the speaker is "far too young to avenge himself properly" (see § 79), he is likely to be not older than 20–21 at the time of the speech. If these events took place not less than 10 years before, the date of the speech is 418 or later.

the rest of the Mytilenians to occupy their territory in peace, he [my father][78] never thereafter did anything wrong or omitted to do any duty or service of which the city, either yours or Mytilene, stood in need. He undertook his chorus-service and paid his taxes. (78) If he likes living in Aenus, ⟨he does⟩[79] so without depriving himself of any ties with the city or taking out citizenship elsewhere (as I observe others doing, some going to the mainland and living among your enemies and trying to enforce contracts made by themselves as allies) or avoiding the popular courts here, but hating informers just as you do. (79) Accordingly, my father cannot fairly be punished as an individual for what he did, as part of a whole city, under compulsion rather than by his own volition. The error of those days is one which all the Mytilenians remember forever. The result was that from exceeding prosperity they changed to exceeding adversity, and saw their own country depopulated.[80] You must not believe the slanders which the prosecution puts upon my father out of private spite. Money is at the bottom of the whole plot which has been directed against him and me. There are many circumstances which favor people who want to lay their hands on other men's goods. He is an old man, too old to help me, and I am far too young to be able to avenge myself properly. (80) But do you come to my aid and do not teach the sycophants to believe that they are stronger than you. If they come into this court and do what they like, it will be taken for granted that it is up to their victims to come to terms with them and keep out of the courts. But if they come here and show their wickedness, but get no advantage from it, then yours will be the honor and power, as is right. So then do you aid me and justice too.

81–84 The speaker claims that the signs from heaven show
his innocence

(81) You have heard everything that human evidence and human witness can demonstrate. You must give your verdict after paying due

---

[78] Thalheim, Gernet, and Maidment omit.
[79] Thalheim and Maidment accept Reiske's insertion of ποιεῖ.
[80] Maidment, "pass into the possession of others." Gernet, "*renversé.*"

attention equally to the signs from heaven on these events. You carry out, indeed, the city's common business in security with due reliance on these signs, both the business which involves risks, and that which does not. You must accordingly regard these signs as of great value and significance also for private business. (82) I expect you are aware that before now many men whose hands were unclean or who had some pollution have joined a ship and involved in destruction both their own lives and the lives of those who were in a state of ritual purity towards the gods. Furthermore, people attending sacrifices have on many occasions been revealed as ritually impure and hindering the completion of the accustomed rites. (83) Well then, the opposite has happened to me on all these occasions. Whenever I have sailed with others, they have had an excellent voyage. Whenever I have attended rites, there has been no occasion when they have not turned out excellently. These things I regard as weighty evidence concerning the accusation, showing that the prosecution's case against me is false. ⟨Let the⟩ witnesses for these statements ⟨stand forth.⟩

(Witnesses)

(84) I am aware of this fact too, men of the jury, that if the witnesses gave any unfavorable evidence to the effect that something unholy happened when I was present on board ship or at a sacred rite, they would be laying the greatest emphasis upon it and would be declaring that this was the clearest support for their accusation, viz., the signs from heaven. As it is, since the signs have turned out to be opposed to their story, and since the witnesses are testifying that what I say is true and that what they accuse me of is false, they tell you to place no reliance on the witnesses, but declare that you must have confidence in the story which they tell. In general, men test the truth of words by facts, but the prosecution tries to establish the untrustworthiness of facts by words.[81]

---

[81] Cf. III (iii) 3; VI (47).

85–96 Final appeal

(85) I have concluded my defense, men of the jury, against all the counts of the prosecution that I can call to mind; and I think . . . [82] give your verdict. There is indeed an identity between what saves me and what is lawful for you and consistent with your oath. You swore that you would give a verdict according to the laws. My case is not covered by the laws under which I was arrested, but recourse is still possible to a legal trial on the charge that has been made against me. If one trial has turned out to be two, that is not my fault but the prosecution's; although it will not happen that, when my worst enemies have arranged two trials for me, you who are fair judges of what is just will condemn me prematurely for murder in this trial. (86) Do no such thing, men of the jury, but allow a little time to elapse, since with the help of time those who seek an accurate account of events find the truest answer. My claim was that, while in such matters the trial should be according to the laws, justice should be established as often as the laws permit. Justice would thus be recognized all the better. Generally, trials are on the side of truth and are directly opposed to slander. (87) [83]A verdict of murder, even if not correctly pronounced, is a stronger thing than justice and truth. If you give an unfavorable verdict it is inevitable, even if a man is not a murderer nor liable to penalty for the deed, that he must accept the judgment and the law. And no one would dare to set aside the verdict once given, confident that he is not liable to it; nor, if he knew that he had committed the crime, would he dare not to observe the law. In fact, it is inevitable that a man should submit to the verdict contrary to the true facts and to the truth itself, particularly if there is no one to avenge the victim. (88) For these very reasons we have laws and preliminary affidavits and sacrifices and public notices and all the other accompaniments of trials for murder—all very different from what happens in other trials, since it is of the utmost importance to discover correctly the facts themselves on which the perils rest. If they are rightly discovered, they

---

[82] A lacuna appears to occur here.

[83] §§ 87–89, cf. VI (4–6).

are a help to the man wronged, while to condemn as a murderer a man who is not guilty is a sin and an act of impiety to the gods and the laws.

(89) A wrong prosecution is not on a par with a wrong decision by you jurymen. The prosecution's accusation is not final, but is subject to you and the trial. But there is no higher court to which a man may refer anything which you do not correctly judge at the actual trial, and thus avoid a miscarriage of justice. (90) How then are you going to give a right decision on the case? You will do so if you allow the prosecution to make its case after swearing the usual oath and allow me to make my defense on the actual charge. How will you allow this? If you now dismiss this case. In this way I do not escape your decision; no, it will be you who decide on my case in that court too. If you spare me now, you will on that later occasion be able to do what you like with me, but once you have put me to death there will no longer be a possibility of deliberating further about my case. (91) See now, if you must make a mistake, it would be a more righteous act to discharge me unjustly than to put me to death unjustly. The former is a mistake, the latter is impious as well. And in such a case you must be very careful, when the thing you are going to do is irretrievable. In a matter where retrieval is possible, it is a smaller matter to make a mistake under the influence of passion and the impact of slander. You can still change your mind and act wisely. But in irretrievable matters it is a further harm to change your mind and realize that you have made a mistake. Some of you perhaps may already have changed your mind after you have put a man to death. Yet where you have changed your mind because you have been deceived, then indeed you ought to put to death those who deceive you. (92) Then again, mistakes which are unintended are venial, but deliberate mistakes are not. An unintended mistake, men of the jury, is a matter of chance, but a deliberate one is a matter of decision. Now could a mistake be more deliberate than when a man puts into immediate execution what he has considered? See now, it comes to the same thing if a man kills another unjustly with his hands as if he kills him with a verdict.

(93) You can be quite sure that I never would have come to this city if I had such a crime on my conscience. In fact, I came trusting in

justice, the best helper a man can have at his side, if he is conscious of having done no unholy deed nor of being guilty of impiety towards the gods. In such a state, though the man's body may be weak, his spirit ensures his salvation, being willing to undergo hardship because his conscience is clear. But on the man who is guilty this very thing wages war. While the body is still strong, the spirit gives up the struggle early, thinking that vengeance is thus come upon it for its impieties. I come into this court with a conscience completely clear of such guilt. (94) That prosecutors should slander is not surprising. This is their function, while your function is not to believe what is not just. If you are persuaded by me you can change your mind, and the cure for acquittal now is punishment later. If, on the other hand, you are persuaded by them and do what they wish, there is no remedy in the future. The time in question is not long, after which you will be able to do legally what the prosecution is trying to persuade you to decide illegally. Decisions are not to be made in haste, but after due deliberation. Now you can give the case a preliminary hearing, later you can be judges with witnesses to assess. Now you can be holders of an opinion, then you can decide the truth.[84]

(95) It is the easiest thing in the world to bear false witness against a man on a murder charge. You only have to persuade the jury to put him to death out of hand, and the possibility of vengeance vanishes with his life. Not even his friends will want to seek vengeance for a dead man. It they should wish it, what good will it do him once he is dead? (96) Rather, you must acquit me now. At a proper trial for murder the prosecution will have to make their case after taking the usual oath; and you will reach your verdict about me in the proper legal way, and I shall not be able to say any more, if I come to grief, that I was condemned unjustly. This then I ask you to do, not disregarding your duty as god-fearing men nor depriving me of what is right. My salvation hangs on your oath. Giving weight to whichever of the arguments you will, acquit me.

---

[84] Cf. III (ii) 2.

186

VI. On the Chorus-boy

A speech written by Antiphon for an unknown defendant who was *chorēgus* at the Thargelia of May 412 B.C. There seems to be good reason for dating the speech in the autumn of 412. The *Prosecution of Philinus* (XIV frr. 48–51 pp. 208–09 below) is mentioned in the speech at 12, 21, and 35, as having been delivered shortly before. One fragment of the *Philinus* (48) speaks of making "all the *thētes* heavy-armed troops" and this statement seems to refer to the arming of the whole Athenian people which, Thucydides says, occurred after fortification of Deceleia by the Spartans in 413 (Thucydides VI 19, 1; VIII 69, 1). Pseudo-Plutarch (A 3 (10) p. 117 above) says that Antiphon "armed those of military age," so that Antiphon may have been responsible for this measure or have claimed responsibility for it (possibly in the speech *On the Revolution*). It looks, in any case, as if the *Prosecution of Philinus* belongs to April 413 and the speech *On the Chorus-boy* to the following autumn. This conclusion seems preferable to the date of 419 B.C. proposed by B. D. Meritt (see *The Athenian Calendar in the Fifth Century* [Cambridge, Mass., 1928], pp. 121–22), on the basis of an elaborate argument from the Athenian calendar, and adopted by Maidment. Maidment admits that the date of 419, which would place the speech earlier than the *Herodes*, is "unsatisfactory in view of the marked difference in style" between the two speeches. As he rightly says, the style of the former is far less stiff than that of the *Herodes* and exhibits to a far less degree "the artificialities of Gorgias and the older generation of rhetoricians."

1–10 Introduction

(1) The highest degree of happiness, men of the jury, consists in escaping personal peril at law;[85] and in our prayers that is what we would pray for. ⟨But⟩ if a man is forced to stand in peril, this is his prime need, in my opinion the most important thing of all in such a

---

[85] Cf. III (ii) 1, ἀπραγμοσύνη. In Aristophanes *Birds* 44 (414 B.C.), the Athenian hero says he is trying to find a τόπον ἀπράγμονα where there will be no lawsuits. In Thucydides II 63, 2 the word is used of quietism in general.

plight, a completely clear conscience. If some misfortune should happen, he prays for it to be without wickedness or shame, and the result not of crime but of chance.

(2) Everyone would approve of the existing code of laws dealing with cases of this kind as the best and most holy of all laws. They have in fact, in the first place, the advantage of being the oldest in the land; a second advantage is that they are always consistent, and consistency is the greatest indication of laws that are well framed, since the passage of time and experience tells us of any deficiencies, with the result that we do not need the words of the prosecution to tell us whether laws are good or not, but it is from the laws that we tell whether the prosecution's words give you a correct and proper account of the matter or not.[86]

(3) This case is of the greatest importance to me, because I am the one who am prosecuted and stand in peril. But I am well aware that you too, the jurymen, regard it as a matter of great importance to decide correctly in trials for murder, particularly because of the gods and your pious duty towards them, and secondly for your own sakes. In matters of this kind there is only one trial, and if this is wrongly decided justice and truth are powerless. (4)[87] If you bring in a verdict of guilty, a man, even if he is not a murderer nor liable to penalty for the act, must needs accept the verdict and be excluded by law from city, from religious rites, from the games, and from sacrifices, the most important and long-established preoccupations of man. The law, indeed, has such a binding force that even if a man kills one of his own chattels, who belongs to him and has no one to avenge him, out of respect for custom and heaven, he purifies himself and will refrain from participation in certain rites prescribed by the law, hoping thereby to have the best fortune. (5) Most things in human life depend on hopes; and if a man is impious and goes against what is due to the gods, he deprives himself of the greatest benefit a man can have, hope itself. No one would dare to set aside the verdict once given, confident that he is not

---

[86] Cf. V (14–15).
[87] Cf. V (87–89).

liable to it; nor, if he knew that he had committed the crime, would he dare not to observe the law. In fact, it is inevitable that a man should submit to the verdict, contrary to the true facts, or submit to the true facts themselves, particularly if there is no one to avenge the victim. (6) For these very reasons we have laws and preliminary affidavits and sacrifices and public notices and all the other accompaniments of trials for murder—all very different from what happens in other trials, since it is of the utmost importance to discover correctly the facts themselves on which the perils rest. If they are rightly discovered they are a help to the man wronged, while to condemn as a murderer a man who is not guilty is a sin and an act of impiety to the gods and the laws. A wrong prosecution is not on a par with a wrong decision by you jurymen. The prosecution's charge is not final, but is subject to you and the trial. But there is no higher court to which a man may refer anything you do not correctly judge, and thus avoid a miscarriage of justice.

(7) My own attitude to the defense, men of the jury, is not the same as the prosecution's attitude to the charge. They assert that they are instituting proceedings because of piety and justice, but the whole case which they have put forward is the outcome of slander and deceit, the most unjust of human motives; and their aim is not to punish me after establishing my guilt; but, by slandering me even if I have done nothing wrong, they aim to inflict penalties upon me and drive me into exile.

(8) I regard it as my first task to answer[88] to the charge and will narrate to you everything that happened. Then, if you permit, I shall wish to make my defense on the other charges the prosecution is bringing. I believe that these facts will bring credit and assistance to my case, but shame to the prosecution and to the slanderers. (9) It is indeed an odd affair, men of the jury. When it was open to them, supposing that I had defrauded the city either in the matter of my *chorēgia* or in anything else, after lodging information and assuring a conviction, to combine punishment of an enemy with aid to the city,

---

[88] I adopt the emendation ἀποκρίνεσθαι proposed by Reiske and accepted by Gernet and Maidment, but not by Thalheim.

not one of them has yet, in this respect, been able to prove me a criminal before your Assembly in any matter either great or small. But in this court, in a prosecution for murder, where the law requires that the charge must refer to the deed itself, they are making a plot against me, concocting lying charges and slandering my public career. They render the city for the ill done to it not compensation but accusation, claiming that they themselves are exacting punishment on their own account for the ill they say the city has suffered. (10) And yet the accusations themselves deserve neither thanks nor credence. The prosecutor does not frame his accusation on grounds whereon the city would obtain satisfaction if it was really wronged, with the result that he would deserve the city's thanks: nor ought a man to be believed, but rather disbelieved, if he makes accusations irrelevant to the charge in a case of this sort. I think, however, that I understand what you feel. You would not bring in a verdict of guilty or not guilty for any other reason than the facts of the case. This attitude accords with justice and with conscience. It is from the facts of the case that I shall begin.

11–14 The facts of the case

(11) When I was appointed *chorēgus* at the Thargelia and had Pantacles allotted to me as poet and the tribe Cecropis in addition to my own [i.e., the Erechtheid],[89] I performed the office as well and conscientiously as I could. In the first place, I provided a room for training in the most convenient part of my house, where I used to train when I was *chorēgus* at the Dionysia. Secondly, I enrolled a chorus in the best way I could, not penalizing anyone nor forcibly exacting security nor making an enemy of anyone; but, as was most agreeable and convenient to both parties, I made my requests and demands, while the parents sent their sons with good grace and willingly. (12) When the boys arrived, I was busy first of all and could not supervise proceedings in

[89] Cf. Harpocration, s.v. διδάσκαλος. "Antiphon in the speech *On the Chorus-boy* says, 'I had Pantacles allotted to me as a poet.'" (Cf. Aristophanes *Frogs* 1036.) See A.W. Pickard-Cambridge, *Dithyramb, Tragedy and Comedy*, 2d ed. (1962), p. 30. The bracketed words are plainly a gloss.

person. I happened to have a case on against Aristion and Philinus;[90] and it was of great importance to me, when I had laid an impeachment, to argue it correctly and properly before the Council and the Assembly. This business occupied my attention, and I appointed Phanostratus to look after the chorus in case they needed anything. Phanostratus is a fellow demesman of the prosecutors and a kinsman of mine, in fact, my son-in-law, and I expected him to look after them well.   (13) I appointed two other men too, Ameinias of the tribe Erechtheis, whom the tribesmen themselves regularly elected to enroll and look after the tribe, a man with a good reputation; and the second man from the Cecropid tribe, who regularly convened that tribe. Then I appointed a fourth, Philippus, who was commissioned to buy and spend any money necessary on the authority of the poet or of any other of the officials, so that the boys should enjoy the best possible *chorēgia* and should go in want of nothing because of my inability to give them my attention.

(14) This then, was how the *chorēgia* was arranged. And if I have told any falsehood in self-excuse, the prosecutor in his final speech can challenge it ⟨and⟩ say what he likes. This is how it is, men of the jury; many of those in the galleries of the court know all the details of the matter and pay attention to the official who administers the oath and listen to the points of my defense. Before them I should like to appear guilty of no perjury myself and, by speaking the truth, to persuade you to acquit me.

15-19 Defense against the main charge

(15) First, then, I shall demonstrate to you that I neither told the boy to drink the poison nor put pressure on him to do so nor administered it, and was not even present when he drank it. I do not lay great emphasis on this point to exculpate myself and inculpate someone else. I do no such thing except to inculpate chance, which I think on many other occasions has brought people to their death. Chance

90 XIV below.

neither I nor anyone else could be expected to prevent bringing each man his. . . .[91]

(Witnesses)

(16) The witnesses have given the evidence I promised you they would about the occurrence. On the basis of this evidence, we must examine the prosecution's sworn testimony and mine, to see which is the truer and more consistent with our oath. The prosecution has testified that I killed Diodotus by contriving his death. I testify that I did not kill him either with my own hand or contriving his death. (17) They base their accusation on the ground that the responsibility rests with whoever told the boy to drink the poison, made him drink it, or administered it. I shall demonstrate from the actual words of their charge that I am not answerable, since I neither told the boy nor made him drink it nor administered it; and I add to these denials that I was not even present when he drank it. If they say that whoever told him to drink it is guilty, I am not guilty because I did not tell him. If they say that whoever made him is guilty, I am not guilty, because I did not make him. And if they say that the man who administered the poison is to blame, I am not to blame, because I did not administer it. (18) Anyone who wants may make accusations and utter slanders. This course is open to each one of us. But that what did not happen should happen, and that the man who is not guilty should be guilty, does not, I believe, depend on these men's eloquence but on justice and truth. Secret doings, murder plots with no witnesses, all these matters must be assessed and investigated from the actual words of the prosecution and defense, and what is said must be examined with scepticism and in detail; and the verdict on the case must be reached by inference rather than clear knowledge.

(19) In a case, however, where, in the first place, the prosecution admits that death came to the boy not from design or prepared plan; and secondly where every particular of the action took place openly and before a number of witnesses, men and boys, free men and slaves, circumstances under which a criminal's action, if there was a criminal,

[91] There appears to be a lacuna in the text.

would be utterly plain, and a false accuser most likely to be shown up
. . . (what doubt can you have on your verdict?)[92]

20–51 Further explanations

(20) You ought, men of the jury, to take two points into consideration, both the intention of my opponents and the way in which
they approach the matter. From the start, their attitude to me has been
quite different from my attitude to them.   (21) Philocrates here, on the
day of the boy's funeral, got up and declared before the Heliaea of the
Thesmothetae that I had killed his brother in the chorus by forcing him
to drink poison. When he said this, I went before the court and
declared to the same jury that Philocrates was improperly using the law
to hinder my proceedings by accusing me and slandering me before the
court, when I had an action pending against Aristion and Philinus on
the two following days, which was the reason why I was speaking;
(22) but that, with regard to the accusations and slanders, he would
easily be shown to be a liar, since there were many witnesses, free men
and slaves, younger and older, in all more than fifty, who would know
what had been said about the drinking of the poison and what had been
done and all the details.   (23) This is what I said in court, and I
challenged him then, at once, and again on the following day, before
the same jury; and I told him to go with as many witnesses as he liked to
those who were present (I mentioned each one by name), and to
question and examine them. I told him to examine the free men in the
proper way, since they would tell the truth and what actually occurred
in their own interests and in the interest of truth. As to the slaves, if any
one of them seemed to answer his inquiry truthfully, well and good;
but if not, I was ready to hand over all my slaves to the examination;
and if he asked for any belonging to other people, I agreed to persuade
their masters and hand them over to him for the examination in whatever way he liked.   (24) Although I challenged him and spoke thus
in the court where there were present as witnesses both the jury them-

___

[92] This appears to be a rhetorical *aposiōpēsis*.

selves and many other private persons, neither then on the spot nor afterwards during the whole time since, have they yet been willing to come to this test, knowing well that the prosecution would not get the proof against me they want, but that I would get one against them to demonstrate that their accusations were not in any way just or true.

(25) You are well aware, men of the jury, that these constraints are the strongest and most powerful that men employ and that examinations give the clearest and most convincing evidence in matters of justice in cases where the witnesses are a number of free men and a number of slaves. The free men can be constrained by oaths and pledges, which are for free men the greatest and most important considerations. The slaves, on the other hand, are compelled by other constraints which force them to tell the truth even if they are likely to die in declaring it. For everyone the immediate constraint is stronger than the future constraint.

(26) I challenged the prosecution to use all these means; and in the investigation they could have used all the methods of discovering truth and right that are open to man. No excuse was left to them. I, who was the accused, and, as they alleged, the criminal, was ready to offer them the fairest investigation against myself, while they, who were making the allegation and saying that they were the wronged party, were the ones who were not willing to have an investigation into their wrongs. (27) If they had been the challengers and I had been the one who had refused to give the names of the bystanders ⟨or⟩ if I had been unwilling to surrender my slaves to their demand or if I had avoided any other challenge, exactly these actions would have been made into the greatest indications against me that the charge was true. But when I am the challenger and it is they who are avoiding the test, it is surely fair that this same fact should be taken as evidence against them that the charge which they bring against me is false.

(28) I know this too, men of the jury, that if the witnesses who were present were giving evidence for them against me, the prosecution would be laying the greatest emphasis on this very fact and would be declaring that this was the strongest guarantee, i.e., the witnesses who were giving evidence against me. But since these very men give evi-

dence that what I say is true and what they say is untrue, they tell you to give no credence to the witnesses who give evidence ⟨on my behalf⟩,[93] but say that you ought to believe the words which the prosecution speak, words which they would assail as false if I uttered them without the support of witnesses. (29) Yet it is strange if the same witnesses were to be trustworthy if they were to give evidence for them but will be untrustworthy if they give evidence for me. If no witnesses were actually present, but I were to produce some, or if I did not produce as witnesses those who were present, but certain others, the words of the prosecution would quite reasonably be more deserving of belief than mine. But where they admit the presence of witnesses and I produce those who were present and, right from the first day, I myself and all the witnesses have been clearly saying what I now say to you, is there any means other than these of making the truth credible or what is not truth incredible? (30) In a case where a man gives an account of an event but produces no witnesses, it could be objected that this account lacked supporting testimony; and where a man does produce witnesses but does not draw conclusions that match the testimony, one could, if one wished, make the same objection.

(31) To conclude: I present you with a likely account and witnesses supporting the account and actions supporting the witnesses and evidence from the actions themselves, and in addition, two of the weightiest and most powerful facts, that the prosecution is convicted of falsehood by their own account, while I am acquitted both by their account and by my own. (32) Insofar as I was willing to submit to an examination on the charge brought against me, but they were not willing to have their claim to injury[94] examined, they surely acquit me, but are become their own witnesses against themselves to the effect that their charge is neither just nor true. And yet if, in addition to my own witnesses, I call my opponents themselves as witnesses on my behalf, can I go any further or is there anywhere else from where I can produce proof that I stand acquitted of the charge?

(33) The conclusion of what I have already said and demonstrated is,

[93] ⟨ἐμοί⟩, Thalheim, Gernet, and Maidment.
[94] ⟨εἴ τι⟩, Thalheim, Gernet, and Maidment.

in my opinion, men of the jury, that you should justly acquit me, and
that you are all aware that this charge does not concern me in any way.
But in order to make the point to you still more effectively, I will
continue and will demonstrate for your benefit that these prosecutors
are the most perjured and godless men alive and deserve, as a result
of this case, the ill will, not of myself only, but of you all and every
other citizen.

(34) On the very day on which the boy died and on the next day
following the prosecution did not even see fit to accuse me of any criminal action in this affair, but actually spent time in my company and
conversed with me. On the day after that, on which the boy's funeral
took place, they were then persuaded by my enemies and prepared a
charge and a ban on my participation in the customary rites. Who then
were the people who persuaded them? And why were they so keen to
persuade them? I must tell you this story too.   (35) I was on the point
of prosecuting Aristion, Philinus, Ampelinus, and the secretary of the
Thesmothetae, in conspiracy with whom the three were embezzling
funds, and had impeached them before the Council. In the circumstances
they had no hope of acquittal, such were the crimes they had committed.
But by persuading the prosecution to make a deposition and to declare
my excommunication, they thought that they would thereby achieve
security and release from all their troubles,   (36) since the law says this,
that when anyone makes a deposition leading to a murder charge, the
defendant is excommunicated. As a result I should not be able to proceed with the prosecution while under a ban of excommunication, and
since I would not be proceeding against them, I who had lodged the
impeachment and knew the facts of the case, they would get an easy
acquittal and would not pay the penalty for their crimes to this court.
I am not the first person against whom Philinus and the others have
practiced this device; they used it against Lysistratus[95] earlier, as you

---

[95] Maidment oddly notes that "nothing further is known of Lysistratus." But
he must be the orator mentioned in Aristophanes fr. 198, which belongs to the
Banqueters of 427 B.C., and also in the *Acharnians* 855, *Knights* 1266, *Wasps* 787,
1302, 1308, and *Lysistrata* 1105. At *Wasps* 1302 he is mentioned as being a guest
at a dinner party with Antiphon.

yourselves have heard.   (37) The prosecution were eager to make a deposition against me straightaway, on the day after the boy's funeral, before the house had been ritually cleaned and the customary rites performed, bearing in mind the particular day on which the first of the four was going to have his case heard, with a view to preventing me proceeding against even one of them and revealing their crimes to the court.   (38) But the king-archon read the laws to them and demonstrated that they could not make a deposition and have the declarations made within the time limits involved, and I brought them to court in spite of their contrivances and secured the conviction of all three. They were fined amounts which you know. When all this happened and the prosecutors were quite unable to give them the help for which they had received payment, then indeed they approached me and my friends in person, asking to be reconciled and even offering to pay the penalty for their errors.   (39) At the instance of my friends I effected a reconciliation with them in the city before witnesses who reconciled us in the temple of Athena. Thereafter they spent time in my company and conversed with me in the temples, in the *agora*, in my house, in their houses, and elsewhere on every occasion.   (40) Finally, Zeus and all the gods, Philocrates himself here, standing with me on the rostrum in the council chamber in front of all the Council, held my hand and spoke (he addressing me by name and I him), so that the Council thought it very strange when it heard that my excommunication had been proclaimed by these men, whom they had seen the day before in my company and speaking with me.

(41) Consider, men of the jury, and reflect. I will demonstrate these points to you not by witnesses alone. You will actually be able to check the truth of what I am saying easily from the actual things which the prosecution have done. In the first place, the accusations they are making against the king-archon, whom they say was not willing to take a deposition for a prosecution because of my influence—this will be a proof against them that their statements are false.   (42) The king-archon, when he had accepted the deposition, had to take three preliminary proceedings, one in each of three months, and bring on the trial itself in the fourth month, as has now occurred. But he had only two

months of his period of office remaining, Thargelion and Skirophorion, and he clearly would not be able to bring on the trial in his own period of office, nor is it permitted for an archon to pass on a murder trial to his successor. No action of this kind has ever been taken by a king-archon in this country. Since he could neither bring on nor hand over the trial, he did not think it was right even to take the preliminary deposition either, which would, in fact, have been illegal.

(43) There is one very striking indication that he was not acting improperly. Philocrates here tried to inform against the other office-holders and blackmail them, but he never came forward to accuse the king-archon before the statutory auditors, although they are dreadful and heinous crimes which they say he has committed. What greater indication than this could I cite you, that Philocrates was not wronged either by me or by the king-archon? (44) When the king-archon came before the auditors, they could have laid depositions against him on any day they pleased, beginning on the first day of Hecatombaion for thirty days of that month. They laid depositions on none of them. And again, during the month of Metageitnion, beginning on the first day, they could have laid a deposition on any day they wished. They have not laid a deposition yet in this month, although twenty days have now passed. Consequently, they have had more than fifty days on which they could have laid a deposition against the king-archon, but they have laid no deposition. (45) All the others, furthermore, for whom there was not sufficient time to have their cases heard under one and the same king-archon,[96] ⟨have made their deposition under the next⟩. The prosecution were fully acquainted with the law. They saw me as a member of the Council and going into the council chamber. In the council chamber itself there is an altar of Zeus Councillor and of Athena Councillor; and at it the councillors make a prayer as they go in. I was a councillor and did this. I took part in all the other rites with the Council, sacrificing and offering prayers on behalf of the city. In addition to this, I was a president for all the first prytany except for two days, and performed rites and offered sacrifices on behalf of the

[96] There appears to be a lacuna in the text at this point.

democracy, and put motions to the vote and gave opinions on the weightiest and most important matters.   (46) The prosecution were present and residing in Athens. They could have laid depositions and excommunicated me from all these duties, but they did not see fit to do so. Yet if they were wronged they ought to have reminded people of it and have borne it in mind both for their own sakes and for the sake of the city. Why then did they lay no depositions? The reason was that they were associating and conversing with me. They met me because they did not think that I was a murderer; and they did not lay a deposition for the same reason, because they did not think that I had killed the boy nor that I was responsible for the murder nor that I had anything at all to do with the affair.

(47) How could men be more wicked or more contemptuous of the law? They see fit to persuade you of things of which they did not persuade themselves, and they bid you adjudicate cases which they themselves by their actions have put out of court. In general, men support their words by actions, but the prosecution seek by words to diminish the credibility of their actions.[97]   (48) And yet, if I said or demonstrated or supported by evidence nothing else, I have shown this at least, that on the occasion when they received money to put me to death they accused me and proclaimed my excommunication; but, when there was no one to give them anything, they associated and talked with me. This point alone is sufficient for you to take note of and acquit me, while recognizing that these are the most perjured and godless of all men.   (49) What trial would they not instigate? What court would they not deceive? What oaths would they not be prepared to break? On this actual occasion, after receiving thirty minas to put me to death from the Boards of Special Finance, of Confiscation, and of Debts, and from the clerks who acted as secretaries to these Boards, and after expelling me from the council chamber, they entered into oaths of such a solemn nature; all because, when I discovered in my office of president that they were guilty of dreadful and heinous crimes, I brought them before the Council and required the Council to deal

[97] Cf. III (iii) 3 ; V (84).

with the matter by an investigation. (50) Now they and their accomplices and those with whom the money was deposited are paying the penalties for their crimes and the affair has been exposed. Not even if they wish, will the prosecution be able to deny it. This is how the business has gone. (51) To what court will these godless men not go, then, with their deceit, or what oaths will they not be prepared to break? They knew you to be the most god-fearing jurymen in all the Greek world, and the most just, and yet they come before you, to deccive you if they can, notwithstanding the great oaths they have sworn.

(ii) FRAGMENTS

(a) SPEECHES BEFORE THE ATHENIAN ASSEMBLY

VII. ON THE TRIBUTE OF THE LINDIANS

Written for delivery by a representative of the Lindians, certainly before 413 B.C., when the tribute was commuted to a 5 percent tax on exports and imports, possibly by as much as twelve years.

1. [*Th.* 25] HARPOCRATION "*Amphipolis*," Antiphon in the speech *On the tribute of the Lindians*.

2. [*Th.* 26] HARPOCRATION "to give up (*apeipein*)" instead of "to weary of and be unable to go on doing," Antiphon in the speech *On the tribute of the Lindians*.

3. [*Th.* 27] HARPOCRATION "which (*hatta*)" instead of *hosa* or *hatina*, Antiphon in the speech *On the tribute of the Lindians*.

4. [*Th.* 28] HARPOCRATION "throughout the year (*di' eniautou*)" instead of "through the whole year," Antiphon *On the tribute of the Lindians*.

5. [*Th.* 29] HARPOCRATION "summons (*epangelia*)." People say "summon" instead of "demand" or "ask," as in Antiphon in the speech *On the tribute of the Lindians*. Cf. SUIDAS II 326, 26 *A*.

6. [*Th.* 30] HARPOCRATION "overseer (*episkopos*)," Antiphon in the speech *On the tribute of the Lindians* and in the speech *Against Laispodias* [B XXII 63]. People seem to have been sent out by the Athenians into the subject cities, overseeing affairs in each city.

7. [*Th.* 31] HARPOCRATION "offering (*prosphora*)" instead of "revenue," Antiphon in the speech *On the tribute of the Lindians*. Cf. SUIDAS IV 235, 25 *A*.

8. [*Th.* 32] HARPOCRATION "advocates (*sunēgoroi*)," Antiphon . . . in the speech *On the tribute of the Lindians*. [See B 31.]

9. [*Th.* 33] HARPOCRATION "practicing evasion (*tribōneuomenoi*)," Antiphon in the speech *On the tribute of the Lindians*, instead of either "interposing delays" or "fiddling," from people being *tribōnes*, "fiddlers," of things.

VIII. ON THE TRIBUTE OF THE SAMOTHRACIANS

"Composed for a delegation which had come to Athens to protest against the new arrangements for tribute," Maidment, *Minor Attic Orators*. A. W. Gomme (*A Historical Commentary on Thucydides* [Oxford, 1945–56], p. 201n) connects this speech, like VII, with the negotiations for raising the tribute which took place in 425/24.

10. [*Th.* 50] DEMETRIUS *On Style* 53 [without specific attributions to Antiphon] "For the island we live in, seen from a distance, is plainly high and rocky. It is small, and the productive and cultivable part of it is small as well, while the incultivable part of it is large."

11. [*Th.* 49] SUIDAS IV 318, 18 *A* Samothrace. They say that the Samians colonized it and gave it this name, and that is what is said in Antiphon's Samothracian speech: "for those who originally colonized the island were Samians, our ancestors. They settled in the island, not because they liked it, but by force of circumstance, since they were driven out of Samos by tyrants, and made the best of what had happened. They actually came to the island after a raid on Thrace."

12. [*Th.* 51] PRISCIAN 18, 280 Hertz Antiphon in the Samothracian speech: "Yet while they were concerned for the sufferings of the other cities, they can hardly have failed to take account of their own safety."

13. [*Th.* 52] HARPOCRATION "collectors (*eklogeis*)," those who collected and exacted what was owed to the public treasury. Antiphon in the speech *On the tribute of the Samothracians:* "Those in our city who appeared to have the most money were appointed collectors."

14. [*Th.* 53] HARPOCRATION "always (*aei*)" instead of "until" in Antiphon's Samothracian speech.

15. [*Th.* 54] HARPOCRATION *BA* 1 p. 427, 18 "exchanging (*apodidomenoi*)," Antiphon in the speech *On the tribute of the Samothracians,* instead of "giving back." He says regularly "we exchanged" instead of "we give back" or "we sell." Cf. SUIDAS 1 295, 23 *A.*

16. [*Th.* 55] HARPOCRATION; SUIDAS 1 324, 9 *A* "setting apart (*apotaxis*)," to set apart those who had previously been classed together for the payment of a fixed tribute. Antiphon in the speech *On the tribute of the Samothracians.*

17. [*Th.* 56] HARPOCRATION "those who join for payment or contribution (*sunteleis*)." The arrangement is called a board, as one can find in the speech of Antiphon's *On the tribute of the Samothracians.*

(b) SPEECHES BEFORE A COURT OF LAW

IX. On the Revolution

This is the famous speech which Antiphon delivered in his own defense at his trial for treason in 412 B.C. Aristotle (A 11 [5]) reports that the tragedian Agathon spoke highly of it to Antiphon himself, and Thucydides (A 11 [2]) gives it exceptional praise. It appears to have been the non-Thucydidean source for the chapters on the constitution of Theramenes in Aristotle *Constitution of Athens* XXIV–XXXII.

18. [*Th*. 1] HARPOCRATION "partisan (*stasiōtēs*)." Antiphon in the speech *On the Revolution:* "On the charges brought by Apolexis that I was a partisan, ⟨both⟩ I and my grandfather before me. . . ." The orator seems in this passage to use the word to mean bodyguard, for in what immediately follows he says: "our forefathers would not have been able to punish those who ruled as tyrants without punishing their bodyguards as well" (i.e., if my grandfather had been a partisan of the tyrants he would have been punished along with their bodyguards).

19. [*Th*. 1a] GENEVA PAPYRUS (publ. J. Nicole, *L'Apologie de Antiphon* [Geneva, 1907]. Text mainly *Th*.) I–IV.

Was this my motive for wanting a revolution, that, being elected to a public office, I had handled [large] sums of money and that there was an audit due which I had cause to fear, or that I had lost my citizen rights or that I had committed some crime or that I had a lawsuit hanging over me? No, this was not the reason, since none of these was the case with me. Was it, then, because you had confiscated my property? Or was it because [you had punished me] for some crime my ancestors had committed against you? [It is for reasons like this that men] begin to yearn for a different kind of political setup to the one they have, either to avoid paying the penalty of their crimes or so that they may take vengeance for some wrong done to them and suffer no compensating attack.

No, I had no such reason. The prosecution does [however] assert that I composed defenses for other people and that I made money out of it.[98] Surely under an oligarchy I should not have had the chance to do this, while it is under a [demo]cra[cy] that I am the powerful man I have become; and whereas under oligarchy I was likely to be of no importance, under a democracy my importance is great. Answer then. What likelihood is there that I should want oligarchy? Am I too stupid to make this calculation? Am I the [only man] in Athens unable to appreciate his own advantage? [*Th.* 1b] Did the . . . think? . . . No, by the gods in heaven, if you are sensible, since Theramenes, who accused me in the Council. . . .

20. [*Th.* 2] HARPOCRATION   "to set at odds (*diastēsai*)" instead of "to disturb, make impotent," as it were; Antiphon in the speech *On the Revolution*.

21. [*Th.* 3] HARPOCRATION   "at hand (*empodōn*)." Antiphon in the speech *On the Revolution:* "and you punished those who happened to be at hand" instead of "those who chanced to turn up."

22. [*Th.* 4] HARPOCRATION   "he denounced (*epeskēpsato*)." The word is on rare occasions used for charges of manslaughter, as Antiphon in the speech *On the Revolution*.

23. [*Th.* 5] HARPOCRATION   "Eetiōneia (a district in Piraeus)," Antiphon in the speech *On the Revolution*.

24. [*Th.* 6] HARPOCRATION   "Four Hundred (*Tetrakosioi*)" (the name of the revolutionary government), Antiphon in the speech *On the Revolution*.

25. [*Th.* 77] SUIDAS II 627, 7 *A* Antiphon: [The prosecutor] "adjured you not to have pity on me, fearing lest I should try to sway you with tears and supplications." (S.v. *hiketeia*.)

---

[98] Text of Gernet.

X. Defense against the indictment of Demosthenes

Cf. A 3 (20): the speech against Demosthenes for moving an illegal measure. Demosthenes was probably the general who was killed in Sicily in 413 B.C., and whom Aristophanes represents in the *Knights* of 424 B.C., together with Nicias, as slave of Demos, recently supplanted in his master's favor by Cleon.

26. [*Th.* 8] HARPOCRATION Alcibiades. There is another Alcibiades whom Antiphon mentions in the speech against Demosthenes' indictment. He is a Phegousian, a guest-friend of Alcibiades. Cf. *BA* 1 p. 378, 22.

27. [*Th.* 9] HARPOCRATION "to wall off (*apoteichisai*)." To wall off is to cut off with a wall. . . . Antiphon in the *Defense against the indictment of Demosthenes.* Cf. *BA* 1 p. 437, 28.

28. [*Th.* 10] HARPOCRATION "tithe collector (*dekateutēs*)" instead of tax-collectors who collect the 10 percent tax, Antiphon in the *Defense against the indictment of Demosthenes.*

29. [*Th.* 11] HARPOCRATION "uprights (*keleontes*)," Antiphon in the *Defense against the indictment of Demosthenes.* "Where he planted the uprights," i.e., properly the upright beams of a loom. By a metaphor the orator would mean in this context just upright beams.

30. [*Th.* 12] HARPOCRATION "bowl (*skaphion*)," Antiphon in the *Defense against the indictment of Demosthenes.* Aristophanes in the *Geras* indicates that the "bowl" was a kind of haircut.

31. [*Th.* 13] HARPOCRATION "advocates (*sunēgoroi*)," Antiphon in the speech *Against the indictment of Demosthenes.* [See B 8.]

32. [*Th.* 14] HARPOCRATION "Andron," Antiphon in the *Defense against the indictment of Demosthenes.* [See A 3 (23).] Crateros in the ninth book of the decrees says that Andron was the man who proposed the decree about the orator Antiphon. Andron was one of the Four Hundred.[99]

XI. Defense against the writ of Callias

This Callias may well be the patron of the "sophists" in whose house the meeting described in Plato's *Protagoras* took place, and whose wife Pericles married.

33. [*Th.* 17] Harpocration "disposition (*diathesis*)," instead of "we have been rendered." Antiphon, in the *Defense against the writ of Callias*, said "we were disposed." The same author uses the word instead of "arrangement" in the book *On Concord* [B 136]. [See also B 82 and B 95.]

34. [*Th.* 18] Harpocration "reef (*herma*)" an underwater rock, Antiphon in the *Defense against the writ of Callias*.

35. [*Th.* 19] Harpocration "we knew (*ēismen*)," instead of *ēideimen*. Antiphon in the *Defense against the writ of Callias:* "We did not know either how much seamanship was needed. . . ."

36. [*Th.* 20] Harpocration "to participate (*moirolonkēsai*)" instead of "to take a share," Antiphon in the *Defense against the writ of Callias*.

XII. Prosecution of Nicocles in a suit about boundaries

The mention of Hyperbolus in B 46 indicates that the speech is probably not before 425 B.C.

37. [*Th.* 36] Harpocration "a place for striking money (*arguro-kopeion*)," Antiphon in the speech *Against Nicocles*, where money is minted, what is sometimes called a "mint" in modern phraseology.

---

[99] Crateros (3d century B.C.) made a collection of decrees of the Athenian Assembly.

38. [*Th.* 37] HARPOCRATION "the wall in the middle (*dia mesou teichos*)," Antiphon *Against Nicocles*. There were three walls in Attica, as Aristophanes says in the *Triphales* [fr. 556 Kock], the northern, the southern, and the Phalerian wall. The one which went in between the other two was called the southern wall, which Plato mentions in the *Gorgias* [456A].

39. [*Th.* 38] HARPOCRATION "Hermai." That there was a porch called "of the Hermai" is shown by Antiphon too in the speech *Against Nicocles*.

40. [*Th.* 39] SUIDAS II 452, 21 *A*; HARPOCRATION "in a straight direction (*euthōron*)," straight, Antiphon in the speech *Against Nicocles*.

41. [*Th.* 40] HARPOCRATION "Kerameikos," Antiphon in the speech *Against Nicocles about boundaries*. That there were two Cerameicuses, as the orator says, one inside and the other outside the city, is shown by Callicrates or Menecles in the book about Athens.

42. [*Th.* 41] HARPOCRATION "places for conversation (*leschai*)," Antiphon in the speech *Against Nicocles*. They called *leschai* public places where people sat about in crowds at leisure.

43. [*Th.* 42] HARPOCRATION "hole-in-a-corner (*parabuston*)." This was the name of one of the lawcourts at Athens in which the Eleven had their sessions, Antiphon in the speech *Against Nicocles about boundaries*.

44. [*Th.* 43] HARPOCRATION "of the presidency (*prytaneias*)," Antiphon in the speech *Against Nicocles*. The presidency was the number of days, either thirty-five or thirty-six, for which each tribe was president.

45. [*Th.* 44] HARPOCRATION; SUIDAS IV 430, 19 *A* "crown-bearer (*stephanēphoros*)," Antiphon in the speech *Against Nicocles*. There was, it seems, a shrine of the Crown-bearer at Athens.

46. [*Th.* 45] HARPOCRATION "Hyperbolus" [an Athenian politician first mentioned by Aristophanes in the *Acharnians* 425 B.C.], Antiphon in the speech *Against Nicocles*. He was a demagogue.

XIII. PROSECUTION FOR AN UNCONSTITUTIONAL PROPOSAL IN THE ASSEMBLY

47. [*Th.* 46] SUIDAS II 27, 7 *A* Antiphon in the *Prosecution for an unconstitutional proposal* "to order the marines (*naumachous*) [cf. PLUTARCH *Cimon* 5] to be summoned before this court on the charge of accepting bribes."

XIV. PROSECUTION OF PHILINUS

This prosecution is mentioned in VI, the extant speech *On the Chorus-boy,* at §§ 12, 21, and 35. It is likely therefore to have been written just before 412 B.C.

48. [*Th.* 61] HARPOCRATION "*thētes, thētikon*" [the lowest of the three property classes at Athens who normally rowed in the fleet], Antiphon in the speech *Against Philinus* says: "to make all the *thētes* heavy-armed troops." Cf. A 3 (10).

49. [*Th.* 62] HARPOCRATION; SUIDAS I 91, 23 *A* "to lend an attentive ear (*akroasthai*)" instead of "to hear," Antiphon in the speech *Against Philinus*. Cf. *BA* I p. 366, 28.

50. [*Th.* 63: *DK* B 116] HARPOCRATION "to obtain a portion by lot (*apolachein*)" instead of merely "to obtain by lot (*lachein*)." Antiphon in the speech *Against Philinus*. SUIDAS I 302, 10–12 *A* "to obtain a portion by lot (*apolachein*)": to divide an inheritance and other common possessions with people and to take one's share. The orators use *dialachein* for division. Antiphon: "when men wish to divide by lot a sum of money." *Apolachein* instead of *dialachein*. So Lysias and Aristophanes and Antiphon. Cf. B 51.

51. [*Th.* 64] HARPOCRATION "division by lot (*dialēxis*)." *Dialankanein* is to divide by lot, *dialēxis* is the action, Antiphon in speech *Against Philinus.*

XV. PROSECUTION OF A PRESIDENT (IF GENUINE) CF. B 44.

52. [*Th.* 48] HARPOCRATION "rhetorical indictment (*rhetorikē graphē*)." Perhaps certain indictments are called rhetorical because indictments are made against orators under certain laws, as Antiphon suggests in the speech *Against the president*, if genuine.

XVI. ON ENSLAVEMENT

53. [*Th.* 7] PHOTIUS *Lexicon* p. 42, 12 Reitzenstein . . . the occurrence in Antiphon in the speech *On enslavement.* . . . He writes thus: "when I went off to Athens and left the cleruchy" [i.e., the farm allocated to an Athenian settler abroad]. Cf. *BA* 1 p. 352, 29.

XVII. IN A CASE OF ⟨ASSAULT⟩ UPON A BOY OF FREE PARENTAGE

54. [*Th.* 60] HARPOCRATION "he claims (*axioi*)" instead of "thinks," Antiphon in the *Case of ⟨assault⟩ upon a boy of free parentage.* Cf. SUIDAS 1 255, 29 *A.*

XVIII. PROSECUTION OF CALLISTRATUS IN A GUARDIANSHIP SUIT

55. [*Th.* 15] HARPOCRATION Antiphon in the *Prosecution of Callistratus in a guardianship suit* and Solon in the twenty-first book of *Laws* says that adopted sons (*poiētoi paides*) may not return to the household of their natural father unless they leave natural sons in the house of their adoptive father.

XIX. Prosecution of Timocrates in a guardianship suit

56. [*Th.* 16] Harpocration "Spartolus," Antiphon in the speech entitled *Prosecution of Timocrates in a guardianship suit.*

XX. Prosecution of Erasistratus in a case about peacocks
Cf. A 3 (20).

57. [*Th.* 57] Athenaeus ix 397cd There is a speech by Antiphon the orator with the title *On the peacocks.* In the speech itself there is no occurrence of the word "peacocks," although he frequently mentions "birds of many hues," saying that Demus, son of Pyrilampes,[100] breeds them, and that many people come from Sparta and Thessaly out of curiosity to see the birds and are keen to have some of their eggs. He writes as follows about their appearance: "if your idea is to set the birds loose in Athens they will fly away. If on the other hand you (loose them but) clip their wings, their beauty will be lost, since their beauty lies not in the body but in the wings." He explains again in the same speech that the sight of them was much sought after. On the first day of the month visitors were admitted, but if anyone came to see them on any other day, he was unlucky. And this is not something which has begun to happen in the last day or two, but has been going on for the last forty years. Cf. Harpocration "Pyrilampes," Antiphon in the speech *On the peacocks,* a proper name.

58. [*Th.* 58] Aelian *On the Nature of Animals* v 21 "... they valued a pair of peacocks at one thousand drachmas," as Antiphon says in the speech *Against Erasistratus.*

59. [*Th.* 59] Harpocration "pleasingly to the eye (*euopthalmōs*)" instead of "becomingly," Antiphon in the speech *About peacocks.* Cf. Suidas ii 462, 6 *A.*

---

[100] See Aristophanes *Wasps* 97, Plato *Gorgias* 481D, Lysias 19 27, Plutarch *Pericles* 13.

XXI. Prosecution of Hippocrates Cf. A 3 (21), A 4 (17).

Hippocrates, the general, was killed at Delium in 424 B.C. He was a nephew of Pericles.

XXII. Prosecution of Laispodias

Laispodias is ridiculed as a general in Aristophanes *Birds* 1569 of 414 B.C. Thucydides says that he was sent on a deputation to Sparta by the Four Hundred in 411 (VIII 86, 9).

60. [*Th.* 21] HARPOCRATION "not to trust (*apistein*)" instead of "to disbelieve," Antiphon *Against Laispodias*.

61. [*Th.* 22] HARPOCRATION "Galepsus," Antiphon *Against Laispodias*.

62. [*Th.* 23] HARPOCRATION "overseer (*episkopos*)," Antiphon . . . in the speech *Against Laispodias*. [See B 6.]

63. [*Th.* 24] HARPOCRATION "Oisume," Antiphon in the speech *Against Laispodias*.

XXIII. In defense of Myrrhus

64. [*Th.* 34] SUIDAS I 397, 14 *A* Antiphon uses *hatta* instead of *hatina* in the *Defense of Myrrhus:* "For I had not yet experienced what (*hatta*) I have since experienced at the hands of my accuser." Cf. B 3.

XXIV. Prosecution of Polyeuctes

65. [*Th.* 47] *BA* I p. 82, 29 "to undertake (*anadexai*)" like "to go surety," Antiphon in the speech *Against Polyeuctes*.

XXV. Defense against Philippus (if genuine) See DK 82 A 5a.

66. [*Th.* 65] Harpocration "being a parishioner (*dēmoteuomenos*)."
Demoteuesthai is to be a member of such and such a parish and to share
in the benefits of membership, Antiphon in the *Defense against Philippus*,
if genuine.

(c) MISCELLANEOUS WORKS

XXVI. On Truth, Books I and II

Book I: Theory of Knowledge

The argument of Book I seems to have been as follows: Mind (*gnomē*)
rules the body, but needs a starting point (B 70, 82). This starting
point is the senses. We all believe what we see with our eyes more than
abstractions (B 68). But when we speak there is no permanent reality
behind our words, nothing in fact comparable to the results of seeing
and knowing (B 67). Antiphon seems to have given at least five
examples of this last assertion:

(1) Time has no reality (B 77).
(2) A circle is a polygon with an infinite number of sides (B 81).
(3) A wooden bed may also be a tree (B 83).
(4) Justice may also be injustice (B 90, 92).
(5) There is no real distinction between Greek and barbarian (B 91).

Nevertheless, although words are deceptive, there is a right and a
wrong way of coining names (B 69). Antiphon also seems to have
denied that there is design in nature, and to have said that God has no
need of us (B 78, 80).

67. [*DK* B 1] Galen *Commentary on Hippocrates' "The Doctor's Workshop"* xviii B 656 Kühn[101]   And in the second book of the *Homiliai*

---

[101] For the text as well as a discussion of this fragment see *Phronesis* VIII 1
(1963) pp. 35–49.

Critias often speaks opposing the cognitive mind to the senses as Antiphon does in the first of the two books of the *Truth*. "When a man speaks he expresses no single thing or single meaning, indeed the subject of his speech is not any single thing either of the things which the most powerful beholder sees with his sight or of the things which the most powerful knower knows with his mind."[102]   Cf. HIPPOCRATES *The Science* 2 "I think, generally speaking, that there is no such thing as a nonexistent science. Indeed, it is absurd to think of one of the things which exist as nonexistent. If some things actually did not exist [as the Eleatics say] how could someone look at them as existing and say that they did not exist. Indeed, if you can actually see what does not exist, just as much as what does exist, I cannot see how anyone could believe that they do not exist, particularly if you can see them with your eyes and know them with your mind as existing.[103] No, this cannot be so. On the contrary, things which exist are always seen and known, while things which do not exist are neither seen nor known. Things which exist are known when the sciences are discovered;[104] and there is no science which is not recognized as the result of some abstract category recognizable by visible characteristics [*eidos*]. I think that the sciences, too, take their names from the visible abstract categories. For it is ridiculous to think that the visible abstract categories spring from their names,[105] and impossible, too. For names are conventional restrictions on nature, but the visible abstract categories of things are not conventional restrictions on, but the offspring of, nature."[106]

---

[102] In Hippocrates' *The Science*, which W. H. S. Jones (*Loeb* ed.) places in the last half of the 5th century B.C., we find the assertion that there are certain *eidē*, or abstract categories of things, which are the "offspring of nature." This is the sort of theory put forward in answer to contemporary Eleatics like Melissus, which Antiphon seems to be denying.

[103] So far the author and Antiphon are in agreement, against the Eleatics, that the senses, including mind (*gnomē*), are the only clue to what exists.

[104] I translate the text of the MSS, omitting the additions of *DK*. Cf. Aristotle *Metaphysics* I 9, 990b12ff.

[105] For this view, see Plato *Cratylus* 391B–427E.

[106] Cf. B 162 for a denial of the visible abstract category, here too in terms of what is natural and unnatural. Also B 72.

68. [*Th.* 35] SUIDAS I 397, 15 *A*   Antiphon [continuation of B 64]. And again, "For whatever [*hatta*] people see with their eyes they regard as more credible than things the evidence for whose existence belongs to what is not seen" from the *Truth*.[107]

69. [*Th.* 76] GALEN *Glossary of Hippocratic Terminology*, Introduction XIX 66 Kühn (A 7 [3])   . . . that each and every one of those concerned with speaking (i.e., the rhetorical teachers) felt entitled to coin new words (or names) is shown sufficiently by Antiphon, too, very clearly, insofar as he taught the best way to coin them. It is shown too by Aristophanes in the same play (the *Banqueters*) in the following passage: fr. 198 Kock. [Galen quotes from the *Truth* in B 67, B 70, and B 101.]

70. [*DK* B 2] GALEN *Commentary on Hippocrates' "The Doctor's Workshop"* XVIII B 656 Kühn (following B 67)   "For in the case of everyone the mind [*gnomē*] is the ruler of the body both in matters of health and disease and in everything else."

71. [*DK* B 3] POLLUX VI 143   Antiphon uses the expression "with unprepared mind" in the books *On Truth* . . . [B 165].

72. [*DK* B 4] HARPOCRATION   "unseen (*aopta*)" instead of "invisible and not actually seen but visible to the inward eye," Antiphon in the first book of *Truth*. Cf. SUIDAS I 256, 15 *A*; B 68; also POLLUX II 58.

73. [*DK* B 5] HARPOCRATION   "not sensible (*apathē*)" instead of "not feeling sensations which really do not exist," Antiphon in the first book of the *Truth*.   SUIDAS I 256, 27 *A* Antiphon uses *apathē* in the plural for feelings which are not real.

74. [*DK* B 6] [*Th.* 161] POLLUX II 58   "to see through (*diopteuein*),"[108] Critias and Antiphon. Antiphon also, "visible (*eisoptoi*)."

---

[107] The last two words, *tēs alētheias*, seem more likely to be indication of provenance than to form part of the quotation as the editors have it.

[108] See Aristophanes *Acharnians* 435.

75. [*DK* B 7] [*Th.* 178] POLLUX II 57   Antiphon also uses the expression "that which is about to see" and "with the sight" [B 67] like "with the eyes" and "witness" [B v 27] and "unseen" [B 72].

76. [*DK* B 8] [*Th.* 173] POLLUX II 76   "scent (*odmē*)" and "sweet-scentedness (*euodmia*)" seem to most people to be fine words, but they are actually poetic. In prose they are Ionic and Aeolic. You will find "scent" and "sweet-scentedness" only in Antiphon.

77. [*DK* B 9] AETIUS I 22, 6 (*D* 318)   Antiphon and Critolaus say that time is thought or measurement, not a real thing.

78. [*DK* B 10] SUIDAS I 46, 20 *A   adeētos*, he who stands in need of nothing and possesses all things (in himself), Antiphon in the first book of the *Truth:* "for this reason he [? God; see A 8 (10)] needs nothing nor expects anything from anyone, but is without limits or needs." Cf. HARPOCRATION, s.v.

79. [*DK* B 11] HARPOCRATION; SUIDAS II 16, 26 *A*   "requests (*deēseis*)" in place of "needs," Antiphon in the first book of *Truth*.

80. [*DK* B 12] ORIGEN *Against Celsus* IV 25   So then if one man were to be a Demosthenes the orator with weaknesses like his and the actions which follow from those weaknesses, or another an Antiphon who had a reputation as an orator and did away with design [in nature] in the works called, like Celsus', *On Truth*, these are nonetheless (Celsus says) worms wallowing in a filthy corner of ignorance and folly.

81. [*DK* B 13] ARISTOTLE *Physics* I 2, 185a14   But at the same time we are also not required to answer every objection, only those that proceed from the principles of geometry, but are wrongly deduced. Those that do not so proceed, we are not required to answer. For example, it is the business of the geometrician to refute the squaring of the circle by means of segments, but it is not his business to refute Antiphon's solution. Cf. *On Sophistical Refutations* XI 172a7. Also SIMPLICIUS *Physics* 54, 12 while many researched into the problem of squaring the circle (i.e., constructing a quadrilateral equal in area to the circle), Antiphon and Hippocrates of Chios believed that they had discovered a solution, but they were mistaken. Antiphon's mistake lay in not proceeding from geometrical principles, as we shall learn, and is not therefore a matter for a geometrician to refute. . . . Antiphon described a circle and inscribed in it one of the polygonal areas that can be so inscribed. Let the inscribed figure then be a quadrilateral. Next he bisected each of the sides of the quadrilateral and, from the point of bisection, drew upright lines straight to the circumference. These lines plainly bisected the relevant segment of the circumference. Then, from the point of bisection of the segment, he drew straight lines to meet the ends of the lines bounding the quadrilateral, so that four triangles were formed from the straight lines, and the whole figure inscribed was an octagon.

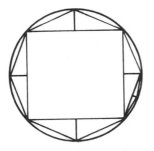

And then again by the same procedure, bisecting each of the sides of the octagon and drawing upright lines from the point of bisection of the sides to the circumference and drawing connecting lines from the points at which the upright lines touched the circumference, he made the inscribed area a figure of sixteen sides. And again by the same procedure bisecting the sixteen-sided figure and drawing connecting lines and doubling the [number of sides of the] inscribed polygon, and going on doing this to infinity, he believed he would reach a point at which, by a process of exhaustion of the area, a polygon would be thus inscribed whose sides will by and large coincide with the circumference of the circle. Then, since we are able to construct a quadrilateral equal to any polygon, as we learned in the *Elements* [EUCLID II 14], because the polygon is equal to the circle which by and large coincides with it, we shall be in a position to construct a quadrilateral equal to a circle. Cf. also THEMISTIUS *Physics* 4, 2 The geometrician would not have anything more to say to refute Antiphon. Inscribing an equilateral triangle in the circle and constructing another equilateral triangle on each of the sides to reach the circumference of the circle, and doing this again and again to infinity, he believed that the side of the ultimate triangle, though a straight line, would coincide with the circumference. This was the process of taking bisection to infinity, which is the geometrician's hypothesis.

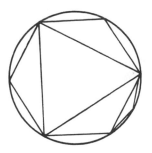

82. [*DK* B 14] HARPOCRATION "disposition (*diathesis*)." [See B 33, B 95, and B 136.] For the word "dispose" is used for "arrange." Antiphon in the first book of the *Truth*: "Without a starting point it [? mind, *gnomē*] would have disposed many good things badly."

83. [*DK* B 15] HARPOCRATION "alive (*embios*)." Antiphon in the first book of the *Truth*: "And the corruption should become alive" instead of "in a living state," i.e., should live and not wither and die. Cf. SUIDAS II 253, 20 *A*. ARISTOTLE *Physics* II 1, 193a9 . . . some take the view that the nature and reality of natural things is the primary inherent stuff, unmodified and by itself, i.e., that the nature of a bed is the wood and of a statue the bronze. Antiphon claims as evidence of this the fact that if you were to dig a bed into the earth, and [it rotted and] the rottenness developed the power to put out a shoot, it would not be a bed but wood, since the bed-ness is merely an incidental attribute, the customary construction and craftsmanship, whereas the reality is that which persists and is constant under these superficial modifications. [Diels-Kranz considered Antiphon's actual words to have been] If you were to dig a bed into the earth and the rottenness of the wood developed the power to put out a shoot, it would not be a bed but wood.

84. [*DK* B 16] [*Th*. 156] *BA* 1 p. 470, 25 "arriving (*aphēkontos*)." Antiphon instead of "reaching to (*diēkontos*)."

85. [*DK* B 17] *BA* 1 p. 472, 14   "Aphrodite" instead of "sex," Antiphon in the first book of *Truth*.

86. [*DK* B 18] Harpocration   "cross-questionings (*anapodizomena*)" instead of "examinings" or instead of "the same things done again and again from the beginning," Antiphon in the first book of the *Truth*. Cf. Pollux II 196.

87. [*DK* B 19] Harpocration   "amounts to (*anhēkei*)" in Antiphon, the first book of the *Truth*, instead of simple "arrives" or something like "ascended" or "advanced."   *BA* 1 p. 403, 5 *A* Antiphon instead of "reaches to (*kathēkei*)." Cf. Suidas I 215, 10 *A*.

88. [*DK* B 20] Harpocration   "interchanges (*epallaxeis*)" instead of "exchanges" or "mixtures," Antiphon in the first book of the *Truth*. Cf. Suidas II 330, 2 *A*.

89. [*DK* B 21] Harpocration   "to yearn for (*orignēthēnai*)" instead of "to desire," Antiphon in the first book of the *Truth*.

90. [*DK* B 44n] Harpocration   Antiphon in the first book of the *Truth*: "were to regard (*agoi*) the laws as important" instead of "were to think (*hēgoito*) [i.e., the laws important]."   Suidas I 39, 6 *A* Antiphon employs *agoi* instead of *hēgoito*. For he says in the work *About Truth* "he were to regard the laws as important."   *POxy* XI no. 1364 ed. H(unt) [Only major supplements are indicated.]

FRAGMENT A

[Col. 1 (1–33 H.)] Justice then consists in not transgressing the customs of the city in which one enjoys citizenship. So a man would employ justice best for his own interests if he were to regard the laws as important[109] when witnesses were present, but, when no witnesses are

---

[109] See Harpocration and Suidas immediately above (90) which provide the identification of this fragment as belonging to the *Truth* of Antiphon. It is assumed that the other papyrus fragments are from the same work and author.

present, he were to regard the demands of nature as important. For the demands of the laws are artificial, but the demands of nature are necessary. And the demands of the laws are the result not of natural disposition but of agreement, but the demands of nature are exactly the opposite.   [Col. 2 (34–66 H.)] So if a man transgresses the demands of law and his transgression is unnoticed by the parties to the agreement, he escapes without either shame or penalty. But if the transgression is noticed he does not. If, on the other hand, a man does what is really an impossibility and violates one of the inherent demands of nature, if all mankind fails to notice it the harm is no less and if everyone is aware of it the harm is no greater. For the injury he suffers is not in appearance but in truth. This is exactly what the present line of argument is about, to demonstrate that many of the things which are just according to the law are at variance with nature. Laws lay down what the eyes may   [Col. 3 (67–99 H.)] see and not see, what the ears may hear and not hear, and what the tongue may say and not say, and what the hands may do and not do, and where the feet may go and where they may not go, and what the heart may desire and what it may not. But as far as nature is concerned, none of these things is more in accord or conformity with nature than any other, either the things from which the laws turn men aside or the things to which they direct them.

Again, life is natural, and so is death, and life is one[110] of the advantages at which men aim, while death is one of the disadvantages. [Col. 4 (100–131 H.)] But the advantages which are prescribed by the laws are fetters of nature, whereas the advantages which are prescribed by nature make for freedom. It is not the case that things which bring pain can truly be said to benefit man's nature more than the things which bring pleasure. Nor indeed is it the case that the things which bring sorrow are advantageous to a greater degree than the things which bring joy. For the things which are truly advantageous ought not to bring harm but help. So then the things which are advantageous in nature are . . . than these.   [Col. 5 (132–64 H.)] And people who act in self-defense when attacked and do not take the offensive themselves,

[110] Taking $ἀπό$ in a partitive sense.

and people who are good to their parents even if their parents act badly to them, and those who offer the other party an oath for them to swear, but do not bind themselves with an oath,[111] many of these cases are examples of conduct against nature, and lead to greater pain when less is possible and to damage which could be avoided. If, on the other hand, the laws afforded protection to those who surrendered their rights[112] in this way and penalties to those who did not surrender them, but hit back instead, [Col. 6 (165–97 H.)] obedience to the laws would have some ⟨profitable aspect⟩. But as things are, it is clear that justice according to the law does not afford sufficient protection to those who submit in this way, since, in the first place, it licenses the sufferer to suffer and the doer to act, and not even when the act has been committed would it attempt to prevent the sufferer from suffering or the doer from acting. When justice is brought in to assist in punishment it is no more on the side of the sufferer than of the doer. For the sufferer must persuade ⟨the jury⟩ that he was the sufferer ⟨and⟩ must ⟨apply⟩ for the opportunity to gain a verdict. It is equally open to the doer to deny the charge. . . .

FRAGMENT B

91. [*DK* B 44] *POxy* XI no. 1364 Hunt [Col. 1 (266–99 H.)] We ⟨respect⟩ and revere those who are of good parentage, but those who are not of good family we neither ⟨respect⟩ nor revere. In this behavior we have become like barbarians one to another, when in fact by nature we all have the same nature in all particulars, barbarians and Greeks. We have only to consider the things which are natural and necessary to all mankind. These are open to all ⟨to get⟩ in the same way, and in ⟨all⟩

---

[111] These are all examples of conduct prescribed by *nomos* in the sense of custom, and the opposite of conduct according to natural self-interest. The third example is explained by Aristotle *Rhetoric* I 25, 1377a8 from which it appears that an honest, god-fearing man offering a dishonest, non-god-fearing adversary an opportunity of affirming on oath gave him an advantage before a jury. Similarly, by not accepting the opportunity of himself affirming an oath offered by a dishonest, non-god-fearing man, the honest man puts himself at a disadvantage before a jury.

[112] Reading προειμένοις of P.

these there is no distinction of barbarian or Greek. For we all breathe out into the air by the mouth and the nose, and we ⟨all eat with our hands⟩. . . .

92. [*DK* B 44] *POxy* XV no. 1797   If justice is taken ⟨seriously⟩, giving true evidence against one's neighbor is considered ⟨just⟩ conduct and no less useful for the various avocations of human society. Now the man who does this is not just, if[113] not wronging anyone who has done you no wrong is considered just conduct. For, necessarily, the man who gives evidence, even if the evidence he gives is true, must nevertheless somehow or other do his neighbor wrong, and lays himself open to suffer wrong thereafter for what he has said, insofar as the man against whom the evidence is given is found guilty because of the testimony of the man in question and loses either money or life through the agency of this man whom he has never wronged. So in this respect he wrongs the man against whom the evidence is given, insofar as he wrongs someone who never did him any wrong, and the result is that he in turn is wronged by the man against whom he gives evidence because he is hated by him by reason of his true evidence. And not only is he wronged by the hatred but also because he must forever afterwards be on his guard against the man against whom he gave evidence. Thus he acquires a lasting enemy, to speak and work him injury whenever he can. In fact, these seem to be no small injustices, both those he suffers and those he commits. Indeed, it is impossible to reconcile the principle that this conduct is just [i.e., giving evidence against one's neighbor] with the other principle, that one should not do any injustice nor suffer it either.[114] No, either one is just or both are unjust. It is clear that the administration of law and justice and arbitration with a view to a final settlement are all contrary to justice. For helping one set of people harms another. And in the process, while those who get help escape injustice, those who get harm are ⟨treated unjustly⟩. . . .

[113] Reading εἶπε ⟩ρ with Diels and with Bignone, *Studi sul pensiero antico*.
[114] Cf. Plato *Republic* I 359A.

Book II: Cosmogony and Zoogony

93. [*DK* B 22] HARPOCRATION; SUIDAS I 62, 3 *A* "Eternity (*aeiestō*)." Antiphon, the second book of *Truth*, eternity and constant immobility, like the word "*euestō* (happiness)." Cf. PHOTIUS *Lexicon* Reitzenstein p. 37, 18. Cf. also *DK* 68 A 167; B 4.

94. [*DK* B 23] HARPOCRATION "separation (*diastasis*)." Antiphon in the second book of *Truth* "concerning the now prevailing separation" [i.e., of the elementary bodies in the present world order] instead of "the ordering of the universe." Cf. SUIDAS II 73, 21 *A*.

95. [*DK* B 24a] [*Th.* 160] SUIDAS II 56, 20 *A* "Disposition (*diathesis*)." [See B 33, B 82, and B 136.] Antiphon used the word "disposition" for mind or thought. He also used it for arranging a speech; i.e., for expressing something. In the second book of the *Truth* the same author uses it for the arrangement of the world. 56, 24 *A diathesis:* Antiphon instead of "arrangement (*dioikesis*)."

96. [*DK* B 24] HARPOCRATION; SUIDAS I 50, 18 *A* "not separated (*adiastaton*)." Antiphon spoke of all that which is not yet separated or distinguished. PHOTIUS *Lexicon* p. 31, 17 Reitzenstein *adiastaton* as Antiphon (?) "and the building is not detached."

97. [*DK* B 25] HARPOCRATION "by means of the whirl (*dinōi*)" instead of "by means of the revolution (*dinēsei*)," Antiphon in the second book of the *Truth*. Cf. ARISTOPHANES *Clouds* 380.

98. [*DK* B 26] AETIUS II 20, 15 (*D* 351) About the sun's nature: Antiphon says it is fire which grazes upon the damp air round the earth and which causes risings and settings by constantly leaving behind the scorched air and in turn going after the air which is dampish.

99. [*DK* B 27] AETIUS II 28, 4 (*D* 358) Antiphon said that the moon shone by her own light, but, it being in the nature of stronger fire to dim the weaker, the moon's light was dimmed and obscured by the sun's light falling upon it, and that this happened also in the case of the other stars.

100. [*DK* B 28] Aetius ii 29, 3 (*D* 359) (About the eclipse of the moon) Alcmaeon [*DK* 24 A 4], Heraclitus [*DK* 22 A 12], and Antiphon said that [the moon was eclipsed] because of the revolution of the bowl-shaped body and the declinations.

101. [*DK* B 29] Galen on Hippocrates *Epidemics* xvii A 681 Kühn So also in Antiphon in the second book of the *Truth* this expression can be found (i.e., *eiloumenon*) in this passage: "Whenever, accordingly, there occurs in the air rain and wind opposed to each other, then the water is compacted and condensed in many places. Whenever any of the colliding bodies is mastered, it is regularly condensed and compacted, packed close by the wind and the force [of the collision]. He, too, seems to express by the word *eiloumenon* what is confined and packed close together.

102. [*DK* B 30] Harpocration; Suidas i 544, 12 *A* "wrinkled (*grupanion*)." Antiphon in the second book of *Truth:* "Scorching the earth and melting it together [the sun, the fire] makes it wrinkled."

103. [*DK* B 31] *Etym. Gen.* "to become wrinkled (*grupanizein*)": the earth quivers and quakes and, as it were, becomes wrinkled by the earthquake, Antiphon. This expression is used by Antiphon.

104. [*DK* B 32] Aetius iii 16, 4 (*D* 381) How the sea arose and how it became salt: Antiphon said that the sweat [cf. *DK* 31 B 55], resulting from the ⟨primal mixture vaporized by the⟩ hot out of which the remaining moisture was separated off⟨and was called the sea⟩, was made salt through evaporation, which happens in the case of all sweat.

105. Lexicon Sabbaiticum (Lexica Graeca Minora K. Latte [1965] p. 41, 19) Antiphon used the word "self-engendered (*autophuton*)."

106. [*DK* B 33] Suidas iv 750, 22 *A*; Harpocration "to be covered with skin (*pephoriōsthai*)": Antiphon in the second book of the *Truth* makes it plain that the word *phorinē* is used of human skin.

107. [*DK* B 34] POLLUX II 41 "headache (*kephalalgia*)" and "heaviness of the head (*karēbaria*)" . . . and food and drink which causes heaviness of the head. Antiphon uses the expression *karoun* ("stupefy") for causing this.

108. [*DK* B 35] POLLUX II 215 "redblooded (*enaimon* and *enaimōdes*)" in Antiphon.

109. [*DK* B 36] POLLUX II 223 Antiphon too has said "that in which the foetus grows and receives nourishment is called the membrane."

110. [*DK* B 37] POLLUX II 224 the word *epiplous*, intestinal membrane, occurs. Antiphon uses it in the masculine and feminine genders.

111. [*Th*. 148: *DK* B 38] POLLUX II 7; PHOTIUS *Lexicon* p. 58, 18 Reitzenstein both *amblosis* as Lysias [fr. 24] and *ambloma* ("abortion") as Antiphon.

112. [*DK* B 39] POLLUX II 61 Antiphon in the books about *Truth* also uses "crippled (*anapēra*)."

113. [*Th*. 158: *DK* B 40] POLLUX VII 169 Antiphon speaks of "tempering (*bapsin*)" of bronze and iron.

114. [*Th*. 159: *DK* B 41] POLLUX VII 189 the helpless, helplessness, "good at self-help (*biomēchanoi*)" as Antiphon.

115. [*Th*. 179: *DK* B 42] POLLUX IX 53 Antiphon's *talantōsis* shows the weight.

116. [*DK* B 43] HARPOCRATION; SUIDAS I 7, 31 *A* "*abios*": Antiphon uses the word for the man who has an ample livelihood, as Homer (*Iliad* XI 155) speaks of a thick forest as *axulos*. . . . Cf. HESYCHIUS s.v. "rich" as Antiphon in the *Truth*.

XXVII. On Concord (See A 6 [12].)

For the title, cf. the decree of Themistocles before Artemisium (*SEG* 18 [1962] no. 153, line 43) by which the exiles were recalled in the interests of the concord of all Athenians in repelling the barbarian. Also Thucydides viii 93, 3 (412 b.c.). The Four Hundred and the hoplites in Piraeus "came to an agreement to hold a meeting of the Assembly on a stated day to discuss concord" (i.e., political reconciliation). For concord as a more abstract idea, cf. Xenophon *Memorabilia* iv 4, 16 [*DK* B 44a] "And again concord is regarded as the greatest asset in political societies; and their upper houses and leading men are constantly advising citizens to live in concord. Indeed, in every city in Greece there is a law that the citizens must swear to live in concord, and everywhere this oath is actually taken. The object of the practice, in my opinion, is not to ensure that they give the prize to the same choruses or approve of the same flute-players or choose the same poets, nor that their tastes should be the same, but that they may obey the laws. For where citizens abide by the laws, cities are strongest and most prosperous; but without concord neither would a city be well governed nor a household well managed." Cf. also Iamblichus *Epistle on Concord* [Stobaeus ii 33, 15; *DK* B 44a] "Concord, as its name goes to show, comprises the bringing together, common activity and unity of similar minds. From that as a beginning, it spreads to cities and households and all public and private societies, and to natural organisms and kinships, similarly both public and private. Furthermore, it embraces also the concordance of each individual with himself. For if a man is governed by one idea and by one mind he is in concord with himself, but if his mind is split and his ideas are at variance with one another, then he is in a state of dissension. In the former case the man, remaining steadfastly in one way of thinking, is full of agreement. In the latter he is infirm in his purpose and is carried away now by one idea and now by another. He is irresolute and at variance with himself." (See also Democritus 68 B 250–55; Plato *Clitophon* 409Eff.; Isocrates 7, 31–35; Aristotle *Nicomachean Ethics* viii 1, 1155a22.)

Apart from the single words which reveal no train of thought (135–45), the fragments of the *Concord* fall under three main headings:

    i. Education (117–22)
    ii. Psychology (123–28)
    iii. Sociology (129–31, possibly leading up to 132–34)

The lines of argument are illuminated by the parallel ideal of (1) *eunomia* in the fragment of an anonymous sophistic writer preserved in Iamblichus (*DK* 89, in particular [7]), an ideal which also seems to be based on the right internal condition of the individual, and (2) *euthumia* in the ethical fragments of Democritus (*DK* 68 B 174, B 191; A 167), which is closely connected with his conception of law. These three contemporary systems of thought exhibit a number of common features. All show an interest in the psychology of the individual as the proper foundation of social and political well-being, and thus foreshadow many of the main positions of Plato's *Republic*.

The clue to the reason for the references to the peculiar peoples (120–22) is likely to be found in the contemporary Hippocratic work *Airs Waters Places* XIV. There the "long-heads" are said to have heads like no other people: "Originally custom was chiefly responsible for the length of the head, but now custom is reinforced by nature." Like the dwellers on Lake Phasis mentioned by the author in the succeeding chapter they have acquired physical peculiarities as a result of their habit of life. "Custom originally so acted that through force such a nature came into being; but as time went on the process became natural, so that custom no longer exercised compulsion." It, literally, became a second nature to them to have long heads. We learn from the scholiast on Aristophanes *Birds* 1553 that the "shady-feet" have immense feet which they use as sunshades when they recline. They are then presumably another people who have acquired a physical peculiarity as a result of a habit of life and of the climate in which they live. Cf. SUIDAS IV 278, 20 A. As to the "people who live beneath the earth," Herodotus (IV 183, 4) says of the cave-dwelling Ethiopians, among other things, that they twitter like bats. This again looks like a physical peculiarity induced by a way of life, since bats also are cave dwellers, and may be the reason for their mention along with the "long-heads" and "shady-feet" in the *Concord*. The idea that nature (*phusis*) is influenced by habit (*meletē, didachē*) appears in Antiphon's contemporaries, Evenus of Paros (fr. 9 *DK* 68 B 33n) and Democritus (*DK* 68 B 33). The peculiar peoples are then likely to have been introduced as evidence for the educational tenet that "by doing good actions we become good men."

i. EDUCATION

117. [*DK* B 60] STOBAEUS II 31, 39   From Antiphon: "First among human activities, I think, is education. For when a man makes a right beginning of any matter whatsoever it is likely that the end, too, will come right. For example, according to the seed which a man sows in the soil so must one expect the crop to be. In the same way, whenever one plants a good education in a young body it lives and increases for the whole of life, and neither rain nor drought destroys it."

118. [*DK* B 61] STOBAEUS II 31, 40   From the same [Antiphon]: "There is nothing worse for men than lack of discipline. With this truth in mind, men of old accustomed their children to discipline [cf. SOPHOCLES *Antigone* 672] and obedience from the beginning, so that when they grew up and came to a great change in their lives they should not be thrown off their balance."

119. [*DK* B 62] STOBAEUS II 31, 41   [Follows 118] A [child] is likely to become similar in his character to the person with whom he spends the greater part of the day.

120. [*DK* B 45] SÜIDAS IV 378, 28 *A*; HARPOCRATION   "Shady-feet (*skiapodes*)," Antiphon in the book *On Concord*. A Libyan tribe.

121. [*DK* B 46] HARPOCRATION   "Long-heads (*makrokephaloi*)." Antiphon in the book *On Concord*. There is a nation so called.

122. [*DK* B 47] HARPOCRATION   "Living beneath the earth (*hupo gēn oikountes*)." [Perhaps the Troglodytes spoken of by Scylax in the *Periplous* (fr. 2 p. 5 Issberner) and the people named "*Katoudaioi*" by Hesiod in the third book of the *Catalog* (p. 150 Merkelbach and West).]

ii. PSYCHOLOGY

123. [*DK* B 49] STOBAEUS IV 22, 66 Cf. III 6, 45. From Antiphon: "Well then, let his life progress further, and let him want marriage and a wife. That day, that night, is the beginning of a new life [*daimon*], a new fate. For marriage is a great gamble for a man. If the wife turns out to be incompatible, how can he deal with the situation? Divorce is difficult, to make enemies of your friends, men who have the same ideas and the same background, who have thought him worthy of alliance, and have been thought worthy by him. But it is difficult, too, to keep such a possession, to have troubles at home when you expected to have joys. Well then, let us not speak of the dark side, but speak of the most compatible of alliances. What is more delightful for a man than a wife after his own heart? What is more pleasant, especially when he is young? Yes, and in that very place where the pleasure lies, dwells close the smart as well. For pleasures do not come alone, but are accompanied by pains and toils. Indeed, even Olympian victories and Pythian victories and contests of that sort, and various skills, and all pleasures, have the tendency only to come after great pains. For honors, prizes, the baits which God has given to mankind, bring them to the necessity of great toil and sweat. For if I had a second body like this one to be responsible for, as I am responsible for myself, I could not endure it, considering all the trouble I give myself, what with health of body and earning a livelihood, and honor, and a good name and reputation. What then if I actually had a second body like this one for which I would be responsible? Is it not then clear that a wife, even if she is after a man's own heart, would nevertheless give him as much pleasure and as much pain as he gives himself, what with the health of two bodies and scraping a livelihood and self-control and a good name? Well then, suppose there are children born. Now indeed is the world full of worries and the mind loses the bounce of youth, and the countenance is no longer the same."

124. [*DK* B 58] STOBAEUS III 20, 66 From Antiphon "A man who goes against his enemy to do him injury, but fears he may fail in his purpose and achieve what he does not intend is more prudent [i.e., than the man who proceeds to action without reflection]. For while he is afraid he puts off action, and while he puts it off frequently the passage of time changes his mind from his purpose. When the deed is done it is too late to change your mind. The man who thinks that he will do his neighbor injury and will suffer no injury himself is a fool. Expectation is not always a good thing. Many people have been cast down by expectations of this kind into irreparable misfortunes. It has turned out that they themselves have suffered what they thought to inflict on their neighbors. Good sense might be said to belong to that man and to no other who makes himself withstand the immediate pleasures of his heart and has succeeded in overcoming and conquering himself. The man who intends to satisfy his heart's desire immediately intends what is worse rather than what is better."

125. [DK B 59] STOBAEUS III 5, 57   From Antiphon: "The man who has neither desired nor had experience of shame or wickedness is not a man of sound mind. For he has had nothing to overcome so as to put himself in a state of harmony."

126. [DK B 55] SUIDAS II 635, 1 A; PHOTIUS *Lexicon* I 294, 4 Naber "Where (*hina, hopou*)." Antiphon in the book *On Concord:* "to delay where there is no need for delay." [DK regards the attribution to the *Concord* doubtful.]

127. [*Th.* 139: DK B 56] SUIDAS III 514, 24 A   "I delay (*oknō*)" ... and the orators did not use the word for timidity or laziness, but for fear and fearing. Antiphon: "He would be a coward who is bold in speech in the face of dangers which are absent or in the future, and presses on with a will, but when it comes to action is afraid."

128. [DK B 57] STOBAEUS III 8, 18   From Antiphon: "For those who shrink from life illness is a holiday," for they do not sally forth to achieve things.

iii. SOCIOLOGY

129. [*DK* B 50] STOBAEUS IV 34, 63   From Antiphon: "Living is like a day-long watch, and the length of life to a single day, so to speak, in which, when we have looked up to the light, we hand over to others who come after."

130. [*DK* B 51] STOBAEUS IV 34, 56   From Antiphon: "The whole of life is wonderfully easy to fault, my friend; it has nothing in it outstanding or great or wonderful, but everything is small and weak and ephemeral and mixed with great sorrows."

131. [*DK* B 52] HARPOCRATION   "to take back (*anathesthai*)." Antiphon *On Concord:* "It is not possible to take back one's life like a man at draughts" instead of "to start one's life over again, repenting of one's former life." The expression is a metaphor from draughts. Cf. SUIDAS I 168 16 *A*.

132. [*DK* B 53] STOBAEUS III 10, 99   From Antiphon "But others in working and exercising thrift and suffering privation and increasing their possessions have as much satisfaction as one would expect them to have. If, on the other hand, they diminish their possessions and use them up, they suffer as much pain as if they lost flesh and blood."

133. [*DK* B 53a] STOBAEUS III 16, 20   From Antiphon: "Some people do not live the life each day brings, but make preparations with great eagerness as if they had another life to live, not the one each day brings. And in the meantime the hours pass by unnoticed."

134. [*DK* B 54] STOBAEUS III 16, 30; IV 40, 19   From Antiphon "There is a story of a man who saw another man getting a large sum of money and asked him to lend it him at interest. But the second man refused. He was the kind of man to distrust others and never help anyone. He took the money and stored it away. A third man heard of what he had done and stole it. Some time later the man who had put it away went and failed to find the money. So in great distress at his misfortune, particularly because he had not lent it to the man who had asked him, since in that case not only would he have had the money safe, but it would have earned interest as well, meeting the man who on the earlier occasion had wanted to borrow, he bewailed his misfortune, saying that he had made a mistake and was sorry he had not done what the other man wanted but had refused [cf. HARPOCRATION, s.v. *acharistein*; SUIDAS I 437, 18 *A*], since the money was now quite lost. The first man told him not to worry, but to believe that he had the money in his possession and had not lost it. He should put a stone in the place the money was. 'For you made absolutely no use of the money when you had it, so there is no need to think you have lost anything.' Indeed, what a man neither uses nor intends to use, it makes no difference whether he possesses it or not, he is not harmed more or less. For if God wishes to bless a man but not without reservation, he gives him plenty of money but poverty of good sense; and by taking away the one he commonly deprives him of both." Cf. AESOP *Fables* 412, 412b Halm and *DK* 89, 7.

135. [*DK* B 48] SUIDAS II 689, 3 *A*; PHOTIUS *Lexicon* I 274, 19 Naber "Most divine-looking (*theeidestaton*)": with the appearance of God. Antiphon in the book *On Concord* says this: "Man, who claims to have been born the most divine-looking of creatures. . . ." Cf. EUSTATHIUS on HOMER *Iliad* III 36.

136. [*DK* B 63] HARPOCRATION "disposition (*diathesis*)" [following B 33]. The same author uses the word instead of "arrangement" in the book *On Concord:* "But knowing the disposition [of the speech; cf. B 95] they listen attentively." Cf. SUIDAS II 56, 24 *A*. Cf. also B 82.

137. [*DK* B 64] EXCERPTA VINDOBONENSIA 44 (Vienna, 1888) [STOBAEUS IV 293, 17 Meineke; cf. H. Schenkl *Florilegia duo* n. 62] Antiphon, "Recent friendships (or friendships among the young) are strong, but longstanding friendships (or friendships among the old) are stronger."

138. [*DK* B 65] SUIDAS II 725, 25 *A* "Flattery (*thōpeia*)," Antiphon in the book *On Concord:* "Many people have friends and do not recognize them, but instead acquire companions who flatter the wealthy and toady to the fortunate."

139. [*DK* B 66] CLEMENT *Miscellanies* VI 19 [II 438, 9 Stählin] Antiphon the orator says: "The care of the old and the care of the young are similar."

140. [*DK* B 67] HARPOCRATION "unviewed (*atheōrētos*)" instead of "unseen," Antiphon in the work *On Concord*.

141. [*DK* B 67a] HARPOCRATION; SUIDAS I 195, 22 *A* "the men's age group (*andreia*)," Antiphon in the work *On Concord*.

142. [*DK* B 68] HARPOCRATION "bivouacking (*aulizomenoi*)" instead of "sleeping." Antiphon *On Concord*. Cf. SUIDAS I 414, 7 *A*.

143. [*DK* B 69] HARPOCRATION "the starting point (*balbis*)." Antiphon *On Concord*, "the beginning." *Etym. Gen. balbis:* . . . and "starting points" instead of "beginnings" [both in dative case].

144. [*DK* B 70] HARPOCRATION "extremely light on the rein (*euēniotata*)." Antiphon in the work *On Concord:* "The man who is quiet and moderate and not troublesome is 'light on the rein'." A metaphor from horses.

145. [*DK* B 71] HARPOCRATION *phēlōmata* for "deceptions (*exapatas*)." Antiphon in the work *On Concord*. *Phēloun* is "to deceive." Cf. SUIDAS IV 718, 3 *A*.

XXVIII. POLITIKOS

146. [*DK* B 72] *BA* I p. 78, 20 "Lack of discipline," Antiphon in *Politikos*.

147. [*DK* B 73] ATHENAEUS X 423A Antiphon in the *Politikos* uses *kataristan* thus: "when a man has *squandered* his own and his friends' livelihood."

148. [*DK* B 74] HARPOCRATION; SUIDAS II 474, 6 *A* "good at sums (*eusumbolos*)" instead of "calculating easily and accurately," i.e., "good at calculation." Antiphon in *Politikos*.

149. [*DK* B 75] HARPOCRATION "adding-half-as-much-again (*hēmioliasmos*)." Antiphon in *Politikos*, "of doubling and adding-half-as-much-again" instead of "⟨adding⟩ half as much in calculations." Cf. SUIDAS II 570, 19 *A*.

150. [*DK* B 76] PRISCIAN 18, 230 Hertz The Greeks speak of "neglecting" with the genitive or accusative case. Antiphon in *Politikos:* "not to be called a drunkard and to have the reputation of neglecting one's livelihood [acc.] because of a weakness for wine."

151. [*DK* B 77] PLUTARCH *Antony* 28 to spend and squander in luxurious living the thing which is the most costly to buy of all, Time, as Antiphon said.

XXIX. ON THE INTERPRETATION OF DREAMS (SEE A 12.)

152. [*DK* B 78] ARTEMIDORUS *On the Interpretation of Dreams* II 14 p. 131, 10 Pack squid: this creature is the only one that helps those who are trying to escape, by means of its ink, which it uses often in flight. Antiphon of Athens mentions this dream.

153. [*DK* B 79] CICERO *On divination* I 20, 39 . . . dreams which Chrysippus argues about with a full and detailed dream-collection in imitation of Antipater, assembling those whose interpretation by Antiphon exhibits the intelligence of the explainer, though he should use less trivial examples. 51, 116 Here there arises a certain significant, but rather unnatural and artificial, interpretation of dreams by Antiphon and similarly of oracles and prophecies. These people are expounders, as the literary scholars are of the poets.

154. [*DK* B 80] CICERO *On divination* II 70, 144 Do not the guesses of the interpreters themselves show their intelligence rather than any force or natural plausibility? The runner planning to run at Olympia seems in sleep to be riding in a four-horse chariot. Next morning he goes to the interpreter who says: "You'll win. That is the significance of the speed and the number of the horses." Then afterwards he goes to Antiphon. But Antiphon says: "You'll be beaten, sure enough. Don't you see that there are four in front of you?" Here is another runner—and Chrysippus' and Antiphon's books are full of these dreams and similar interpretations—but to return to the runner. He told the interpreter that in his sleep he seemed to be an eagle. The man replied: "You are the winner, no bird is stronger on the wing than the eagle." Antiphon, in the same vein, tells him: "Fool, don't you see you're the loser? That particular bird pursues other birds and harries them, while itself always coming last."

155. [*DK* B 81] SENECA *Controversies* II 1, 33 Otho Junius . . . edited four books of *Styles* which our friend Gallio aptly called Antiphon's books; they are so full of dreams.

156. [*DK* B 81a] MELAMPUS *On palpitations* 18, 19 If the right eye ticks, the man will have the upper hand over his enemies, according to Phemonoe, the Egyptians, and Antiphon. And he'll have people coming home from abroad. If the upper eyelid of the right eye ticks, it is a manifest indication of a gain, according to Antiphon success and health; for a slave an attack, for a widow a journey abroad.

XXX. INVECTIVE AGAINST ALCIBIADES

Maidment (*Minor Attic Orators*) dates this work about 418 B.C. when Alcibiades appears to have been at the center of a political struggle. Cf. also *Classical Quarterly*, XXXV (1941), pp. 14–16.

157. [*Th.* 66] PLUTARCH *Alcibiades* 3 In Antiphon's *Invective* we find the story that when Alcibiades was a boy he absconded from home and went to one of his admirers, Democrates; and that when Ariphron wished to make a public announcement Pericles would not allow it, saying: "If the boy is dead we shall only know a day earlier if we make an announcement, but if he is safe the rest of his life will be past recovery." We also find the story that he killed one of his attendants in the palaestra of Siburtius by a blow with a piece of wood. But perhaps we should not give credence to such tales, which we are told by someone who is confessedly abusing him.

158. [*Th.* 6] Athenaeus xii 525b Antiphon in the speech of invective against Alcibiades: "When you had been presented by your guardians to your parish, they gave you your inheritance and you went off by sea to Abydus, not to recover some debt owing to you or to establish some official connection, but by reason of your lack of discipline and depravity of your character (*gnomē*), to learn from the women of Abydus ways of behavior befitting your mentality, so that you could spend the rest of your life putting them in practice."

XXXI. Introductions

159. [*Th.* 68] Suidas ii 180, 16 *A* Antiphon in the *Introductions:* "I lodged this indictment because I had suffered, by heaven, many wrongs at the hands of this man, and because I perceived that you and the rest of the citizens had suffered still more wrongs than I had."

160. [*Th.* 69] Suidas i 130, 28 *A* In the *Introductions:* "But if the matter seems to be more on my side, and I shall turn out to provide a detailed confirmation."

161. [*Th.* 70] Suidas iii 417, 10 *A*; Photius *Lexicon* i 430, 3 Naber Antiphon, the earliest of the orators, uses the word *mochthēros*, not for a criminal who is brought to court for trial, but for a father who has obtained leave to bring a suit on behalf of his son who had been killed; and he speaks thus in the *Introductions and perorations:* "And I, *the miserable man* who ought to be dead, am alive to be mocked by my enemies."

XXXII. The Art of Speaking, Books I, II, and III
(See A 3 [6], A 10 [2].)

162. [*Th.* 71] Longinus *On the Art, Rh.Gr.* 1 318, 9 (IX 576 W) Antiphon in the *Art of Speaking* says: "It is natural for us to perceive things present, at hand and beside us. It is unnatural to keep a clear image of them when we are not actually looking at them."

163. [*Th.* 72] Ammonius *On differences of expression* p. 127 Valckenaer There is a difference between "clue (*sēmeion*)" and "indication (*tekmērion*)." Antiphon in the *Art* says that past events are confirmed by clues, future events foreshadowed by indications.

164. [*Th.* 73] *BA* 1 p. 78, 6 "lack of affection (*astorgia*)," "love of affection (*philostorgia*)," "affection (*storgē*)," Antiphon in the second book of the *Art of Speaking*.

165. [*Th.* 74] *BA* 1 p. 79, 1 "unprepared (*aparaskeuaston*)," Antiphon in the third book of the *Art of Speaking*. [The book seems not to be genuine. Cf. Pollux v 143.]

166. [*Th.* 75] *BA* 1 p. 110, 33 "paucity of friends (*oligophilian*)," Antiphon in the third [book of the *Art of Speaking*]. Cf. Pollux III 63.

(d) FRAGMENTS NOT ATTRIBUTABLE TO ANY PARTICULAR WORK

167. [*Th.* 78] Suidas IV 69, 5 *A* "handed down from ancestors (*patroōn*)." Antiphon: "and knowing that your laws were handed down to you from your fathers and were ancient."

168. [*Th.* 79] Suidas IV 524, 14 *A* "temporarily (*teōs*)" Antiphon: "For temporarily the long period seemed more credible than the short."

169. [*Th.* 178: *DK* B 82] *BA* I p. 114, 28; PHOTIUS *Lexicon* II 203, 4 Naber "to be accomplished (*telesthlēnai*)." Antiphon for "to be spent." Cf. SUIDAS IV 18, 2 *A:* "to be spent (*telesthlēnai*)," Antiphon.

170. [*Th.* 143: *DK* B 83] PHOTIUS *Lexicon* p. 34, 21 Reitzenstein; *BA* I p. 345, 26 "impotence (*adunasia*)" like Antiphon and Thucydides [VII 8, 2; VIII 8, 4]. [So Sauppe at V 3.]

171. [*Th.* 147: *DK* B 84] *BA* I p. 367, 31; PHOTIUS *Lexicon* p. 62, 25 Reitzenstein "following (*akoloutha*)," Antiphon, things which follow or agree.

172. [*Th.* 150: *DK* B 85] *BA* I p. 418, 6 "impracticable (*apalamnon*)." So Antiphon.

173. [*Th.* 152: *DK* B 86] *BA* I p. 419, 18 "he departed" instead of "he died." So Antiphon and Thucydides [II 34, 2 and passim].

174. [*Th.* 145: *DK* B 87] HARPOCRATION *BA* I p. 363, 31; PHOTIUS *Lexicon* p. 58, 18 Reitzenstein "tiny (*akarē*)" instead of "small" or "nothing" in Antiphon. Cf. SUIDAS I 76, 6 *A*.

175. [*Th.* 157: *DK* B 88] HARPOCRATION "touchstone (*basanos*)," Antiphon: a stone so called is one by which gold is tested by rubbing on it. Cf. SUIDAS I 456, 24 *A*.

176. [*Th.* 163: *DK* B 89] HARPOCRATION; SUIDAS II 147, 19 *A* "soon-vexed (*dusanios*)," Antiphon: the man who is vexed at everything even if it is small and negligible. Cf. *DK* 88 B 42.

177. [*Th.* 164: *DK* B 90] HARPOCRATION "to take in (*eisphrēsein*)," Antiphon, for "to bring in, accept" [all future tenses].

178. [*Th.* 165: *DK* B 91] HARPOCRATION; SUIDAS II 254, 33 *A* "in short (*em brachei*)" instead of "simply" and "in sum," Antiphon.

179. [*Th.* 170: *DK* B 92] Moeris 203, 2 Bekker "stonemasons" Thucydides [e.g., IV 69, 2], "stone-cutters" Antiphon.

180. [*Th.* 185: *DK* B 93] Philodemus *On Poetry* C 187, 3 "The folly of others is clear who believe that either the same things please and annoy or that different things do, as of Antiphon, one of the ancients, whether he preferred to be called orator or philosopher."

181. [*Th.* 144: *DK* B 93a] Photius *Lexicon* p. 66, 4 Reitzenstein "not shared in common (*akoinōnētos*)," Plato in the *Laws* VI [768B], and *akoinōnēta* [neuter plural]. But Antiphon and Euripides [*Andromache* 470] too.

182. [*Th.* 144a: *DK* B 93b] Photius *Lexicon* p. 87, 25 Reitzenstein "in unwitnessed fashion (*amarturētōs*)" for "without witnesses (*amarturōs*)," so Antiphon. Suidas I 134, 22 *A amarturētous* instead of *amarturous*, so Antiphanes [?].

183. [*Th.* 181: *DK* B 94] Photius *Lexicon* II 215, 20 Naber "honorable (*timion*)" instead of "honored (*entimon*)," so Antiphon.

184. [*Th.* 171: *DK* B 95] Pollux I 34 "post-festival days (*metheortoi hēmerai*)" in Antiphon.

185. [*Th.* 176: *DK* B 96] Pollux I 98 Let him be called the helmsman. . . . and in Antiphon "holder of the sheet (*ho podochōn*)," or rather, as I think, "the guide (*ho podēgōn*)."

186. [*Th.* 141: *DK* B 97] Pollux II 109 "tonguelessness (*aglottia*)" says Antiphon.

187. [*Th.* 149: *DK* B 98] Pollux II 120 But Antiphon "contradicting (*antilogoumenoi*)."

188. [*Th.* 151: *DK* B 99] Pollux II 120 But Antiphon, "an even number (*apartilogia*)" like Herodotus [VII 29, 2]. [But] Harpocration, *apartilogia*: Lysias in the speech against Aresandros [fr. 23 *Orat.Att.* II 177] and Herodotus instead of "a complete and full number."

189. [*Th.* 172: *DK* B 100] POLLUX II 123 *kakologos, kakēgoros* and, as Antiphon, *hēdulogos* "sweet-spoken" and *metriologos* "mild-spoken."

190. [*Th.* 168: *DK* B 101] POLLUX II 229 Antiphon "ingenious idea (*epinoēma*)."

191. [*Th.* 145: *DK* B 102] POLLUX II 230 "They are disheartened (*athumousin*)" as Antiphon.

192. [*Th.* 182: *DK* B 103] POLLUX III 113 "to transact business" and, as Antiphon, "to love money (*philochrematein*)."

193. [*Th.* 142: *DK* B 104] POLLUX IV 9 *anepistēmosunē, agnoia, agnōsia* [different words for "ignorance"]. Antiphon for this adds *agnōmosunē*.

194. [*Th.* 162: *DK* B 105] POLLUX IV 9 "a man who thinks he knows everything (*dokēsisophos*)" as Antiphon said. Cf. ARISTOPHANES *Peace* 44.

195. [*Th.* 178: *DK* B 106] POLLUX IV 167 "of proportion (*symmetrias*)," Antiphon, and "with bad proportion (*dusmetrēton*)," Antiphon.

196. [*DK* B 106a] POLLUX V 145 "being ignorant (*agnoōn*)." But Antiphon also says *agnōmōn*. Cf. B 193.

197. [*Th.* 155: *DK* B 107] POLLUX V 441 And the action is lack of feeling, ingratitude, injustice, folly, and, as Antiphon, fraud (*aposterēsis*).

198. [*Th.* 175: *DK* B 108] POLLUX VI 163 But Antiphon also said: "to be banished with all his household (*exalasthai panoikesiai*)."

199. [*Th.* 169: *DK* B 109] POLLUX VI 169 "of evil mind (*kakonous*)" as Antiphon.

200. [*Th.* 167: *DK* B 110] POLLUX VI 183 But Antiphon "object of desire (*epithumēma*)."

201. [*Th.* 153: *DK* B 111] POLLUX VIII 68 In the case of the defendant, "he made his defense," "he was acquitted (*apeluthē*)," as Antiphon.

202. [*Th.* 166: *DK* B 112] Pollux VIII 103   And in the distribution of corn there were corn-registrars (*epigrapheis*), as Antiphon.

203. [*Th.* 117: *DK* B 113] Pollux IX 26   "to catch votes (*politokopein*)," as Antiphon.

204. [*Th.* 140: *DK* B 114] Lesbonax p. 180 Valckenaer   Clazomenian [dialect], e.g., "I go with the contest" instead of "I go to the contest." As the phrase, "He went with his country" instead of "to it," so Antiphon.

205. [*Th.* 154: *DK* B 115] Suidas I 301, 5 *A*   "to answer," . . . and "answer," i.e., the defense speech. *BA* I p. 429, 18   So Lysias [fr. 305 *Orat.Att.* II 214a23] and Antiphon "answer (*apokrisis*)."

206. [*Th.* 183: *DK* B 117] Suidas IV 823,24 *A*   "of things (*chrēmatōn*)": the expression is applied to an action or a character or a speech, as Antiphon.

Note: Athenaeus XIV 650E (*DK* B 118) speaks of a work of Antiphon *About Agriculture*. Kaibel reads "Androtion" for "Antiphon." It seems very unlikely that this Antiphon is Antiphon of Rhamnus.

88. CRITIAS

translated by DONALD NORMAN LEVIN

Critias of Athens was descended from Dropides, a kinsman of Solon, and was related also to Plato via the latter's mother, Perictione. Both he and Alcibiades, similarly brilliant and unscrupulous, spent much time in Socrates' company. Probably the reckless behavior of both had not a little to do with the later charge that Socrates was guilty of corrupting the young men of Athens—this despite the fact that the sage himself had refused to countenance either Alcibiades' treachery or Critias' outrageous behavior as a member of the oligarchical Thirty.

Even before the overthrow of the democracy, Critias, like Alcibiades, had been implicated rightly or wrongly in the affair of the defacement of the Hermae. Later he became active in the pro-Spartan faction at Athens. How many times he was forced into exile is uncertain. But on one such occasion he took refuge in Thessaly, where he seems to have fallen into disreputable company and to have engaged in additional intrigues.

The thesis that power corrupts seems only too well demonstrated in the case of Critias. When the Thirty seized control at Athens, Critias himself was in the forefront of what amounted to a reign of terror. Perhaps there is a certain poetic justice in his demise in the aftermath of Thrasybulus' coup. At any rate, Critias' fame went into a lengthy eclipse, from which it might never have emerged, were it not for the merit of his writings.

Critias produced both prose and verse. Into the former category fall several *Commonwealths* (or *Constitutions*), also *Aphorisms, Lectures* (or *Conversations*), *On the Nature of Desires or of Virtues*, and *Proems for Public Speaking*. His poetic production includes hexameters and elegiacs (among the latter a work addressed to Alcibiades) and the *Well-Balanced Commonwealths*. He may have written dramas also, but the authorship of the *Tennes, Rhadamanthys, Pirithus*, and even of the *Sisyphus* remains controversial: all four plays have been ascribed both to Critias and to Euripides.

Only if the *Sisyphus* is really his, do Critias' published thoughts depart from the conventional. Elsewhere he does not question the reality of the divine, but recommends moderation—a policy which he would have done well to follow in his own life.

A. LIFE AND WRITINGS

1. PHILOSTRATUS *Lives of the Sophists* I 16   Even if Critias the sophist brought down the democracy of the Athenians, still he had not yet turned evil. For the democracy would have collapsed on its own; it had become so overconfident that it failed to heed even those who held office in accordance with the laws. Yet Critias obviously sided with the Spartans, betrayed what was sacred, leveled the fortifications through the agency of Lysander. By declaring Sparta at war against all, [and in effect forbidding] anyone to take in the Athenian in exile, he deprived those of the Athenians whom he had banished even of a stopping place anywhere in Greece. In cruelty and in bloodthirstiness he outdid the Thirty. He also collaborated with the Spartans in absurd resolution in order that Attica, emptied of its flock of men, might become a grazing-ground for sheep. Hence it seems to me that he is the worst of all the men who have gained a reputation for wickedness. Had Critias been misled through lack of education, there would be corroborated the claim of those who allege that he became corrupted by Thessaly and by association with it. Uninstructed natures are quite easily led astray in the matter of a choice of life. But since [Critias] had been extremely well educated, expounding many judgments and referring them to Dropides, who, after Solon, governed the Athenians [593–592 B.C.], he could not escape responsibility in the eyes of many for having committed these mistakes through the wickedness of his nature. In fact, it is absurd that he not be compared with Socrates, son of Sophroniscus, whom he joined especially in the pursuit of wisdom, Socrates seeming the wisest and most honorable of his contemporaries. And it is absurd that he be compared with the Thessalians, among whom unadulterated arrogance exists and tyrannical pursuits are carried on under the influence of wine. Still, not even the Thessalians were uninterested in wisdom. Rather, small and larger cities in Thessaly professed Gorgian doctrines, looking toward Gorgias the Leontinian, and would have shifted to professing Critian doctrines, had Critias undertaken among them some exposition of his own wisdom. Instead, he rendered their oligarchies the more grievous by conversing with those in power there and by attacking all democracy. He slandered the Athenians, claiming that they, of all mankind, erred the most. Consequently, upon reflection, Critias would have corrupted the Thessalians rather than the converse. He perished at the hands of Thrasybulus' associates, who were bringing back the democratic faction from Phyle. It appears to some that he became a good man toward the end of his life, inasmuch as he employed tyranny as his winding-sheet. But let it be declared on my part that none among men died well in behalf of a poor choice. And it seems to me that for this reason the man's wisdom and his thoughts were taken less seriously by the Greeks. Unless speech corresponds to character, we shall appear to be discoursing in an alien language, as though we were playing flutes.

Being a sententious person and very sagacious, Critias is highly competent to render solemn the shape of his discourse. His solemnity is not dithyrambic, nor one which takes refuge in terms derived from poetic speech. Rather, it is put together from ordinary words and holds to the natural. I envision the man both expressing himself with sufficient brevity and attacking wondrously in the guise of defense, speaking Attic not purely, yet not unidiomatically (for want of taste in speaking Attic is barbarous): Attic terms shine, rather, through his utterance like sunbeams. To join ⟨passage⟩ to passage without connectives is elegance of style for Critias; to reason via paradoxes, and via paradoxes to declaim, is Critias' battle plan. The spirit of his utterance is rather elliptical, yet pleasant and smooth, like the breeze of the west wind.

243

2. DIOGENES LAERTIUS III 1   Plato, the Athenian, son of Ariston and of Perictione (or Potone), who traced her lineage back to Solon. Solon had a brother Dropides, whose son was Critias, father of Callaeschrus. The sons of Callaeschrus were Critias, the member of the Thirty, and Glaucon, father of Charmides and of Perictione. Plato was her son and Ariston's in the sixth generation after Solon.   PLATO *Charmides* 154B [Critias is the speaker] Charmides, son of our divine Glaucon, and my cousin.   157E [Socrates addresses Charmides] Your paternal house, that which has been celebrated by both Anacreon and Solon and by many other poets, has been handed over to us.   SCHOLIUM on AESCHYLUS *Prometheus Bound* 130 [Anacreon] took up residence in Attica out of fondness for Critias.

3. PLATO *Timaeus* 20A   All of us here perhaps know that Critias is not unversed in any of the matters which we are discussing.   20D [Critias is the speaker] Listen, Socrates, to a statement which is quite outlandish, yet altogether true, as Solon, wisest of the Seven Sages, once said.   E He was a kinsman and extremely dear to our great-grandfather Dropides, as even he himself says in many places in his poetry. To Critias, our grandfather, he said, as the old man kept calling to our attention, that the great and wondrous old deeds of this city had become obscured through time and men's destruction. . . .   21A I shall tell you, having heard an ancient statement of a not-so-young man. Critias [the tyrant's grandfather] was close to ninety years old at the time, while I was about ten.   SCHOLIUM ad loc.   Critias had a noble and sturdy nature. He joined philosophical fellowships and was termed a layman among philosophers, a philosopher among laymen. Even he himself exercised tyrannical power, since he was one of the Thirty.

4. XENOPHON *Memorabilia* I 2, 12   But, stated the accuser, Critias and Alcibiades became disciples of Socrates and did the city much harm. For, in the oligarchy, Critias turned into the most thievish and violent and murderous of all, while Alcibiades, in the democracy, was of all men the most uncontrolled and wanton and violent.   (13) If the two of them did the city harm, I shall not offer a defense. But I shall explain how their association with Socrates came about. (14) These two men were born to be the most eager for honors of all the Athenians: they wanted to do everything on their own and to become most renowned of all. . . . (16) And they became illustrious as a result of what they did. They thought it desirable to become more powerful than their associates as quickly as possible. Turning away from Socrates forthwith, they engaged in politics, the very reason for their having reached out to Socrates. . . . (24) As long as both Critias and Alcibiades remained in Socrates' company, they were able, by employing him as an ally, to control their ignoble inclinations. But once they got free of him, Critias fled to Thessaly and there consorted with men subject to lawlessness rather than to a sense of justice. . . . (29) But even if, without doing anything base himself, he praised them, though he saw that they were carrying on worthless activities, he would rightly be blamed. Aware that Critias was in love with Euthydemus and was attempting exploitation, just as those do whose enjoyment consists in sexual pleasures of the body, [Socrates] tried to deter him by declaring that it was unworthy of a free man and ungentlemanly to make demands of a beloved, to whom one wishes to appear very worthy, by supplicating as beggars would and by pleading for concessions. These are the actions of one who is worthless. (30) But since Critias paid no heed to such statements and was undeterred, it is said that Socrates in the presence of many others, Euthydemus included, remarked that Critias seemed to him to be suffering from a swinelike malady and that in his desire he was rubbing himself against Euthydemus just as piglets rub against stones. (31) As a consequence Critias came also to hate Socrates, so that when, as a member of the Thirty, along with Charicles, he became lawgiver, he felt a grudge against him and included in the laws a provision against teaching the art of speech.

5. ANDOCIDES *On the Mysteries* I 47 Come now, I shall read to you the names of the men whom he entered into the register. . . . Critias: he too is a cousin of my father [Leogoras]. Our mothers are sisters. (68) My father was saved, as were my father-in-law, three cousins, and seven other kinsmen on the verge of dying unjustly. They now see the light of the sun through my efforts.

6. [DEMOSTHENES] *Against Theocrines* 6   Aristocrates, son of Scelius, ... performed many fine deeds when his city was at war with the Spartans and destroyed utterly Eetionia, the place where the entourage of Critias expected to welcome the Spartans [411 B.C.]. He pulled down the fortress and brought home the populace. Cf. THUCYDIDES VIII 92.

7. LYCURGUS *Against Leocrates* 113   The public voted, at Critias' suggestion, to bring the corpse [of Phrynichus, assassinated in 411] to trial for treason. If it were acknowledged that, though a traitor, he had been buried in the region, they would exhume his bones and banish them beyond the frontiers of Attica.

8. ARISTOTLE *Rhetoric* I 15, 1375b32   Even Cleophon employed Solon's elegies against Critias, stating that the household was licentious long since. Never would Solon have composed, "Tell red-haired Critias for me to listen to his father" [fr. 18 Diehl].

9. XENOPHON *Hellenica* II 3, 1–2   The following year [404–403] ... it seemed advisable to the public to choose thirty men to codify the inherited laws in accordance with which they would administer the state.

10. ——— ——— II 3, 15   The first time, Critias shared Theramenes' opinions and was friendly to him. But when he himself became prone to put multitudes to death, inasmuch as he had been forced into exile by the democratic faction [407 B.C.], Theramenes resisted, saying. . . .   (18) After this, however, Critias and the rest of the Thirty, already afraid of Theramenes and not a little apprehensive lest the citizenry coalesce around him, reckon[ed] the prospective participants in public affairs at three thousand.   (36) [Speech of Theramenes] Still, I am not surprised at Critias' having transgressed the law. When this was underway [the trial after the battle of Arginusae], he happened not to be present. Rather, along with Prometheus, he was setting up a democracy in Thessaly and was arming the serfs against their overlords.

11. LYSIAS 12, 43   When the sea battle [at Aegospotami] and the disaster to the city had taken place, since a democratic regime was still in power, whence they inaugurated civil strife, five men were appointed ephors by their so-called comrades. They were to be conveners of the citizenry, leaders of the conspirators working against your multitude. Members included Eratosthenes and Critias. They appointed tribal leaders for the tribes and announced that it was necessary to hold an election and that whoever must, should lead and that if they wished to do anything else, they had authority.

12. XENOPHON *Hellenica* II 4, 8   After this [Thrasybulus' attack from Phyle] the Thirty, adjudging matters no longer safe for themselves, wished to win over Eleusis, so that they would have a refuge there, should it prove necessary. Issuing orders to the cavalry, Critias and the rest of the Thirty arrived at Eleusis [arrest of the Eleusinians follows]. (10) After this Thrasybulus took along the thousand or so men who had been assembled from Phyle and arrived during the night at the Piraeus. . . . (11) The men from Phyle . . . marched in close order to Munichia. . . . (19) Of the Thirty, Critias and Hippomachus were slain there [May 403].

13. SCHOLIUM on AESCHINES I 39 p. 261 Schultz   Here is an example of the government of the Thirty. When Critias, one of the Thirty, had been slain, they erected by way of memorial Oligarchy wielding a firebrand and igniting Democracy; and they inscribed the following:

This is a memorial to good men who restrained the accursed populace of the Athenians from arrogance for a brief period.

14. ARISTOTLE *Rhetoric* III 16, 1416b26   The many do not demand a statement of the case if you wish to extol Achilles (for all know his deeds); yet it is necessary to make use of them. Also, if you wish to extol Critias, it is necessary. For not many know *his* deeds.

15. ATHENAEUS IV 184D   At least Chamaeleon of Heraclea states in his treatise entitled *Protrepticus* that all Spartans and Thebans learn to play the flute and that the inhabitants of Heraclea Pontica still do so individually, while among the Athenians the most conspicuous are Callias, son of Hipponicus, and Critias, son of Callaeschrus.

16. [PLUTARCH] *Lives of the Ten Orators* p. 832 DE   However, one would find that all (if we trace back to the earliest) who tried their hand at recording this type of speech have attacked Antiphon [the Rhamnusian], although he was already an old man. Thus did Alcibiades, Critias, Lysias, and Archinus, for example.

17. CICERO *On the orator* II 23, 93   Hard upon them [the orators Pericles, Alcibiades, and Thucydides] came Critias, Theramenes, and Lysias. Much was written down by Lysias, some things by Critias; we hear of Theramenes. All even then retained that Periclean flavor, though with a somewhat richer quality.   PHILOSTRATUS *Epistles* 73 Critias and Thucydides are not unknown; they have taken over from him [Gorgias] loftiness of sentiment, also pride, and they refashion them into their own, the one via fluency of speech, the other via vigor.

18. DIONYSIUS OF HALICARNASSUS *Lysias* 2   He [Lysias] is clear in expression altogether and the best model of the Attic dialect, not of the old type which Plato and Thucydides employ, but of that fashionable at the time, as one can attest from the speeches of Andocides and from those of Critias and from numerous others. Cf. *Isaeus* 20. [See *DK* 85 A 13.]

19. HERMOGENES *On Kinds* [*of Literary Composition*] B 401, 25 Rabe   On Critias: For he too is stately, much like Antiphon, and sublime, verging on majesty, and says much in the negative, yet is rather pure in style and, when he resorts to circumlocution, careful in arrangement, with the result that he is clear and distinct in conjunction with his loftiness. In many places he manifests both truthfulness and persuasiveness, particularly in his *Proems for Public Speaking*. Though careful, still he employs this sort of ornament not moderately, nor simply, nor, after the fashion of Antiphon, tediously and with obvious refinements, but in such a way that he partakes even thus of the truth. He does not go to extremes in utilizing types of character such as reasonableness or simplicity or the like.

20. PHRYNICHUS *Praeparatio sophistica* [PHOTIUS *Bibliotheca* cod. 158 p. 101b4] He says that the standards and yardsticks and best model of unalloyed and pure Attic speech are . . . [Plato, the Ten Orators, Thucydides, Xenophon, Aeschines the Socratic, Critias, son of Callaeschrus, and Antisthenes.]

21. PHILOSTRATUS *Lives of the Sophists* II 1, 14 [Herodes] was devoted to all the ancients, and was taken up with Critias and introduced him, hitherto neglected and disregarded, into the usage of the Greeks.

22. PHILOPONUS on ARISTOTLE *de Anima* 89, 8 [on A 23] It makes no difference to us whether he means Critias, one of the Thirty, who heard Socrates also, or someone else. They say that there was also another Critias, a sophist, author of the writings in question, as Alexander states: the member of the Thirty has not written anything other than *A Well-Balanced Commonwealth.*

23. ARISTOTLE *de Anima* I 2, 405b5 Others, like Critias, claim that [the soul is] blood, since they assume that sensation is most closely related to soul and that this is the case due to the nature of blood. PHILOPONUS on ARISTOTLE *de Anima*, Introduction 9, 19 Cf. 89, 12. Critias, one of the Thirty. For he stated that the soul was blood. "For blood flowing around the heart," he says, "is what perception is for men" [=Critias fr. 8 Bach].

B. POETIC FRAGMENTS

HEXAMETERS

1. [7 Bach (1827), 8 Diehl] ATHENAEUS XIII p. 600D [Eros], celebrating whom in song, wise Anacreon is in everyone's mouth. Thus even mighty Critias says the following about him:

Teos brought to Greece sweet Anacreon, who once wove songs of womanly melody, a source of stimulation at drinking fests, a cajolement for women, opposed to flutes, fond of the lyre, sweet, painless. Affection for you will not grow old nor will it perish, so long as a servingboy carries around water mixed with wine in goblets, handing out toasts as he moves toward the right, and as long as feminine dancing-troupes conduct sacred all-night festivities, and as long as the disc, daughter of bronze, sits atop the cottabus, ⟨struck⟩ by lofty drizzles of wine. . . .

CRITIAS' *ELEGIES*

2. ATHENAEUS (*Epitome*) I 28B Critias thus [i.e., lists peculiarities from each city]: "the cottabus . . . of the furnace." Attic pottery is really praised also. XV 666B First of all, the game of cottabus is a Sicilian invention, since the Sicilians were first to contrive it, as Critias, son of Callaeschrus, states in his *Elegies* thus: "the cottabus . . . wine-drop missiles." *BA* I p. 382, 19 [PHOTIUS A 73, 3 Reitzenstein] aid to discourse: so Critias the tyrant referred to letters [line 10]:

The cottabus, a distinguished achievement, comes from Sicily. We set it up as target for wine-drop missiles. Next there is a Sicilian wagon, outstanding in beauty and expense. * * * The throne is Thessalian, a most luxurious resting-place for the limbs. Miletus and Chios, the sea-girt city of Oenopion, possess ⟨especially⟩ the beauty of a conjugal couch. And the gold-wrought Etruscan bowl prevails and all bronze that decorates a home, whatever its use. The Phoenicians invented letters as an aid to discourse. Thebe[s] was first to construct a chariot, while the Carians, stewards of the sea, created cargo ships. But she who set up the fine victory emblem at Marathon devised the potter's wheel and highly celebrated pottery useful for household management, a product both of the earth and of the furnace.

3. MALLIUS THEODORUS *On Meters* VI 589, 220 Keil Critias avers that the dactylic hexameter was invented originally by Orpheus. Cf. *DK* 68 B 16.

TO ALCIBIADES

4. HEPHAESTION 2, 3 (on vowel mixture) or two shorts into one short, as is found in other meters . . . but rarely in epic. Similarly, Critias in his elegy addressed to Alcibiades did not think that Alcibiades' name could fit:

Even now I shall garland Cleinias' son, Athenian Alcibiades, hymning him in a new fashion. For it was impossible to fit his name into an elegiac verse. But now it will be placed, not unmetrically, in an iamb.

5. PLUTARCH *Alcibiades* 33 The vote for recall, which Critias, son of Callaeschrus, had proposed, had already taken place. He himself has written thus in his *Elegies*, reminding Alcibiades of the favor as follows:

The opinion which brought you back—I expressed it amid all the people and, having set forth a proposal, did this deed. The seal made by my tongue lies upon it. Cf. B 75.

WELL-BALANCED COMMONWEALTHS

COMMONWEALTH OF THE LACEDAEMONIANS

6. ATHENAEUS X 432D It was not customary at Lacedaemonian drinking parties to make toasts or to pass lovingcups around. Critias makes this clear in his *Elegies:*

And it is a habit and established practice at Sparta to drink from the same winecup and not to give toasts mentioning someone by name and not to pass it around, as is customary at Athens, moving to the right in a circle around the company. * * * An Asiatic-born Lydian hand invented pitchers as well as the practice of extending toasts to the right and of challenging by name whomever one wishes to toast. Then, as a result of such drinking, they loosen their tongues for shameful tales and render the body weaker. And a sight-blunting fog sits before one's eye and forgetfulness wastes recollection away from one's heart and reason is tripped up. But servants have an undisciplined character. Extravagance ruinous to the home bursts in.

Lacedaemonian youths, however, drink only enough to direct the thinking of all toward cheery hopefulness and the tongue toward friendliness and temperate laughter. This sort of drinking is beneficial to body and thought and property. And it is well suited to the works of Aphrodite and to sleep, haven from toils, and to Health, most delightful of the gods for mortals, and to Piety's neighbor, Moderation.

And next he says:

For toasting from cups beyond due measure, though momentarily pleasurable, confers permanent harm. The way of life of the Lacedaemonians is evenly ordered: to eat and drink the appropriate amount to render them capable of thought and labor. No day is set apart for soaking the body with wine through immoderate draughts.

7. SCHOLIUM on EURIPIDES *Hippolytus* 264 A saying of one of the Seven Sages is "Nothing in excess," which, according to Critias, they attribute to Chilon. DIOGENES LAERTIUS I 41 [without the author's name]:

It was a Lacedaemonian, Chilon the Sage, who said this: "Nothing in excess." All that is beautiful proves appropriate [only] at the right time.

8. PLUTARCH *Cimon* 10 [after *DK* 82 B 20] Critias, one of the Thirty, prays in his *Elegies* [as follows]:

[I should wish upon myself] the wealth of the Scopadae, the high-mindedness of Cimon, the success of Arcesilas, the Lacedaemonian.

9. STOBAEUS III 29, 11 Of Critias:

More persons are good as a result of practice than from nature.

DRAMAS

10. ANONYMOUS *Life of Euripides* p. 135, 33   Of these [dramas of Euripides], three are considered spurious: *Tennes, Rhadamanthys, Pirithus.*[1]

TENNES

11. On Tennes as eponym of Tenedos, cf. CONON 28 [PHOTIUS *Bibliotheca* cod. 126 p. 135b19].

12. [EURIPIDES fr. 695, *TGF* p. 578 (2d ed.)] STOBAEUS III 2, 15 Euripides in his *Tennes:*

Alas! there is no justice in the present generation.

RHADAMANTHYS

12a. Conclusion of a hypothesis preserved on papyrus and published by Carlo Gallavotti, *Rivista di Filologia e di Istruzione Classica,* n.s. XI (1933), p. 179; cf. A. Körte, *Archiv für Papyrusforschung,* XI (1935), p. 258. Fighting alone, he was slain ⟨by Po⟩lydeuces. While ⟨Rh⟩adamanthys rejoiced at the victory, yet grieved over the daughters, Artemis, making an appearance, commanded Helen to establish honors for ⟨both⟩ deceased brothers and affirmed that his daughters would become goddesses.

13. [EURIPIDES fr. 660 Nauck] *BA* 1 p. 94, 1   "Remove (*exairein*)" in place of "take away (*aphairein*)."   Euripides in the *Rhadamanthys:*

For there is no one ⟨who⟩ will remove us.

[1] See Athenaeus XI 496A, cited below, B 17 ad init. U. von Wilamowitz-Moellendorff, *Analecta Euripidea* (Berlin, 1875), p. 166, adds *Sisyphus,* a satyr-play. The rationale for attributing these works rather to Critias is briefly discussed by K. Freeman, *Companion to the Pre-Socratic Philosophers* (Oxford, 1946), p. 411.

14. [EURIPIDES fr. 658 Nauck] STRABO VIII p. 356   Euripides . . . in the *Rhadamanthys:*

Who hold the land of Euboea, the neighboring state. . . .

15. [EURIPIDES fr. 659 Nauck]   STOBAEUS II 8, 12; IV 20, 61   Euripides' *Rhadamanthys:*

In life we have all sorts of desires. This one yearns to gain nobility; that one has no concern for such, but wishes to be called lord over many possessions at home. It gratifies yet another to persuade those near him through evil daring, even if from his thoughts he conveys nothing healthy. Still others among mortals seek out shameful gains in preference to the beautiful. To such an extent does the life of men consist in wandering astray. ⟨But⟩ I desire to attain none of these things: I should like to have a reputation for the right kind of glory.

PIRITHUS

15a. *POxy* XVII 36ff., consisting here of five fragments from *POxy* no. 2078 with remains of 85 verses, published by A. S. Hunt. Cf. A. Körte, *Archiv für Papyrusforschung,* X (1932), p. 5 off.; W. Morel, *Bursians Jahresber,* LIX (1933), p. 159ff.   Fr. 1 probably comes from the Prologue, with Pirithus himself as the speaker (Körte). The first five verses preserve beginnings only: "I tripped up" (1), "under" (or "by") (2), "(?) down" (3), "gone" (4), "Greek" (5). Add "altar" (6). Lines 7–20 follow:

A divine madness . . . sent disaster. ⟨Indeed, having possessed once the woman Nephele,[2] he disseminated to the The⟨ssalians⟩ a rumor full of wantonness. ⟨He said⟩ that [?] had copulated with ⟨Cronos'⟩ daughter, . . . for such boasts he paid penalties to the gods. . . . Around the cycle of madness . . . he proceeded unheard by men whom a gadfly tortured.[3] Not even

---

[2] Possibly Kathleen Freeman is right in understanding the context rather as, "He had a cloud for wife." On the other hand, she has personified ἄτη and ὕβρις whereas I have been content to translate the one as "disaster," the other as "wantonness." *Ancilla* (Oxford, 1946), p. 156.

[3] Miss Freeman's "driven by a gadfly" refers to Ixion himself. Yet the somewhat restored original shows οἰστρη⟨λ⟩άτοισιν apparently in agreement with ἀνθρώποι⟨σιν⟩. Ibid.

a grave hid him, but . . . the father, erring against the gods, was torn to pieces ⟨by the⟩ sons of the North Wind. But I . . . his woes.[4]

2) and 3) = dialogue of Heracles and Theseus. Only the ends of lines 22–23 are preserved: in line 23 "[?] of labor." Lines 24–39 follow:

HERACLES: . . . would . . . now seems pleasant.

THESEUS: I shall ⟨not⟩ blame ⟨you⟩, Heracles. ⟨Yet one must stay⟩; for it is ⟨disgraceful⟩ to betray a trustworthy man and friend who has been hostilely received.

HERACLES: Theseus, you said what was appropriate ⟨for you⟩ and for the city of the Athenians. For you are always at some point an ally to the unfortunate. It is unseemly ⟨for me⟩ to go to my homeland on a pretext. Do you think that Eurystheus, were he to find out that I had collaborated with you, would gladly note that the task undertaken remains unfinished?

THESEUS: Still, for what you desire you have my good will entirely, not capricious, ⟨but⟩, as befits a free man, inimical to foes and well disposed ⟨toward friends⟩.[5] Before to me . . . discourse. You would make . . . [?] statements.[6]

In the remaining verses no connection is recognizable. Line 47, however, supplies the clausula, "Each die is cast," comparable to Aristophanes [fr. 673 Kock], and Menander [fr. 65, 4 Kock]. Thus Caesar's remark upon crossing the Rubicon was not a quote from Menander, but a proverbial phrase.[7] Cf. the *Nachtrag* to *DK* II 165, 7.

16. IOANNES DIACONUS on HERMOGENES ed. Rabe [from Codex Vaticanus graecus 2228, 14th century, *Rheinisches Museum,* n.s. LXIII (1908)] p. 144   GREGORY OF CORINTH on HERMOGENES B 445–47 Rabe (Even Euripides' "Zeus, as has been said" is a reference, "out of truth"

---

[4] Restorations are supplied by Hunt, only line 17 by Körte. In line 15 the papyrus preserves ωχ or ωλ.

[5] B 27 (see below) apparently originates from this dialogue.

[6] Restorations by Hunt, only lines 25 ("not," οὔτοι), 26, and 30 by Körte.

[7] Possibly both Shakespeare's "All the world's a stage" and Caesar's "Veni, vidi, vici" owe something to the Democritean (or Democratean) "The universe is a stage-setting, life an entry upon stage: you came, you saw, you departed."

a confirmation): This verse has been found in two plays of Euripides, both in the so-called *Pirithus* and in *Wise Melanippe*. It is not untimely to expose both their arguments and their locales to those who welcome erudition. The argument of the *Pirithus* is as follows: Pirithus, having descended into Hades along with Theseus in order to court Persephone, gained appropriate punishment. Shackled to an immovable seat of rock, he himself was guarded by a serpent's yawns, while Theseus, thinking it disgraceful to abandon his friend, preferred existence in Hades to life. When, however, Heracles was dispatched against Cerberus by Eurystheus, he prevailed over the beast by force and, through the favor of earthly deities, rescued Theseus' entourage from the constraint which held them at the time. In a single action he subdued his opponent both because he had gained a favor from the gods and because he had taken pity on friends suffering misfortune. In this play Aeacus is introduced, addressing himself to Heracles:

Ha! what is this? I espy someone proceeding this way in haste and with a very bold attitude. Stranger, it is right that you tell me who you are who approach these sites and [that you tell me] for what reason [you have come].

Then Heracles [replied] to him [*TGF* p. 547; EURIPIDES fr. 591]:

No squeamishness [restrains me] from revealing the whole story. My homeland is Argos; Heracles is my name. I am descended from Zeus, father of all the gods. Zeus came to my mother's noble bed, as has been truthfully stated. I have arrived here by compulsion, in deference to the sovereignty of Eurystheus, who sent me with orders to lead Hades' hound alive to the Mycenaean gates. [He gave the order] not because he wished to see [the beast]; rather, he thought that he had contrived thereby a task impossible of fulfillment. Tracking down such employment, I have traveled around Europe in a circle and have come to the remotest parts of all Asia.

17. [EURIPIDES fr. 592 Nauck] ATHENAEUS XI 496A An earthen vessel . . . they use (the apparatus) at Eleusis on the last day of the mysteries, which they name "Plemochoae" after it. . . . Of the same matters also the author of the *Pirithus* reminds us, whether he be Critias the tyrant or Euripides, as he says the following:

That we [the Chorus] may void these earthen vessels into a cleft in the ground in reverent silence.

18. [EURIPIDES fr. 594 Nauck] CLEMENT *Miscellanies* V 35 [II 349, 18 Stählin] Concerning these matters, what is recorded on the holy ark reveals aspects of the intelligible universe, though it has been hidden away and shut off from the multitude. Indeed, even those golden ornaments, six-winged, each of them, whether they show the two bears, as some wish, or, preferably, the two hemispheres, still the name "Cherubim" is likely to indicate considerable knowledge. But the two together have twelve wings and show the perceptible universe through the circle of the zodiac and the time sequence connected with it. Discoursing on nature, I think, the tragedy says "untiring . . . celestial vault." SCHOLIUM on ARISTOPHANES *Birds* 179 The ancients employ the word "pole" not, as do the moderns, as a defining term for "axle," but as that which embraces all. Euripides in his *Pirithus* writes "and guarding Atlas' celestial vault," as if it circled around and everything passed through it.

Untiring time wanders around the everflowing stream. In its fullness it keeps reproducing itself, and twin bears borne on swift-flappings of wings keep watch over Atlas' celestial vault.

Atlas can be the unaffected celestial vault and the unstraying sphere, but is better understood, perhaps, as immovable time.

19. [EURIPIDES fr. 593 Nauck] CLEMENT *Miscellanies* V 115 [II 403, 14 Stählin] In his play *Pirithus*, the same author [Euripides] also writes the following tragic verse: "You . . . dance about." [SCHOLIA on APOLLONIUS RHODIUS IV 143 and on EURIPIDES *Orestes* 982 quote lines 1–2; SATYRUS *Life of Euripides* (*POxy* IX) p. 140, cites 1–4, "who . . . of the s(tars)"]:

[I call on] you, self-begotten, who interwove all things in a heavenly whir, around whom light, around whom spangled murky night and the numberless horde of stars continually dance about.

Here he has called "self-begotten" the creative mind. The sequel has to do with the universe, including even the oppositions of light and darkness.

20. [Euripides fr. 595 Nauck] Plutarch *On Friendships* 7 p. 96c Some, though they derived no benefits from friends whose fortunes were good, join them in ruin when they meet mischance. And especially philosophers and men of taste suffer thus, as Theseus along with Pirithus, when the latter was punished and tied up:

[Theseus] has been yoked [to Pirithus] in shackles of awe not forged by any smith.

21. [Euripides fr. 598 Nauck] Stobaeus ii 8, 4   In Euripides' *Pirithus:*

Not with unpracticed mind did the first speaker make his contribution, he who originated the statement that chance becomes ally to men of understanding.

22. [Euripides fr. 597 Nauck] Stobaeus iii 37, 15   In the *Pirithus:*

An honest manner is more steadfast than a law. No orator could ever distort the one; but, stirring the other up and down with speeches, he frequently does dishonor.

23. [Euripides fr. 596 Nauck] Stobaeus iv 53, 23   In Euripides' *Pirithus:*

Is it not true that it is better not to live than to live ill?

24. From the *Pirithus*, according to Welcker, come the following fragments of Euripides, fr. inc. 865 d:

Fame points out the good man even in the far corners of the earth.

and 936,

No, but while I was still living Hades received me.

and, according to Wilamowitz, fr. 964 also.[8] Cf. PHOTIUS *Lexicon* p. 91, 18 Reitzenstein: "Motherless (*amētoros*)": Euripides:

O Aphidnus, scion of motherless Earth!

SISYPHUS (SATYR-PLAY)

25. [EURIPIDES (1 p. 770 Nauck)] SEXTUS *Against the Schoolmasters* IX 54 And Critias, one of those who held tyrannical power at Athens, appears to come from the rank[s] of the atheists, since he says that ancient lawgivers fabricated the deity as an overseer of men's successes and failures in the interest of no man's secretly injuring his neighbor, guarding against retribution on the part of the gods. So goes the statement in his writings: "There was . . . race." AETIUS I 7, 2 (*D* 298) And Euripides, the tragic poet, out of fear of the [Council of the] Areopagus, was unwilling to lay the truth bare, yet gave indications in the following manner. For he introduced Sisyphus as the champion of this opinion and shared in advocacy. "There was a time," he says, "when . . . subservient" [lines 1–2]. Then he avers that lawlessness was undone through the introduction of laws. For since law could restrain the obvious among injustices, whereas many men acted unjustly in secret, at that point some sage established that it was necessary to obscure the truth with false discourse and persuade mankind "that there is . . . with life, who hears and sees these things and is extremely thoughtful" [lines 17–18]. AETIUS I 6, 7 (*D* 294) Whence also Euripides says "and the starry brightness of heaven, wise . . . Time" [lines 33–34].

There was a time when the life of men was uncivilized and bestial and subservient to brute force, a time when neither was there any prize for the good
5 nor for the wicked did any chastisement arise. It seems to me that men next set up laws as chastisers, that Justice might become tyrant ⟨equally of all⟩ and might have Arrogance as a slave. Should anyone commit an error, he
10 was penalized. Next, since laws hindered them from committing obvious

---

[8] The fragment is cited in connection with Anaxagoras, *DK* 59 A 33.

crimes by force, yet they acted secretly; it seems to me that at this point some clever and wise man ⟨for the first time⟩ invented fear ⟨of the gods⟩ for
15 mortals, that the wicked might experience fear, even if they act or say or think ⟨something⟩ in secret. As a consequence he introduced the divine: "There is a deity flourishing with indestructible life. Through mind it hears, sees, is extremely thoughtful, and attends to these things, bearing divine
20 nature [in itself]. It will hear all that is said among mortals and will be able to see all that is done. If in silence you plan some evil, this will not escape the notice of the gods. For thought is in it ⟨to too great a degree⟩." Making
25 these statements, he introduced the most pleasant of doctrines and with false discourse obscured the truth. He claimed that the god inhabited a place where, merely by mentioning it, he could have frightened men extremely.
30 He recognized that from this source there were fears for mortals and benefits for their wretched way of life, coming from heavenly revolution, where he saw that there existed lightning flashes and frightful thunderclaps and the star-spangled frame of heaven, the lovely embroidery of Time, wise crafts-
35 man. From here the bright mass of the star proceeds and damp storm moves out toward earth. With such fears did he encircle men, through whom he
40 settled the deity well via discourse and in a suitable location; and through laws he quelled lawlessness.

And, going a bit further, the poet adds:

And I think that it was in this way that someone first persuaded mortals to think that there existed a race of deities.

FROM UNDETERMINED DRAMAS

26. STOBAEUS I 8, 11:

After the shadow time grows old very quickly.

27. ——— III 14, 2   Of Critias:[9]

[One must be able to oppose even friends.] Whoever in dealing with friends does everything in order to gain favor causes immediate pleasure to turn into enmity for a later time.

[9] Cf. B 15a above.

28. ——— III 23, 1   Of Critias:

But it is frightening when someone who lacks understanding believes that he understands.

29. ——— IV 33, 10   Of Critias:

Is it better to have wealthy gaucherie as an inmate in the home rather than wise poverty?

PROSE FRAGMENTS

⟨COMMONWEALTH OF THE ATHENIANS⟩

30. Possibly B 53–73 belong here.

COMMONWEALTH OF THE THESSALIANS

31. ATHENAEUS XIV 662F   "It is admitted that the Thessalians have become the most extravagant of the Greeks, so far as dress and mode of life are concerned. This turned out to be the reason for their bringing in the Persians against Greece, for the latter envied them their extravagance and luxury." Critias makes observations concerning the Thessalians' extravagance in his *Commonwealth of the Thessalians*.

COMMONWEALTH OF THE LACEDAEMONIANS

32. CLEMENT *Miscellanies* VI 9 [II 428, 12 Stählin]   Aware that Euripides wrote, "Offspring are superior if from a mother and father who labor to provide an austere mode of life" [fr. 525, 4–5] Critias writes: "I start, you see, from a man's hour of birth. How might he become physically supreme and strongest? [He could,] if his sire would exercise and eat manfully and harden himself physically and if the mother of the child-to-be would grow physically strong and exercise."

33. ATHENAEUS XI 463E From city to city there are peculiar fashions of drinking, as Critias shows in his *Commonwealth of the Lacedaemonians* through these words: "The Chian and the Thessalian drink out of large cups passed to the right, the Athenian out of small cups passed to the right, while the Thessalian proposes grandiose toasts to whomever they [*sic*] wish. But the Lacedaemonians drink, each, the cup placed at his side, and the wine-pourer ⟨pours in⟩ just so much as one [is likely to] drink."

34. ————483B Critias in his *Commonwealth of the Lacedaemonians* writes thus: "Apart from these things the most modest for daily living: Laconian shoes are best ⟨and⟩ Laconian cloaks are most pleasing to wear and most useful. The Laconian beaker is the most suitable drinking vessel for military activity and easiest to carry in a knapsack. On what account it is fit for soldiers ⟨I shall explain⟩. It often becomes necessary ⟨for a soldier⟩ to drink impure water. Thus the first consideration is the liquid's not being very clear. Next the beaker, having rims which curve inward, causes the impurity to keep to itself." PLUTARCH *Lycurgus* 9, 7 On that account, the handy and necessary among utensils—couches, stools, tables—were best crafted in their midst. And the Laconian beaker was especially popular for military campaigns, as Critias states. For water which had to be drunk, though unpleasant to the sight, became obscure in color. Since mud rubbed against the interior and clung to the incurving rims, what was swallowed down approached the mouth in a purer condition. POLLUX VI 97 The beaker is a Laconian [s.c., drinking cup]. And the beaker's sides, like those also of the pot, are called "rims (*ambōnes*)." Cf. PHOTIUS *Lexicon* s.v. "beaker (*kōthōn*)" [I 364, 11 Naber].

35. ATHENAEUS XI 486E Critias in his *Commonwealth of the Lacedaemonians:* "Milesian-made bed and Milesian-made stool, Chian-made bed and Rheneian-made table." HARPOCRATION s.v. "Lycian-made (*Lukiourgeis*)" [following a quotation from Didymus]: The grammarian seems not to know that one would derive such a formation, not from names of persons, but rather from names of cities and peoples.

Critias says "Milesian-made bed" in his *Commonwealth of the Lacedae-monians.*

36. EUSTATHIUS on HOMER *Odyssey* VIII 376 1601, 25 [from SUETONIUS *On Games*?]   And it was an old custom to play thus and, they say, the Lacedaemonians had a local contest, the "ball-match". . . . note that such a game played with a ball was also a kind of dance, as he makes clear likewise who wrote thus: "The tong-dance involves vehement leg movements." In any event, Critias says the following: "Leaping up to a high point before dropping down to earth, they executed many alternations with their feet. They called it 'doing the tong-dance'." Cf. ATHENAEUS XIV 629D.

37. LIBANIUS *Orations* 25, 63 [II 567 Förster]   The Lacedaemonians [are] those who keep open to themselves the license of slaughter against the Helots and concerning whom Critias speaks [when he notes that] in Lacedaemon especially there are slaves and freemen. What else is there than what Critias himself says? "On account of mistrust toward these Helots the Spartan at home strips off the sling from the Helot's shield. Since he cannot do this on campaign because of the frequent necessity for speed, he always travels around with spear in hand in order to prove stronger in this particular than the Helot, should the latter, relying on his shield alone, essay an uprising. They have devised bolts as well, which they deem stronger than any treachery coming from the Helots."   (64) This would be the situation of men living with fear and not allowed a respite by those who are terrible in their expec-tations. Thus, when they breakfast and go to sleep and proceed about any other business, fear of their householders arms them. How could they, O son of Callaeschrus, derive enjoyment from a freedom which is pure, if slaves attacked them in alliance with Poseidon and were furnished as an example that on similar occasions they would act similarly? Just as their kings, therefore, were not very free, inasmuch as it was granted the ephors to shackle a king and put him to death, so all the Spartans together were stripped of freedom, living as they did with the hatred coming from their householders.

FROM AN UNDETERMINED *COMMONWEALTH*

38. POLLUX VII 59   They call trousers also "breeches (*skeleai*)." The name occurs also in Critias' writings, specifically in his *Commonwealths*.

APHORISMS (BOOKS I, II, ETC.)

39. GALEN *Commentary on Hippocrates' "The Doctor's Workshop"* I 1   (What it is to perceive with sight, touch, hearing, smell, taste, and thought)   XVIII B 654 Kühn Such is the Stoic explanation [namely, of perception] as that which is indicated. On that account Quintus' disciple Aephician accepted Stoic philosophy itself and welcomed it. . . . 655, 7 He says that Hippocrates availed himself of the expression "perceiving," as opposed to "thought." 656, 2 And he recalls, in discussing the term "thought," that in the time of the ancients it was on a par with "mind" or "intelligence," unless "consideration" too was mentioned. Though there are many testimonia to it, I shall cite as evidence only a few.

Critias in Book I of his *Aphorisms* writes as follows: "Neither what one perceives through the rest of one's body nor what one knows through thought."

And again: "Men come to know if they are accustomed to be healthy in their thought."

LECTURES (BOOKS I–II)

40. ——— ——— [directly after the last passage cited above] Also in Book I of the *Lectures:* "But if you yourself were to become practiced in order to be competent for thought, you would thus be least wronged by them."[10] And often in the same book and in Book II of the *Lectures,*

---

[10] Kathleen Freeman, like Diels before her, conjecturally identifies the unspecified agent as "the sense-perceptions," *Ancilla to the Pre-Socratic Philosophers: A Complete Translation of the Fragments in Diels' "Fragmente der Vorsokratiker"* (Oxford, 1948), p. 160. Cf. Diels's "*Sinneswahrnehmungen.*"

in making a logical distinction between thought and perceptions he has spoken much as did Antiphon. . . . [DK 87 B 1 = Morrison B 67]

41. HERODIAN *On Anomalous Words* p. 40, 14   The substitution in Critias' *Lectures* of "impulsitude" for "impulse" is incorrect.

41a. PLATO *Charmides* 161B   I just remembered having heard someone say already, that moderation would be attending to one's own affairs. Cf. 162A.

ON THE NATURE OF DESIRE OR OF VIRTUES

42. GALEN *Glossary of Hippocratic Terminology* XIX 94 Kühn (*On Epidemics* III 17, 11 [III 134 Littré] a woman named Dysenius) s.v. "*dysaniēs*": Critias in his *On the Nature of Desire or of Virtues* explains the noun thus: "An 'ill-pleased' (*dysanios*) person is one who becomes distressed over small and large matters to a greater degree or for a longer time than other men." Cf. 87 B 176.

PROEMS SUITABLE FOR PUBLIC SPEAKING

43. HERMOGENES *On Kinds* [*of Literary Composition*] B 401, 25 Rabe Cf. A 19 above.

FROM UNDETERMINED PROSE WORKS

44. AELIAN *Miscellaneous History* X 13   Critias censures Archilochus for having spoken very ill of himself: "If he had not publicized such an opinion of himself among the Greeks, we should have found out neither that he was the son of Enipo, the slave-woman, nor that, having abandoned Paros due to poverty and need, he came to Thasos, nor that upon his arrival he became an enemy to the residents, nor even that he reviled friends and foes alike. In addition, we should not have known either that he was an adulterer, unless by learning it from him, or that he was lecherous and wanton and—what is most disgraceful even among these things—that he threw away his shield. Thus, in leaving behind such a reputation and such renown for himself, Archilochus was not a good witness in his own behalf." Not I, but Critias laid these criticisms upon Archilochus.

45. ———— ———— x 17 Critias states that Themistocles, son of Neocles, before he inaugurated political activity, had as his inheritance three talents. But when be became leader of the democracy, then fled and suffered confiscation of his goods, it was discovered that he possessed property worth more than one hundred talents. Similarly, Cleon, before his entry into public affairs, was not encumbered with possessions, but left an estate of fifty talents afterward.

46. ARISTIDES *Art of Rhetoric* II 15 Schmid [on XENOPHON *Symposium* ad init.: "But it seems to me"] Had his discourse started from a declarative expression, such as "It seems to me, at least," his utterance would have become stronger and would have seemed to be rather like that of Critias than of any such persons.

47. ———— ————II 50 Schmid [on XENOPHON *Symposium* 1 4: "Rather to them, as if to generals and cavalry-commanders and office seekers"] But if, incorporating the contrary, you said something such as "All who choose such men, whom they observe excelling in offices and honors and such powers more than the rest, do not seem to me to be doing correctly," such a manner would have seemed to be rather that of Critias than of any of the ancient sophists.

48. DIO CHRYSOSTOM 21, 3 [II 267 Arnim] Or do you not know that Critias, the member of the Thirty, said the following: "Among males the feminine form is most beautiful, among females the opposite"? Therefore, the Athenians justly chose him as a legal expert for the revision of old laws, since he left not one of them [alone]. Cf. A 4.

49. [DIONYSIUS] *Art of Rhetoric* [3d century, A.D.] 6 II 277, 10 Usener-Radermacher   For a man who comes into the world, according to Callaeschrus' son, one of the Thirty, "Nothing is secure, save dying for him who comes into the world and the impossibility of a living man's making his way outside the range of disaster. . . ."

50. PHILOSTRATUS *Lives of the Sophists* p. 1, 9   For I am indeed aware that Critias the sophist also did not make mention of paternity, but allowed an exception in the case of Homer, since he was intending to disclose the marvel of Homer's having as his father a river.

51. PLANUDES on HERMOGENES *Rh. Gr.* V 484 Walz   Like "the contest of the Pythians." This is common and easy; but Critias, employing an inverted word order, said: "Of the Pythians the contest."

52. PLUTARCH *Cimon* 16   Critias says that, whereas Ephialtes hindered and protested against aiding and raising up a city to rival Athens, but [advised] allowing the pride of Sparta to lie low and be trampled under, Cimon, having placed the aggrandizement of his homeland after the advantage of the Spartans and having convinced the populace, went forth to the rescue with numerous heavily armed troops.

53. POLLUX II 58   Critias and Antiphon [*DK* 87 B 6 = Morrison B 74] [employ the expression] "look into (*diopteuein*)."

54. ——— II 122   In the works of Critias, a rhetorician is also a "speaker (*logeus*)."

55. ——— II 148   "Nimble (*tachycheir*)," as Critias [says].

56. ——— III 116   And, as Critias [says], "sordidness (*rhyparia*)."

57. ——— IV 64   Critias is satisfied to call lyre-accompanied odes "songs sung to instrumental music (*prosōidiai*)."

58. ——— IV 165   In the works of Critias [there occurs the expression] "priced at two drachmas (*didrachmiaioi*)."

59. —— vi 31 Critias explains "beakerize further (*epikōthōnid-zesthai*)" as "go on drinking (*peraiterō pinein*)."

60. —— vi 38 Critias said both "catering (*opsōniai*)" and "purchase victuals (*opsōnein*)," but identified the latter also as "be a cook (*opsonomein*)."

61. —— vi 152–53 "False witnesses (*pseudomartyres*)" have been mentioned in the works of Critias, also the "false witness (*pseudomartys*)," I know not where. The same author, I suppose, employs also the verb "bear false witness (*pseudomartyrein*)."

62. —— vi 194 "To be scattered (*diaskedannusthai*)" ... or "to have been spread abroad (*diapephorēsthai*)," as Critias [says].

63. —— vi 195 Also part of themselves, all that is beside them, that which is according to them, that which comes upon them, that which is ⟨directed⟩ against them. Critias possibly says: "insofar as they are worthy."

64. —— vii 78 Those who sell garments are called "clothes-dealers (*himatiopōlai*)," inasmuch as Critias used the name.

65. —— vii 91 Cf. ii 196. Critias calls them "socks (*podeia*)," whether one is to think of them as felt shoes or as a wrapping for feet. In his *Phrygians* [fr. 259 Nauck] Aeschylus calls them "ankle-bandages (*pellutra*)."

66. —— vii 108 "Gem-engravers (*daktulioglyphoi*)." The word occurs in the writings of Critias.

67. —— vii 154 "Lyre-string-dealer (*chordopōlēs*)," as Critias says.

68. —— vii 177 "Perfumer (*myrepsos*)." For so Critias used the name.

69. ——— VII 179 "Hairnet (*kekryphaloplokos*),"[11] as Critias said.

70. ——— VII 196–97 Critias mentions most of the series, much of it chosen rather for euphony:

> bronze-dealers (*chalkopōlai*)
> iron-dealers (*sideropōlai*)
> vegetable-dealers (*lachanopōlai*)
>
> . . .
>
> cheese-dealers (*turopōlai*)
>
> . . .
>
> emetic-dealers (*surmaiopōlai*)
> oakum-dealers (*styppeiopōlai*)
> wool-dealers (*eriopōlai*)
> frankincense-dealers (*libanotopōlai*)
>
> . . .
>
> root-dealers (*rhidzopōlai*)
> silphium-dealers (*silphiopōlai*)
> cabbage-dealers (*kaulopōlai*)
> equipment-dealers (*skeuopōlai*)
> scrap-pickers (*spermologoi*)
> seed-dealers (*spermatopōlai*)
> pot-dealers (*chytropōlai*)
>
> . . .
>
> drug-dealers (*pharmakopōlai*)
>
> . . .
>
> needle-dealers (*belonopōlai*)
>
> . . .
>
> plucked-bird-on-a-board dealers (*pinakopōlai*)

Critias calls them "bird-retailers (*ornithokapēloi*)" and so on.

---

[11] Kathleen Freeman, however, interprets the term as "hairnet-maker" (wrongly?), *Ancilla*, p. 161.

71. —— VIII 25   Critias explained "acquit (*apodikasai*)" as dissolving the trial or denying it a victory, just as we would say "refuse to condemn (*apopsēphisasthai*)." The same [authority understood] "hold inquiry (*diadikadzein*)" [to signify] giving judgment throughout the year.

72. —— IX 17   Also in the writings of Critias, "one who lives always in the city (*astutrips*)" [is considered] a "city-protector (*astunomos*)."

73. —— IX 161   Both in the writings of Euripides [fr. 1100] and in the writings of Critias, "scholarship (*eupaideusia*)" is called "shrewdness (*euxunesia*)."

SPURIOUS OR DOUBTFUL FRAGMENTS

74. [The sayings in Ryssel's Graeco-Syrian collection (*Rheinisches Museum*, LI [1896], p. 531ff., n. 4, 11, 15) are uncertain as to form of the name and in their content have nothing to do with the sophists.]

75. PLATO *Republic* II 368A   Not badly, O sons of that man, did Glaucon's lover[12] direct the start of his elegies toward you, since you had gained renown in connection with the battle at Megara. He said:

Sons of Ariston, divine progeny of a famous man.

---

[12] Schleiermacher surmises that the reference is to Critias.

89. ANONYMUS IAMBLICHI

translated by MARGARET E. REESOR

The *Anonymus Iamblichi* is found in the *Protrepticus* of Iamblichus. It is the work of an unknown writer of the late fifth or early fourth century B.C. In a recent article, A. T. Cole ("The *Anonymus Iamblichi* and His Place in Greek Political Theory," *HSCP*, LXV [1961], pp. 127–63) pointed out the similarities between the *Anonymus* and the second book of Cicero's *De Officiis*, which is based on Panaetius, as well as the parallels between the *Anonymus* and the fragments of Protagoras and Democritus. He concluded that the *Anonymus* was an Athenian follower of Democritus, and that he and Panaetius found a common source in Democritus' *Peri Andragathias. Untersteiner,* on much weaker grounds, attributes the *Anonymus* to Hippias.

Other than Cole's and Untersteiner's, the most important works on the *Anonymus Iamblichi* are R. Roller's *Untersuchungen zum Anonymus Iamblichi* (Tübingen, 1931), and Q. Cataudella's "Nuove Ricerche sull' Anonimo di Giamblico e sulla Composizione del Protreptico," *Rendiconti della Classe di Scienze morali, storiche e filologiche delle' Accademia dei Lincei* (1937), pp. 182–210.

1. p. 95, 13 Pistelli   (1) Whatever one wishes to bring to the best conclusion, whether it be wisdom, manliness, fluency, or virtue, and whether all of it or part of it, it will be possible for him to accomplish if he takes what follows as his starting point.   (2) First, he must have a good natural endowment. Although this may be credited to chance, the other characteristics which follow are already in the power of the man himself: to be an earnest seeker after what is honorable and good, to be industrious, both learning at the earliest possible moment and continuing in the pursuit of these things over a long period of time.

(3) But if even one of these be absent, it will not be possible for him to carry anything through to the supreme excellence; but if he has all of these, whatever he may attempt will not be surpassed.

2. p. 96, 1   (1) Therefore, if anyone wishes to receive a good reputation among men, and if he wants to appear such as he is, he must start immediately while he is still young and practice uniformly and consistently.   (2) For everything which has been of long standing, started early, and perfected, receives a sure reputation and fame for the following reasons: because it is already trusted unequivocally, and because the envy of people generally does not attach itself to it. It is because of envy that in some things men withhold their praise and do not make the achievement known as would be reasonable, and in others they make false accusations attaching blame unjustly.   (3) For it is not pleasant for people to honor somebody else (for they think that they themselves are being deprived of something), but, if they are overpowered by necessity itself, and gradually over a long period of time have been won over, they offer their praise although it may be much against their will.   (4) At the same time, they do not doubt that, even if a man is such as he appears, he is ensnaring and pursuing a good reputation for the purpose of practicing deceit, and that in whatever he is doing he is making a show and leading men on for his own advantage. But if virtue is practiced in that way which I mentioned before, it creates belief in itself and a good reputation.   (5) For when they are already firmly convinced, men cannot employ envy or think that they are being deceived. (6) What is more, time, if it is present in every activity and in public business for a long period, establishes what is being practiced; but a short period of time cannot accomplish this.   (7) A man could learn skill in words, and when he had mastered it he might be in no way inferior to his teacher in a short time; but it is not possible for a man who has started late to bring to fruition in a short time the virtue which has its origin in many activities, but it is necessary for him to be nurtured with it and to grow with it, keeping away from what is wrong in both speech and habits, practicing other things and bringing them to fruition over a long period of time and with great care.   (8) And, at the same time, the following detraction is added to a good reputation which has been acquired in a short time: men do not receive gladly those who have become wealthy, wise, good, or manly suddenly and in a short period of time.

3. p. 97, 16   (1) When anyone who desires any of these has brought it to fruition and has acquired a firm grasp of it, whether it be fluency, wisdom, or strength, he must employ it to the full for ends which are good and lawful; but if anyone uses the good which belongs to him for wrong and unlawful ends, a proficiency of this sort must be the most base of all, and it would be better for him not to have it at all. (2) And just as the man who possesses any of these is absolutely good, if he uses them for good ends, so, on the other hand, the man who uses them for bad ends is utterly vicious.   (3) Again, we must consider by what kind of speech or action a man who desires complete virtue would become best. He would become this if he benefited as many people as possible.   (4) But if anyone benefits his neighbors by gifts of money, he will be forced to be nasty again if he collects the money. Secondly, he could not bring together such an abundance that his resources would not fail while he is making gifts and presentations. Then, too, this second disadvantage is added after he has collected the money, if, having been rich, he becomes poor and has nothing, although he once had possessions.   (5) How, then, can anyone be beneficent towards others, if he does not distribute money but uses some other means, and that not with vice but with virtue? And, in addition, how can he give presents and not lose the power of giving?   (6) This will come to pass in the following way—if he should stand by the laws and what is just—for it is this which unites cities and men and binds them together.

4. p. 98, 17   (1) And surely it is necessary for every man to be very self-disciplined to a special degree. He would be particularly self-disciplined if he should be superior to the influence of money, for it is in respect to this that all are corrupted, and if he should be unsparing of his own soul, with an earnest purpose fixed on what is right, and if he should be intent upon the pursuit of virtue. With regard to both of

these most men are lacking in self-discipline.   (2) Because of some such thing as this they are affected in the following way: they are over-anxious about their souls, because it is the soul that is life; they are oversparing of it; and they are concerned about it because of their love of life and because they are so closely connected with the soul with which they grew up. And they love possessions because of the following things which frighten them.   (3) What are these? Sickness, old age, sudden penalties or losses—I do not mean penalties of the laws, for it is possible to take precautions and be on one's guard against incurring these, but such penalties or losses as conflagrations, the deaths of members of one's household, of animals, and other misfortunes, of which some pertain to the body, others to the soul, and others to one's estate. (4) Because of all these misfortunes, in order that he may be in a position to use his money to meet these contingencies, every man desires wealth.   (5) But there are some other factors which no less than those already mentioned drive men on to money-making—I mean, ambitious rivalry with one another, jealousy, and the exercise of political power-situations in which they consider money of great importance, because it is helpful for such purposes.   (6) The man who is really good does not seek out a reputation clad in the ornaments belonging to another man but by his own virtue.

5. p. 99, 18   (1) With regard to love of one's own soul we might believe as follows: if it fell to a man's lot to be ageless and immortal for all future time, provided that he were not killed by another man, there might be a ready pardon granted to the man who is oversparing of his soul.   (2) But since it falls to a man's lot, if his life is lengthened, to suffer old age, which is a greater evil, and not to be immortal, it shows great ignorance and the use of bad judgment and goals if a man preserves this soul into dishonor and does not leave an immortal glory to take its place—an everlasting and immortal fame in place of a soul which is only mortal.

6. p. 100, 5   (1) Furthermore, we must not rush towards a consideration of our own advantage, nor should we consider either that the power which is based on a consideration of one's advantage is virtue, or that obeying the laws is cowardice. For this attitude is most base, and from it arises everything which is just the reverse of what is good, namely immorality and the inflicting of injury. If men were given such a nature that they were not able to live alone, but formed an association with one another under pressure of necessity, and found out our general way of life and the skills related to it, and cannot associate and live with one another without observance of law (for this would be a greater punishment than living alone), we can conclude, then, that because of these necessities Law and Justice are kings among men, and that they could in no way change, for by nature they have been firmly fixed. (2) If there should be anyone who had from the beginning of his life a nature such as we shall describe: if he should be invulnerable, not subject to disease, free from emotion, extraordinary, and hard as adamant in body and soul, perhaps someone might believe that the power based on consideration of one's own advantage would be suffi-cient for such a man, on the grounds that a man of that type is invulner-able even if he does not submit to the law. The man who believes this is wrong.   (3) If there should be such a man, as in fact there could not be, such a man would be preserved if he placed himself on the side of the laws and what is just, strengthening these and using his strength to support these and what confirms them, but otherwise he could not endure.   (4) For it would appear that all men would be in a state of hostility to a man formed of such a nature, and because of their own observance of law and their numbers, they would surpass such a man in skill or force and they would get the better of him.   (5) Accordingly, it appears that power itself, the real power, is preserved by law and justice.

7. p. 101, 11   (It is right to learn this, too, in regard to the observance of law and the lack of such observance, and to understand how they differ from one another, and that ⟨the⟩ observance of law would be best for the state and for the individual, and the failure to observe law would be worst, for immediately ⟨serious⟩ consequences result from the failure to observe law. Let us begin by pointing out first the true nature of the observance of law.)

(1) An atmosphere of trust is the first result of the observance of law. It benefits all men greatly and may be classed among those important things which are called good. Community of property has its origin in this, and accordingly, even if the property is small, it is still sufficient since it is shared, but without mutual trust it is not sufficient even if it is great. (2) And the changes of fortune which affect wealth and one's life, whether good or bad, are most suitably directed by men if they observe the law. Those who have good fortune enjoy it in safety and with no fear of attack; those who have bad fortune receive help from those who enjoy good fortune because of their common dealings and mutual trust, since both of these have their basis in the observance of law. (3) Because of the observance of law, time lies fallow with respect to public business, but it is tillable in regard to the activities of life. (4) Under the observance of law, men are freed from the most unpleasant concern, but they enjoy the most pleasant; for a concern about public business is most unpleasant, but a concern about the activities of life is most pleasant. (5) If they go to sleep, for this is a rest from trouble for men, they approach it without fear and without painful anxieties; when they rise from it, they enjoy the same state of mind. They are not seized with sudden fright, nor after this most pleasant change do they expect the day to be. . . .[1] Pleasantly,[2] forming thoughts which feel no anxiety about the activities of life, they lighten the burden of their search for good things with hopes and expectations which are credible. For all this the observance of law is responsible. (6) And as for that which brings the greatest trouble to men, war which leads to subjugation and slavery, to face this is more difficult for those who do not observe law and less difficult for those who do observe it. (7) And there are many other good things in the observance of law which provide assistance in life and a consolation for the hardships which arise from it; but the evils which result from a failure to observe law are as follows: (8) First, men have no leisure for the

---

[1] The text is mutilated at this point. It has been restored by M. Untersteiner (*I Sofisti, Testimonianze e Frammenti,* Fasc. III [Florence, 1954], p. 134) to read: "nor, after a most pleasant sleep, do they await [anxiously] the outcome of the day."

[2] Reading ἡδέως with the MS.

activities [of life] and are concerned about what is most unpleasant—
public business rather than these activities; they hoard money because
of the lack of mutual trust and the lack of common dealings but they
do not share it, and in this way money becomes scarce, even if it exists
in large quantities.   (9) Changes of fortune, both bad and good, serve
opposite purposes; for good fortune is not safe when there is no observance of law, but is subject to plots; and ill fortune is not driven
away but grows stronger as the result of lack of trust and lack of
common dealings.   (10) External war is kindled all the more, and
internal strife for the same reason, and if it has not happened earlier, it
happens then; it happens that men are involved in public business
continually because of plots arising among themselves, which force
them to be on their guard continuously and to plot against one another.
(11) When they are awake their thoughts are not pleasant; and when they
have gone to sleep, they do not find a pleasant place of refuge but one
that is filled with fear. An awakening which is full of fear and dread
leads them to a sudden recollection of their troubles; these and all
other evils which I have mentioned previously result from a failure to
observe law.   (12) Tyranny, an evil of such proportions and so mon-
strous, arises from nothing else than the nonobservance of law. Some
men think, although they are wrong in their opinion, that a tyrant is
established from some other cause, and that men who are deprived of
their freedom are not themselves responsible, since they have been
overpowered by the tyrant who has been established. In this they are
wrong.   (13) Whoever thinks that the rise of a king or of a tyrant is
due to any other cause than nonobservance of law and consideration
of one's own advantage is stupid. For when everybody turns to evil
practices, this result follows, for it is not possible for men to live
without laws and justice.   (14) Whenever these two, law and justice,
depart from the people, then the guardianship and protection of these
people pass into the hands of one man. For how otherwise could sole
authority pass into the hands of one man, unless the law which was in
the interests of the people had already been driven out?   (15) This
man, who is to depose justice and take away the law which is common
to all and expedient for all, must be as hard as adamant, if he is going

to strip this away from the people, since he is one and they are many. (16) If he were only human and like everybody else he would not be able to do this; but, on the contrary, if he were to reestablish what had already ceased to exist, he could be sole ruler. That is why some men have not observed this happening.

90. DISSOI LOGOI OR DIALEXEIS

translated by ROSAMOND KENT SPRAGUE

The *Dissoi Logoi*[1] is an anonymous sophistic treatise written in literary Doric at some time subsequent to the end of the Peloponnesian War. (See I [8].)

I. CONCERNING GOOD AND BAD

(1) Twofold arguments concerning the good and the bad are put forward in Greece by those who philosophize. Some say that the good is one thing and the bad another, but others say that they are the same, and that a thing might be good for some persons but bad for others, or at one time good and at another time bad for the same person. (2) I myself side with those who hold the latter opinion, and I shall examine it, using as an example human life and its concern for food, drink, and sexual pleasures: these things are bad for a man if he is sick but good if he is healthy and needs them. (3) And further, incontinence in these matters is bad for the incontinent but good for those who sell these things and make a profit. And again, illness is bad for the sick but good for the doctors. And death is bad for those who die but good for the undertakers and gravediggers. (4) Farming, too, which produces good

[1] A preliminary version of this translation was distributed to the members of the Society of Ancient Greek Philosophy for criticism. The translator wishes to thank Professors George A. Kennedy, William O'Neill, Thomas M. Robinson, Gilbert Ryle, Friedrich Solmsen, and Leonard Woodbury for their valuable suggestions. The present version appeared in *Mind*, n.s. 306, LXXVII (Apr. 1968), pp. 155–67, and is reprinted with the permission of the editor.

crops, is good for the farmers but bad for the merchants. Again, if trading vessels are staved in or smashed up, this is bad for the master and owner but good for the shipbuilders. (5) ⟨And⟩ further, if a tool is corroded or blunted or broken, this is good for the blacksmith but bad for everyone else. And, certainly, if a pot gets smashed, this is good for the potters but bad for everyone else. And if shoes are worn out and ripped apart, this is good for the cobbler but bad for everyone else. (6) And further, take the case of various contests, athletic, musical, and military; in a race in the stadium, for instance, victory is good for the winner but bad for the losers. (7) The same holds true for wrestlers and boxers, and for all those who take part in musical contests: for instance, ⟨victory⟩ in lyre-playing is good for the winner but bad for the losers. (8) In the case of war (and I shall speak of the most recent events first) the victory of the Spartans which they won over the Athenians and their allies was good for the Spartans but bad for the Athenians and their allies. And the victory which the Greeks won over the Mede was good for the Greeks but bad for the barbarians. (9) And, again, the capture of Ilium was good for the Achaeans but bad for the Trojans. And the same is true of the disasters of the Thebans and the Argives. (10) And the battle between the Centaurs and the Lapiths was good for the Lapiths but bad for the Centaurs. And, what is more, the battle which we are told took place between the gods and the giants (with the resulting victory for the gods) was good for the gods but bad for the giants.—(11) But there is another argument which says that the good is one thing and the bad another, and that as the name differs, so does the thing named. And I, too, distinguish in this fashion; I think it ⟨would⟩ not be clear what was good and what was bad if they were just the same and one did not differ from the other; in fact, such a situation would be extraordinary. (12) And I think a person who says these things would be unable to answer if anyone should question him as follows: "Just tell me, did your parents ever do you any good?" He would answer, "Yes, a great deal." "Then you owe them for a great deal of evil if the good is really the same as the bad." (13) "Well then, did you ever do your kinsmen any good?" ⟨"Yes, a great deal."⟩ "Then you were doing your kins-

men harm. Well then, did you ever do your enemies harm?" "Yes, a
⟨great⟩ deal." "Then you did them the greatest goods."—(14) "Come
and answer me this: isn't it the case that you are both pitying beggars
because they have many evils, ⟨and⟩ again counting them lucky because
they have many goods, if good and bad are really the same thing?"
(15) There is nothing to prevent the Great King from being in the same
state as a beggar. His many great goods are many great evils if good and
bad are the same. We can consider that these things have been said in
every case. (16) I shall go through the individual cases, beginning
with eating, drinking, and sexual pleasures. For the sick these things
are ⟨bad to do and again⟩ they are good for them to do, if good and bad
are really the same. And for the sick it is bad to be ill and also good, if
good is really the same as bad. (17) And this also holds for all the
other cases which were mentioned in the previous argument. And I
am not saying what the good is, but I am trying to explain that the bad
and the good are not the same but that each is distinct from the ⟨other⟩.

II. CONCERNING SEEMLY AND DISGRACEFUL

(1) Twofold arguments are also put forward concerning the seemly
and the disgraceful. Some say the seemly is one thing and the disgraceful
another, and that as the name differs, so does the thing named, and
others say that the seemly and disgraceful are the same. (2) And I
shall try my hand by expounding the matter in the following way: for
example, it is seemly for a boy in the flower of his youth to gratify a
lover, but for him to gratify one who is not a lover is disgraceful.
(3) And for women to wash themselves indoors is seemly, but for them
to do so in the palaestra is disgraceful (although for men to do so in the
palaestra and gymnasium is seemly). (4) And to have intercourse
with a man in a quiet place where the action will be concealed behind
walls is seemly, but to do so outside, where someone will see, is disgraceful. (5) And for a woman to have intercourse with her own
husband is seemly, but to do so with another woman's husband is most

shameful; and for a man to have intercourse with his own wife is seemly, but to do so with the wife of another is disgraceful. (6) And to adorn and powder oneself and wear gold ornaments is disgraceful in a man but seemly in a woman. (7) And it is seemly to do good to one's friends but disgraceful to do so to one's enemies. And it is disgraceful to run away from the enemy but seemly to run away from one's rivals in the stadium. (8) To murder one's friends and fellow citizens is wicked but to slaughter the enemy is admirable. And examples like this can be given on all topics. (9) I go on ⟨to⟩ the things which cities and peoples regard as disgraceful. For instance: to the Spartans it is seemly that young girls should do athletics and go about with bare arms and no tunics, but to the Ionians this is disgraceful. (10) And to ⟨the former⟩ it is seemly for their children not to learn music and letters, but to the Ionians it is disgraceful not to know all these things. (11) To the Thessalians it is seemly for a man to select horses and mules from a herd himself and train them, and also to take one of the cattle and slaughter, skin, and cut it up himself, but in Sicily these tasks are disgraceful and the work of slaves. (12) To the Macedonians it appears to be seemly for young girls, before they are married, to fall in love and to have intercourse with a man, but when a girl is married it is a disgrace. (As far as the Greeks are concerned it is disgraceful at either time.) (13) To the Thracians it is an ornament for young girls to be tattooed but, with others, tattoo marks are a punishment for those who do wrong. And the Scythians think it seemly that who⟨ever⟩ kills a man should scalp him and wear the scalp on his horse's bridle,[2] and, having gilded the skull ⟨or⟩ lined it with silver, should drink from it and make a libation to the gods. Among the Greeks, no one would be willing to enter the same house as a man who had behaved like that. (14) The Massagetes cut up their parents and eat them, and they think that to be buried in their children is the most beautiful grave imaginable, but in Greece, if anyone did such a thing, he would be driven out of the country and would die an ignominious death for having committed such disgraceful and terrible deeds. (15) The

---

[2] The Greek says "carry it in front of his horse," but see Herodotus IV 64, 2.

Persians think it seemly that not only women but men should adorn
themselves and that men should have intercourse with their daughters,
mothers, and sisters, but the Greeks regard these things as disgraceful
and against the law.   (16) And, again, it strikes the Lydians as seemly
that young girls should first earn money by prostituting themselves and
then get married, but no one among the Greeks would be willing to
marry a girl who did that.   (17) Egyptians do not think the same
things seemly as other people do: in our country we regard it as seemly
that the women should weave and work ⟨in wool⟩ but in theirs they
think it seemly for the men to do so and for the women to do what the
men do in ours. To moisten clay with the hands and dough with the
feet is seemly to them, but we do it just the other way round.   (18) And
I think that if someone should order all men to make a single heap of
everything that each of them regards as disgraceful and then again to
take from the collection what each of them regards as seemly, not a
thing ⟨would⟩ be left, but they would all divide up everything, because
not all men are of the same opinion.   (19) And I shall offer some verses
on the subject [*TGF* 844 adesp. 26]:

And if you investigate in this way, you will see another law for mortals:
nothing is always seemly or always disgraceful, but the right occasion takes
the same things and makes them disgraceful and then alters them and makes
them seemly.

(20) To sum up, everything done at the right time is seemly and everything done at the wrong time is disgraceful. What have I then worked
out? I said I would show that the same things are both disgraceful
and seemly, and I have done so in all these cases.—(21) But there is
also an argument about the disgraceful and ⟨the⟩ seemly which says
that each is distinct from the other. Since, if anyone should ask those
who say that the same thing is both disgraceful and seemly whether
they have ever done anything seemly,[3] they would admit that they have
also done something disgraceful, if disgraceful and seemly are really
the same thing.   (22) And if they know any man to be handsome, they

---

[3] Supply, "and they should say 'yes'."

would also know the same man to be ugly.[4] And if they know any man to be white, they would also know the same man to be black. And it is seemly to honor the gods and, again, disgraceful to honor the gods, if disgraceful and seemly are really the same thing. (23) We can take it that I have made the same points in absolutely every case, and I shall turn to the argument which they put forward. (24) If it is seemly for a woman to adorn herself, it is ⟨also⟩ disgraceful for a woman to adorn herself, if disgraceful and seemly are really the same thing. And all the other cases can be treated in the same way. (25) In Lacedaemon it is seemly for girls to do athletics; in Lacedaemon it is disgraceful for girls to do athletics, and so forth. (26) And they say that if a group of people should collect from all the nations of the world their disgraceful customs and then should call everyone together and tell each man to select what he thinks is seemly, everything would be taken away as belonging to the seemly things. I would be surprised if things which were disgraceful when they were collected should turn out to be seemly and not what they were when they came. (27) At least if people had brought horses or cows or sheep or men, they would not have taken away anything else. Nor, again, if they had brought gold, would they have taken away brass, nor if they had brought silver, would they have taken away lead. (28) Do they then take away seemly things in exchange for disgraceful ones? Now really, if anyone had brought an ugly ⟨man⟩, would he take him away handsome? They give as witnesses the poets—⟨who⟩ write to give pleasure, and not for the sake of truth.

III. CONCERNING JUST AND UNJUST

(1) Twofold arguments are also put forward concerning the just and the unjust. And some say that the just is one thing and the unjust another, and others that the just and the unjust are the same. And I shall try to support this latter view. (2) And, in the first place, I shall

---

[4] The Greek words are still *kalon* and *aischron*, but the seemly-disgraceful antithesis seems unsuitable here.

argue that it is just to tell lies and to deceive. My opponents would
declare that it is ⟨right and just⟩ to do these things to one's enemies but
disgraceful and wicked to do so ⟨to one's friends⟩. ⟨But how is it just
to do so to one's enemies⟩ and not to one's dearest friends? Take the
example of parents: suppose one's father or mother ought to drink or
eat a remedy and is unwilling to do so, isn't it just to give the remedy in
a gruel or drink and to deny that it is in it? (3) Therefore, from this
one example, it is ⟨just⟩ to tell lies and to deceive one's parents. And,
in fact, to steal the belongings of one's friends and to use force against
those one loves most is just. (4) For instance, if a member of the
household is in some sort of grief or trouble and intends to destroy
himself with a sword or a rope or some other thing, it is right, isn't it,[5]
to steal these things, if possible, and, if one should come in too late and
catch the person with the thing in his hand, to take it away by force?
(5) And how is it not just to enslave one's enemies ⟨and⟩ to sell a whole
city into slavery if one is able to capture it? And to break into the
public buildings of one's fellow citizens appears to be just. Because, if
one's father has been imprisoned and is under sentence of death as a
result of having been overthrown by his political rivals, then isn't it
just to dig your way in to remove your father stealthily and save him?
(6) And what about breaking an oath: suppose a man is captured by the
enemy and takes a firm oath that, if he is set free, he will betray his
city: ⟨would⟩ this man do right if he kept his oath? (7) I don't think
so, but rather if he ⟨should⟩ save his city and his friends and the temples
of ⟨his⟩ fathers by breaking it. Thus it follows that it is right to break
an oath. And it is right to plunder a temple. (8) I'm not talking about
the civic temples, but about these common to the whole of Greece,
such as the ones at Delphi and Olympia: when the barbarian was on the
point of conquering Greece, and the safety of the country lay in the
temple funds, wasn't it right to take these and use them for the war?
(9) And to murder one's nearest and dearest is right: in the case of
Orestes and of Alcmaeon, even the god answered that they were right

---

[5] An affirmative answer is clearly required, although the Greek does not make
this plain.

to have done as they did. (10) I shall turn to the arts and to the writings of the poets. In the writing of tragedies and in painting, who⟨ever⟩ deceives the most in creating things similar to the true, this man is the best. (11) I want also to present the testimony of older poetry, of Cleobulina, for instance [fr. 2 *ALG* 1 47]:

> I saw a man stealing and deceiving by force,
> And to do this by force was an action most just.

(12) These lines were written a long time ago. The next passages are from Aeschylus [frr. 301, 302]:

> God does not stand aloof from just deceit,

⟨and⟩

> There are times when god respects an opportunity for lies.

(13) But to this, too, an opposite argument is put forward: that the just and the unjust are different things, and that as the name differs, so does the thing named. For instance, if anyone should ask those who say that unjust and just are the same whether they have yet done anything just for their parents, they will say yes. But then they have done something unjust, because they admit that unjust and just are the same thing. (14) Just take another case: if you know some man to be just, then you know the same man to be also unjust, and again if you know a man to be large, you also know him to be small, by the same argument. And ⟨if⟩ the sentence is pronounced, "Let him die the death for having done many acts of injustice," then let him die the death for having done ⟨many acts of justice⟩. (15) Enough on these topics: I shall go on to what is said by those who claim to prove that just and unjust are the same. (16) To state that to steal the enemy's possessions is just would also show the same action to be unjust if their argument is true, and so in the other cases. (17) And they bring in the arts, to which just and unjust do not apply. As for the poets, they write their poems to give men pleasure, and not for the sake of truth.

IV. CONCERNING TRUTH AND FALSEHOOD

(1) Twofold arguments are also put forward concerning the false and the true, concerning which one person says that a false statement is one thing and a true statement another, while others say the true statement is the same as the false. (2) And I hold the latter view: in the first place, because they are both expressed in the same words, and secondly, because whenever a statement is made, if things ⟨should⟩ turn out to be as stated, then the statement is true, but if they should not turn out to be as stated, the same statement is false. (3) Suppose the statement accuses a certain man of temple-robbery: if the thing actually happened, the statement is true, but if it did not happen, it is false. And the same argument is used by a man defending himself against such a charge. And the lawcourts judge the same statement to be both true and false. (4) And, again, suppose we are all sitting in a row and each of us says, "I am an initiate," we all utter the same words, but I would be the only person making a true statement, since I am the only person who is one. (5) From these remarks it is clear that the same statement is false whenever falsehood is present in it and true whenever truth is present (just the way a man is the same person when he is a child and a young man and an adult and an old man).[6]

(6) But it is also said that a false statement is one thing and a true statement another, and that as the name differs ⟨so does the thing named⟩. Because, if anyone should ask those who say that the same statement is both false and true whether their own statement is false or true, if they answer "false" then it is clear that the true and false are two different things, and if they answer "true," then this same statement is also false. And if anyone ever says or bears witness that certain things are true, then these same things are also false. And if he knows some man to be true, he knows the same man to be false. (7) As a result of the argument they say that if a thing comes to pass, the statement they make is true, but if it does not, then the statement is false. If so, ⟨it isn't the name that differs in these cases but the thing named.

---

[6] According to DK's notes, Wilamowitz places the contents of this parenthesis at the end of V (4). I cannot see that it makes much better sense there.

(8) And,⟩ again, ⟨if anyone should ask⟩ jurymen what they are judging (because they are not present at the events), (9) even they themselves agree that that in which falsehood is mingled is false, and that in which[7] truth is mingled is true. This constitutes a total difference. . . .

V. [NO TITLE]

(1) "The demented and the sane and the wise and the foolish both say and do the same things. (2) And, in the first place, they use the same names for things, such as 'earth' and 'man' and 'horse' and 'fire' and all the rest. And they do the same things: they sit and eat and drink and lie down, and so forth. (3) And furthermore, the same thing is larger and smaller and more and less and heavier and lighter. Thus all things are the same. (4) A talent is heavier than a mina and lighter than two talents; therefore, the same thing is both heavier and lighter. * * *[8] (5) And the same man both is alive and is not alive, and the same things both are and are not: the things that are here are not in Libya, nor are the things in Libya in Cyprus. And the same argument takes care of the other cases. Therefore, things both are and are not." (6) Those who say these things (that the demented ⟨and the sane, and⟩ the wise and the foolish, do and say the same things) and maintain the other consequences of the argument are mistaken. (7) Because, if you ask them this sort of question, whether madness differs from sense, or wisdom from folly, they say "yes." (8) For each of them makes it pretty well clear even from his actions that he will agree. Therefore, if they[9] do the same things, both the wise are demented and the demented wise, and everything will be thrown into confusion. (9) And we ought to bring up the question whether it is the sane or the demented who speak at the right moment. For whenever anyone asks this question they answer that the two groups say the same things, but that the wise

---

[7] *DK* has ᾧ, which appears to be a misprint for ᾧ.

[8] See above, n. 6.

[9] I.e., the wise and the demented.

speak at the right moment and the demented at the wrong one. (10) And in saying this, they appear to be making a small addition, "⟨the⟩ right moment" or "the wrong one," so that the situation is no longer the same. (11) I, however, think that things are not altered by such a small addition, although they can be altered by a change of accent, for instance: Γλαῦκος ("Glaucus") and γλαυκός ("white"), or Ξάνθος ("Xanthus") and ξανθός ("blonde"), or Ξοῦθος ("Xuthus") and ξουθός ("nimble"). (12) These examples differ from each other by a change in accent, the next ones by whether they are pronounced with a long or short vowel: Τύρος ("Tyre") and τῡρός ("cheese"), σάκος ("shield") and σᾱκός ("enclosure"), and still others differ by a change in the order of the letters: κάρτος ("strength") and κρατός ("of the head"), ὄνος ("ass") and νόος ("mind"). (13) Since there is such a great difference in cases in which nothing is taken away, what about those in which someone does add or take away something? And I shall show in this next example what sort of thing I mean. (14) If someone takes one from ten, ⟨or adds one to ten⟩, the result is no longer either ten or one, and so forth. (15) With respect to the assertion that the same man both is and is not, I put the following question: "Does he exist with respect to some particular thing, or just in general?" Then if someone denies that the man exists, he is mistaken, because he is treating ⟨the particular and⟩ universal senses as being the same. Because everything exists in *some* sense.

VI. CONCERNING WISDOM AND VIRTUE, WHETHER THEY ARE TEACHABLE

(1) A certain statement is put forward which is neither true nor new: it is that wisdom and virtue can neither be taught nor learned. And those who say this use the following proofs: (2) That it is not possible, if you were to hand a thing over to someone else, for you still to have this thing; this is one proof. (3) Another proof is that, if they had been teachable, there would have been acknowledged teachers of them, as in the case of music. (4) A third proof is that the men in Greece who

became wise would have taught their art to their friends. (5) A fourth proof is that, before now, some have been to the sophists and derived no benefit from them. (6) A fifth proof is that many who have *not* associated with the sophists have become notable. (7) But I think this statement is very simpleminded: I know that teachers teach letters, these being the things a teacher knows, and that lyre-players teach lyre-playing. In answer to the second proof, that there are in fact no acknowledged teachers, whatever else do the sophists teach except wisdom and virtue? (8) And what were the followers of Anaxagoras and Pythagoras? With respect to the third point, Polycleitus taught his son to be a sculptor. (9) And even if a particular man did *not* teach, this would not prove anything, but if a single man *did* teach, this would be evidence that teaching is possible. (10) With respect to the fourth point, that some do not become wise in spite of associating with the sophists, many people also do not succeed in learning their letters in spite of studying them. (11) There does exist also a natural bent by means of which a person who does not study with the sophists becomes competent, if he is well endowed, to master most things easily after learning a few elements from the very persons from whom we also learn our words. As for our words, one man learns more from his father and fewer from his mother, and another man the other way around. (12) And if someone is not persuaded that we learn our words but thinks we are born knowing them, let him form a judgment from what follows: if someone should send a child away to the Persians as soon as he was born and should bring him up there, hearing nothing of the Greek tongue, he would speak Persian. And if one were to bring a Persian child here, he would speak Greek. We learn our words in this fashion, and we don't know who our teachers are. (13) Thus my argument is complete, and you have its beginning, middle, and end. And I don't say that wisdom and virtue are teachable, but that these proofs do not satisfy me.

VII. [NO TITLE]

(1) Some of the popular orators say that offices should be assigned
by lot, but their opinion is not the best.   (2) Suppose someone should
question the man who says this as follows: Why don't you assign your
household slaves their tasks by lot, so that if the teamster drew the
office of cook, he would do the cooking and the cook would drive the
team, and so with the rest?   (3) And why don't we get together the
smiths and cobblers, and the carpenters and goldsmiths, and have them
draw lots, and force each one to engage in whatever trade he happens
to draw, and not the one he understands?   (4) The same thing could
also be done in musical contests: Have the contestants draw lots and
have each one compete in the contest he draws; thus the flute-player
will play the lyre if that falls to his lot, and the lyre-player the flute. And
in battle it may turn out that archers and hoplites will ride horseback
and the cavalryman will use the bow, with the result that everyone will
do what he does not understand and is incapable of doing.   (5) And
they say that this procedure is also not only good but exceptionally
democratic, whereas I think that democratic is the last thing it is.
Because there are in cities men hostile to the *demos*, and if the lot falls
to them, they will destroy the *demos*.   (6) But the *demos* itself ought to
keep its eyes open and elect all those who are well disposed towards it,
and ought to choose suitable people to be in command of the army and
others to be the law officers, and so on.

VIII. [NO TITLE]

(1) I think it belongs to ⟨the same man⟩ and to the same art to be
able to discourse in the brief style and to understand ⟨the⟩ truth of
things and to know how to give a right judgment in the lawcourts and
to be able to make public speeches and to understand the art of rhetoric
and to teach concerning the nature of all things, their state and how they
came to be.   (2) And, first of all, how will it not be possible for a man
who knows about the nature of all things to act rightly in every case

and ⟨teach the city⟩ to do so too?   (3) And, further, the man who knows the art of rhetoric will also know how to speak correctly on every subject.   (4) Because it is necessary for the man who intends to speak correctly to speak about the things which he knows, it follows that he will know everything.   (5) The reason for this is that he knows the art of all forms of speech, and all forms of speech have for their subject matter everything that ⟨exists⟩.   (6) It is necessary for the man who intends to speak correctly to have a knowledge of whatever things he might discuss and to give the city correct instruction in doing good things and thus prevent it from doing bad ones.   (7) If he knows these things, he will also know the things which differ from them, because he will know everything. For the same things are the elements of everything, and ⟨a man⟩ confronted with the same thing will do what is necessary if occasion arises.   (8) And if he knows how to play the flute, he will always be able to play the flute, whenever it is necessary to do this.   (9) And a man who knows how to give a judgment ought to have a right understanding of the just, because this is what cases are about. And if he knows the just, he will also know its opposite and the things which differ from ⟨both of these⟩.   (10) It is also necessary for him to know all the laws; if, therefore, he is not going to know what goes on, he won't know the laws either.   (11) The same man who knows the rules of music is the one who knows music, but if he doesn't know music he won't know its rules.   (12) If a man ⟨nevertheless⟩ knows the truth of things, the argument readily follows that he knows everything;   (13) and so he is ⟨also⟩ ⟨able to discourse⟩ in the brief style on all subjects, ⟨whenever⟩ he has to answer questions. Therefore, it must be that he knows everything.

IX. [NO TITLE]

(1) The greatest and fairest discovery has been found to be memory; it is useful for everything, for wisdom as well as for the conduct of life.   (2) This is the first step: if you focus your attention, your mind, making progress by this means, will perceive more.   (3) The second

step is to practice whatever[10] you hear: If you hear the same things many times and repeat them, what you have learned presents itself to your memory as a connected whole.   (4) The third step is: whenever you hear something, connect it with what you know already. For instance, suppose you need to remember the name "Chrysippos," you must connect it with *chrusos* ("gold") and *hippos* ("horse").   (5) Or another example: if you need to remember the name "Pyrilampes," you must \ connect it with *pyr* ("fire") and *lampein* ("to shine"). These are examples for words.   (6) In the case of things, do this: if you want to remember courage, think of Ares and Achilles; or metalworking, of Hephaistos; or cowardice, of Epeios. . . .

---

[10] Reading ἄ κα with Blass.

APPENDIX

EUTHYDEMUS OF CHIOS

translated by ROSAMOND KENT SPRAGUE

The historicity of Euthydemus may be inferred from two passages in Aristotle (see below 20) in which a fallacious argument not mentioned in Plato's dialogue *Euthydemus* is attributed to the sophist. Euthydemus' very nearly inseparable brother, Dionysodorus, receives an independent mention in Xenophon *Memorabilia* III 1, 1. When we consider that the characters in Plato's dialogues are almost invariably historical, there seems no doubt that Euthydemus and his brother really did exist. Why then does Diels omit Euthydemus while including an obscure figure such as Xeniades? The most likely explanation is that at the time of compiling the sophist section he accepted the prevailing view that many of Plato's characters were really masks for his contemporaries, in this case for Antisthenes. It may be too that in common with many historians of ancient thought he underestimated the importance of the eristical side of sophistry. If this is the case, however, he is out of step with both Plato, who saw in eristic of the Euthydemian type an Eleatic attack on his own theory of Forms (see especially below 17), and Aristotle, who realized that an analysis of sophistical arguments was a necessary part of his newly constructed *Organon*.

In employing a Platonic dialogue as a source of information about a particular sophist I am following the custom of Diels, as may readily be seen from an inspection of the Platonic passages cited in the index. If this is thought to be an illegitimate method of supplying Euthydemus with a respectable body of "doctrines," I would be willing to call the Platonic material "Euthydemian" rather than to attribute it to the sophist himself. Certainly there can be no doubt that there did exist a large stock of eristic arguments, and that considerable attention was paid to these arguments by Plato and Aristotle. These two factors alone would seem to me to justify the inclusion of a collection of eristic arguments in a book entitled *The Older Sophists*.

The best that can be done to date Euthydemus is to take him as an older contemporary of Socrates with a possible birthdate of 475, perhaps earlier.

It should be noted that I have made no special attempt to distinguish Dionysodorus from his brother. These Heavenly Twins seem to have spoken with a single voice, and there would, I think, be little philosophical value in treating them separately.

1. PLATO *Euthydemus* 271Aff. [Crito and Socrates] Who was it, Socrates, you were talking to in the Lyceum yesterday? . . . Euthydemus is the man you mean, Crito, and the one sitting next to me on my left was his brother, Dionysodorus—he, too, takes part in the discussions. —— I don't know either of them, Socrates. They are another new kind of sophist, I suppose. Where do they come from, and what is their particular wisdom? —— By birth, I think, they are from this side, from Chios. They went out as colonists to Thurii but were exiled from there and have already spent a good many years in this region. As to your question about the wisdom of the pair, it is marvelous, Crito! The two are absolutely omniscient, so much so that I never knew before what pancratiasts really were. They are both absolutely all-round fighters, not like the two battling brothers from Acarnania who could only fight with their bodies. These two are first of all completely skilled in body, being highly adept at fighting in armor and able to teach this skill to anyone else who pays them a fee; and then they are the ones best able to fight the battle of the lawcourts and to teach other people both how to deliver and to compose the sort of speeches suitable for the courts. Previously these were their only skills, but now they have

put the finishing touch to pancratistic art. They have now mastered the one form of fighting they had previously left untried; as a result not a single man can stand up to them, they have become so skilled in fighting in arguments and in refuting whatever may be said, no matter whether it is true or false. Cf. XENOPHON *Memorabilia* III 1, 1, and PLATO *Sophist* 226A and 231DE.

2. —— —— 272Bff.   [Socrates] The two men [Euthydemus and Dionysodorus] . . . were already pretty well advanced in years when they made a start on this wisdom I want to get; I mean the eristic sort. Cf. *Sophist* 251BC.

3. —— —— 273D   [Euthydemus] . . . we think we can teach [virtue] better than anyone else and more quickly.   274AB We are here . . . to give a demonstration, and to teach, if anyone wants to learn.

4. —— —— 275Dff.   [Euthydemus and Cleinias] Cleinias, which are the men who learn, the wise or the ignorant? . . . —— . . . the wise [are] the learners. —— . . . Are there some whom you call teachers, or not? —— Yes. —— And the teachers are teachers of those who learn, I suppose, in the same way that the music master and the writing master were teachers of you and the other boys when you were pupils? —— [Yes.] —— And when you were learning you did not yet know the things you were learning, did you? —— No. . . . —— And were you wise when you did not know these things? —— By no means. . . . —— Then if not wise, ignorant? —— Very much so. —— Then in the process of learning what you did not know, you learned while you were ignorant? —— [Yes.] —— Then it is the ignorant who learn, Cleinias, and not the wise, as you suppose.   Cf. *Theaetetus* 199A . . . if anyone enjoys dragging about the expressions "know" and "learn." . . . and ARISTOTLE *Metaphysics* IX 8, 1049b33. This is the source of the sophistical refutation that a person engages in a science of which he does not have the knowledge, because the person who is learning a science does not have it.

5. PLATO *Euthydemus* 276Cff. [Dionysodorus and Cleinias] Well then, Cleinias, when the writing-master gave you dictation, which of the boys learned the piece, the wise or the ignorant? —— The wise. . . . —— Then it is the wise who learn, and not the ignorant. . . . ARISTOTLE *On Sophistical Refutations* IV 165b30 Arguments like these are based on equivocation: the knowing are those who learn, because it is those who know letters who learn what is dictated. The word "learn" is equivocal, meaning both "understand by using knowledge" and "getting knowledge." Cf. PLATO *Euthydemus* 277Eff.

6. PLATO *Euthydemus* 276Dff. [Euthydemus and Cleinias] Do those who learn learn the things they know or the things they do not know? . . . —— . . . the learners [learn] what they do not know. —— What then, . . . don't you know your letters? —— Yes. . . . —— Then you know them all? —— [Yes.] —— Whenever anyone dictates anything, doesn't he dictate letters? —— Yes. —— Then doesn't he dictate something you know, if you really know them all? —— [Yes.] —— Whenever anyone dictates anything, doesn't he dictate letters? —— [Yes.] —— Then doesn't he dictate something you know, if you really know them all? —— Yes. —— Well, then, . . . you are not the one who learns what someone dictates, are you, but the one who doesn't know his letters is the one who learns? —— No, . . . I am the one who learns. —— Then you learn what you know . . . if you in fact do know all your letters. ARISTOTLE *Rhetoric* II 24, 1401a29 [immediately following the trireme argument] . . . when a person knows his letters, he knows the word [composed of them]. Cf. *On Sophistical Refutations* IV 166a31 And, "he now understands his letters, if he has really understood what he knows."

7. PLATO *Euthydemus* 283Cff. [Dionysodorus and Socrates] —— . . . you say you want [Cleinias] to become wise? —— Very much so. —— And at the present moment . . . is Cleinias wise or not? —— [No.] —— But you people wish him to become wise . . . and not to be ignorant? —— Yes. —— Therefore you wish him to become what he is not, and no longer to be what he is now? . . . Then since you wish him no longer to be what he is now, you apparently wish for nothing else but his death. Cf. *DK* 90, 5 (15).

8. ——— ——— 283Eff. [Euthydemus and Ctesippus] —— Why Ctesippus, . . . do you think it possible to tell lies? —— Good heavens, yes. . . . —— When one speaks the thing one is talking about, or when one does not speak it? —— When one speaks it. . . . —— So that if he speaks this thing, he speaks no other one of things that are except the very one he speaks. —— Of course. . . . —— And the thing he speaks is one of those that are, distinct from the rest? —— Certainly. —— Then the person speaking that thing speaks what is. . . . —— Yes. —— But surely the person who speaks what is and things that are speaks the truth—so that Dionysodorus, if he speaks things that are, speaks the truth and tells no lies about you.

9. ——— ——— 285Eff. [Dionysodorus and Ctesippus] ——Well, you, at any rate, could not prove that you have ever heard one person contradicting another. . . . Are there words to describe each thing that exists? —— Certainly. —— And do they describe it as it is or as it is not? —— As it is. —— . . . we showed a moment ago that no one speaks of things as they are not, since it appeared that no one speaks what does not exist. —— Well, what about it? . . . Are you and I contradicting each other any the less? —— Now would we be contradicting . . . if we were both to speak the description of the same thing? . . . But when neither of us speaks the description of the thing, whereas you speak another description of another thing, do we contradict then? Or is it the case that I speak it but that you speak nothing at all? And how would a person who does not speak contradict one who does? Cf. ARISTOTLE *Topics* I 104b21; *Metaphysics* V 24, 1024b32.

10. ——— ——— 293Bff. [Euthydemus and Socrates] —— Would you prefer, Socrates, to have me teach you this knowledge you have been in difficulties over all this time, or to demonstrate that you possess it? —— . . . for heaven's sake, demonstrate that I possess it. . . . —— Then come answer me this . . . is there anything you know?

—— Oh, yes . . . many things, though trivial ones. . . . —— Then you are knowing, if you really know? —— Of course, as far as concerns that particular thing. —— That doesn't matter, because mustn't you necessarily know everything, if you are knowing? —— How in heaven's name can that be, . . . when there are many other things I don't know? —— Then if there is anything you don't know, you are not knowing.

11. —— —— 295Eff. [Euthydemus and Socrates]   —— Do you know what you know by means of something or not? . . . —— [Yes.] —— And do you always know by this same means? . . . —— Always. . . . —— Then you always know, by this means.

12. —— —— 297Eff. [Dionysodorus and Socrates] —— And Patrocles . . . is your brother? —— Yes indeed, . . . we have the same mother, though not the same father. —— Then he both is and is not your brother.

13. —— —— 298Eff. [Dionysodorus and Ctesippus] —— Tell me, have you got a dog? —— Yes, and a brute of a one too. . . . —— And has he got puppies? —— Yes indeed, and they are just like him. —— And so the dog is their father? —— Yes, I saw him mounting the bitch myself. —— Well, then, isn't the dog yours? Certainly. . . . —— Then since he is a father and is yours, the dog turns out to be your father, and you are the brother of puppies, aren't you? ARISTOTLE On Sophistical Refutations xxiv 179a33 All the arguments of the following type are fallacies of accident. . . . "Is the dog your father?" Cf. 179b15.

14. PLATO Euthydemus 299Bff. [Euthydemus] Since you admit that it is a good thing for a man to drink medicine whenever he needs it, then oughtn't he to drink as much as possible? And won't it be fine if someone pounds up and mixes him a load of hellebore? ARISTOTLE Rhetoric ii 24, 1401a32 And since a double amount is unhealthy, one could say that the original amount is not healthy either. Because it would be ridiculous to say that two goods make an evil.

15. PLATO *Euthydemus* 300Aff. [Euthydemus and Ctesippus] —— Tell me, . . . do the Scythians and the rest of mankind see things capable of sight or incapable? —— Capable, I suppose. —— And do you do so, too? —— Yes, so do I. —— And do you see our cloaks? —— Yes. —— Then these same cloaks are capable of sight. Cf. ARISTOTLE *Metaphysics* IX 1, 1046a19ff.

16. —— —— 300Bff. [Dionysodorus and Ctesippus] —— But surely it is not possible for there to be a speaking of the silent. . . . —— Entirely impossible. —— Then neither is there a silence of the speaking? —— Still less so. . . . —— But whenever you mention stones and wood and pieces of iron, are you not speaking of the silent? Cf. ARISTOTLE *On Sophistical Refutations* IV 166a12; X 171a8, 171a20, 171a28ff.

17. —— —— 300Eff. [Dionysodorus and Socrates] —— Why, Socrates, have you ever yet seen a beautiful thing? —— Yes, indeed, . . . and many of them. —— And were they different from the beautiful, . . . or were they the same as the beautiful? —— . . . different from the beautiful itself but at the same time there [is] also some beauty present with each of them. —— Then if an ox is present with you, you are an ox? And because I am present with you now, you are Dionysodorus? —— Heaven forbid. . . . Cf. *Parmenides* 130Eff.

18. —— —— 301Dff. [Dionysodorus and Socrates] —— Now if a man does his proper business, . . . he will do rightly? —— Very much so. —— And the proper business in the case of the cook is . . . to cut up and skin? . . . —— Yes. . . . —— Then it is clear . . . that if someone kills the cook and cuts him up, and then boils him and roasts him, he will be doing his proper business.

19. —— *Cratylus* 386Dff. [Socrates] But surely you don't hold the view of Euthydemus that all things belong equally to everyone at the same time and for all time. . . .

20. ARISTOTLE *Rhetoric* II 24, 1401a26   There is another [fallacy] which takes either the divided as combined or the combined as divided. For since, on many occasions, a thing which is not the same [as something else] appears to be so, one has the option of choosing whichever alternative seems more useful. There is an argument of Euthydemus like this: a man knows that there is a trireme in the Piraeus because he knows each of the two things ["a trireme" and "in the Piraeus"] separately.   *On Sophistical Refutations* XX 177b12   Then there is Euthydemus' argument: do you know now, being in Sicily, that there are triremes in the Piraeus? [or] do you know now, being in the Piraeus, that there are triremes in Sicily?

21. SEXTUS *Against the Schoolmasters* VII 13   Panthoides and Alexinus and Eubulides and Bryson and Dionysodorus and Euthydemus busied themselves with the logical part [of philosophy].

22. ——— ——— VII 64   . . . and Euthydemus and Dionysodorus are also said to have held these views, because they too rejected existence and truth as being relative things.

23. ——— ——— VII 48   Besides which [the criterion] has been rejected by Xenophanes of Colophon and Xeniades of Corinth and Anacharsis the Scythian and Protagoras and Dionysodorus. . . .

INDEX

OF PERSONS AND PLACES

The following have not been indexed: Athens, Athenians, Greece, Greeks, Plato, and places of origin regularly attached to the name of a particular person, e.g., "Leontini" in Gorgias of Leontini. A single page number may indicate more than a single occurrence of the entry in question; the whole page should be consulted. The major section of each sophist appears in bold face, e.g., Prodicus **70–85**. For the authors of the various citations, consult the index of passages.

INDEX
OF PASSAGES

Each entry is followed, first, by a reference number (e.g., 82 A 7) and, second, by the number of the page in this book on which the passage (or a mention of it) appears. The reference numbers coincide with those of *DK* with the exception of section 87 (Antiphon) and of the Appendix (Euthydemus of Chios). In the case of Antiphon three different types of numbers occur: 1) 87 B 150 (B 76) indicates that *DK* B 76 appears as B 150 in Morrison's numbering; 2) 87 B 12 (M) indicates that the passage is a new citation not appearing in *DK*; 3) 87 B XXVII (M) refers to the introductory matter of a particular section. For a complete concordance of the *DK* numbers with those of Morrison, see pp. 112-14. The passages in the Euthydemus section are cited as App. 1, App. 2, and so forth. For explanation of *FHG*, *FGrHist*, etc., consult the abbreviation list on pp. ix–x.

AELIAN
Miscellaneous History

II 35	82 A 15	37
X 13	88 B 44	265
X 17	88 B 45	266
XII 32	82 A 9	35

On the Nature of Animals

V 21	87 B 58 (M)	210

AESCHINES THE SOCRATIC
Callias

fr. 16 p. 50 Krauss	80 C 5	28
fr. 16 p. 50 Krauss	84 A 4b	73

Thargelia

fr. 22 Dittmar	82 A 35	42

AESCHYLUS
Phrygians (TGF)

fr. 259	88 B 65	268

Seven Against Thebes [Wilamowitz]

———	82 B 24	65

ANECDOTA GRAECA (*BA*)

[*Antiatticistes*]

I p. 78, 6	87 B 164 (M)	236
I p. 78, 20	87 B 146 (B 72)	232
I p. 79, 1	87 B 165 (M)	236
I p. 82, 29	87 B 65 (M)	211
I p. 94, 1	88 B 13	253
I p. 110, 33	87 B 166 (M)	236
I p. 114, 28	87 B 169 (B 82)	237

[*Synagoge Lexeon Chresimon*]

I p. 345, 26	87 B 170 (B 83)	237
I p. 352, 29	87 B 53 (M)	209
I p. 363, 31	87 B 174 (B 87)	237
I p. 366, 28	87 B 49 (M)	208
I p. 367, 31	87 B 171 (B 84)	237
I p. 378, 22	87 B 26	205
I p. 382, 19	88 B 2	250
I p. 403, 5	87 B 87 (B 19)	218
I p. 418, 6	87 B 172 (B 85)	237
I p. 419, 18	87 B 173 (B 86)	237
I p. 427, 18	87 B 15 (M)	202
I p. 429, 18	87 B 205 (B 115)	240
I p. 437, 28	87 B 27 (M)	205
I p. 470, 25	87 B 84 (B 16)	217
I p. 472, 14	87 B 85 (B 17)	218

ANECDOTA PARISIENSIA [Cramer]
Cf. A. Bohler, *Sophistae anonymi Protreptici fragmenta* (Leipzig, 1903).

I 171, 31	80 B 3	20

ANONYMUS TRAGICUS (*TGF*)

fr. 26 p. 844	90, 2	283

ANTIPHON (the tragic poet) (*TGF*)

p. 792	87 A 13 (A 4)	128

APOLLODORUS (*FGrHist* 244)

F 33	82 A 10	35
F 70	80 A 1	4
F 71	80 A 1	6

APULEIUS
Florida

18	80 A 4	7

HARPOCRATION

[*Lexicon of the Ten Orators*]

327

Index of Passages

METRODORUS
  On Poems (A. Körte)
    fr. 20ff.   85 B 7a   92

MINUCIUS FELIX
  Octavius
    21, 2   84 B 5   83

MOERIS (Bekker)
    203, 2   87 B 179 (B 92)   238

MOSCHION (*TGF*)
    fr. 6 p. 813   80 C 1   27

OLYMPIODORUS [on PLATO]
  Gorgias (Jahn)
    p. 112   82 A 10   35
    ———   82 B 2   42
    p. 131   82 A 27   40

ORIGEN
  Against Celsus
    IV 25   87 B 80 (B 12)   215

PANAETIUS (Fowler)
    fr. 50   80 B 5   21

PAPYRI
  Geneva Papyrus (Nicole)
    cols. I–IV   87 B 19 (M)   203
  Oxyrhynchus (POxy) (Grenfell-Hunt)
    I no. 68   80 A 30   18
    IX [no. 1176]   88 B 19   257
    XI no. 1364   87 B 90 (B 44n)   218
    XI no. 1364   87 B 91 (B 44)   220
    XV no. 1797   87 B 92 (B 44)   221
    XVII no. 2078   88 B 15a   254
  Petrograd Papyrus (Jernstedt)
    (*Journal des Unterrichtsmin* [Russian])
    no. 13 col. 2, 11   86 B 19   103
    ed. Carlo Gallavotti, *RFIC*, n.s. XI (1933),   88 B 12a   253
      p. 179

PAUSANIAS
    V 25, 4   86 B 1   100
    V 27, 8   86 B 1   100
    VI 17, 7ff.   82 A 7   34
    X 18, 7   82 A 7   34

Index of Passages

SOLON
   Laws 21
   fr. 18 (*ALG*)

87 B 55 (M)		209
88 A 8		246

SOPATER
   Commentary on Hermogenes (*Rh. Gr.,* Walz)
     V 6ff.
     VIII 23

82 *ad* B 12–14		63
82 B 31		67

SOPHOCLES
   Antigone
     672

87 B 118 (B 61)		227

STEPHANUS BYZANTIUS
   Abdera

80 A 21		13

STOBAEUS
   [*Anthology* Wachsmuth]

Reference	Passage	Page
I 8, 11	88 B 26	260
II 8, 4	88 B 21	258
II 8, 12	88 B 15	254
II 31, 39	87 B 117 (B 60)	227
II 31, 40	87 B 118 (B 61)	227
II 31, 41	87 B 119 (B 62)	227
II 33, 15	87 B XXVII (B 44a)	225

   [Hense]

Reference	Passage	Page
III 2, 15	88 B 12	253
III 5, 57	87 B 125 (B 59)	229
III 6, 45	87 B 123 (B 49)	228
III 8, 18	87 B 128 (B 57)	229
III 10, 99	87 B 132 (B 53)	230
III 14, 2	88 B 27	260
III 16, 20	87 B 133 (B 53a)	230
III 16, 30	87 B 134 (B 54)	230
III 20, 66	87 B 124 (B 58)	228
III 23, 1	88 B 28	261
III 29, 11	88 B 9	252
III 29, 80	80 B 10	24
III 37, 15	88 B 22	258
III 38, 32	86 B 16	103
III 42, 10	86 B 17	103
IV 20, 61	88 B 15	254
IV 20, 65	84 B 7	84
IV 22, 66	87 B 123 (B 49)	228
IV 29, 24	83, 4	69
IV 33, 10	88 B 29	261

IV 34, 56	87 B 130 (B 51)	230
IV 34, 63	87 B 129 (B 50)	230
IV 40, 19	87 B 134 (B 54)	230
IV 53, 23	88 B 23	258
[Meineke]		
IV 293, 17	87 B 137 (B 64)	231

STRABO [Casaubon]

VIII p. 356	88 B 14	254

SUETONIUS

On Games (?)	88 B 36	263

SU[I]DA[S]

abios I 7, 31 *A*	87 B 116 (B 43)	224
acharistein I 437, 18 *A*	87 B 134 (B 54)	231
adeētos I 46, 20 *A*	87 B 78 (B 10)	215
adiastaton I 50, 18 *A*	87 B 96 (B 24)	222
aeiestō I 62, 3 *A*	87 B 93 (B 22)	222
agoi I 39, 6 *A*	87 B 90 (B 44n)	218
akarē I 76, 6 *A*	87 B 174 (B 87)	237
akroasthai I 91, 23 *A*	87 B 49 (M)	208
amarturētous I 134, 22 *A*	87 B 182 (B 93b)	238
anathesthai I 168, 16 *A*	87 B 131 (B 52)	230
andreia I 195, 22 *A*	87 B 141 (B 67a)	232
anhēkei I 215, 10 *A*	87 B 87 (B 19)	218
Antiphon I 245, 21–28 *A*	87 A 1 (M)	114
aopta I 256, 15 *A*	87 B 72 (B 4)	214
apathē I 256, 27 *A*	87 B 73 (B 5)	214
apodidomenoi I 295, 23 *A*	87 B 15 (M)	202
apokrisis I 301, 5 *A*	87 B 205 (B 115)	240
apolachein I 302, 10–12 *A*	87 B 50 (B 116)	208
apotaxis I 324, 9 *A*	87 B 16 (M)	202
aulizomenoi I 414, 7 *A*	87 B 142 (B 68)	232
axioi I 255, 29 *A*	87 B 54 (M)	209
———— I 130, 28 *A*	87 B 160 (M)	235
basanos I 456, 24 *A*	87 B 175 (B 88)	237
chrēmatōn IV 823, 24 *A*	87 B 206 (B 117)	240
deēseis II 16, 26 *A*	87 B 79 (B 11)	215
diastasis II 73, 21 *A*	87 B 94 (B 23)	222
diathesis II 56, 20 *A*	87 B 95 (24a)	222
diathesis II 56, 24 *A*	87 B 95 (24a)	222
———— II 56, 24 *A*	87 B 136 (B 63)	231
diathesis II 689, 3 *A*	87 B 136 (B 63)	231
dusanios II 147, 19 *A*	87 B 176 (B 89)	237

CORRIGENDA

for *The Older Sophists*

(based on G. B. Kerferd in *Classical Review* Nov '75)

p. 1, line 2 — *Name & Notion* (O'Neill) for "what the very term ... with this subject": "how the very term "philosophy" was used by the Greeks and what it meant, nor in general anything at all of matters relating to these questions"

p. 36, next to last line — *Gorgias* (Kennedy) for "survived to the time of Socrates": "outlived Socrates"

p. 37 end of A 18 — ——— ——— for "ten thousand": "a thousand"

p. 41 end of A 32 — ——— ——— for "native country": "traditional usage" [presumably "exiled" would need to be e.g. "departed from" (the) trad. usage] RKS.

p. 41 next to last line (in A35) — ——— ——— for "were not unaware of how to inquire": "are known to have acquired"

p. 46 next to last line of (86) — ——— ——— for "multiplicity": "majority"

p. 47 line 3 — ——— ——— for "you tell an old man what he must answer": "you impose on an old man the troublesomeness of answering"

p. 79 line 4 — *Prodicus* (Stewart) for "in systematic fashion": "in prose"

p. 244 line 7 — *Critias* (Levin) for "divine": "paternal uncle"

p. 246 line 7 (end of A6) — ——— ——— for "brought . . . populace": "restored the democracy"

p. 247 line 7 — ——— ——— K. says that at the end of A11 "construction has been misunderstood"

p. 248 line 2 — ——— ——— for "still do so individually": "still do so in his own day"